MW01098363

# Practicing Medicine in Difficult Times

## Protecting Physicians from Malpractice Litigation

**Marjorie O. Thomas**
Senior Vice President
Risk Management and Underwriting
Administrators for the Professions, Inc.

**Christine J. Quinn**
Vice President
Risk Management Services
Administrators for the Professions, Inc.

**Geraldine M. Donohue**
Associate Director
Risk Management Education
Administrators for the Professions, Inc.

JONES AND BARTLETT PUBLISHERS
*Sudbury, Massachusetts*
BOSTON     TORONTO     LONDON     SINGAPORE

*World Headquarters*

| Jones and Bartlett Publishers | Jones and Bartlett Publishers | Jones and Bartlett Publishers |
| 40 Tall Pine Drive | Canada | International |
| Sudbury, MA 01776 | 6339 Ormindale Way | Barb House, Barb Mews |
| 978-443-5000 | Mississauga, Ontario L5V 1J2 | London W6 7PA |
| info@jbpub.com | CANADA | UK |
| www.jbpub.com | | |

Jones and Bartlett's books and products are available through most bookstores and online booksellers. To contact Jones and Bartlett Publishers directly, call 800-832-0034, fax 978-443-8000, or visit our website www.jbpub.com.

Substantial discounts on bulk quantities of Jones and Bartlett's publications are available to corporations, professional associations, and other qualified organizations. For details and specific discount information, contact the special sales department at Jones and Bartlett via the above contact information or send an email to specialsales@jbpub.com.

This publication is designed to provide accurate and authoritative information in regard to the subject matter covered. It is sold with the understanding that the publisher is not engaged in rendering legal, accounting, or other professional service. If legal advice or other expert assistance is required, the service of a competent professional person should be sought.

**Library of Congress Cataloging-in-Publication Data**
Thomas, Marjorie O.
  Practicing medicine in difficult times : protecting physicians from malpractice litigation / by Marjorie O. Thomas, Christine J. Quinn, and Geraldine M. Donohue.
      p. ; cm.
  Includes bibliographical references and index.
  ISBN-13: 978-0-7637-4856-2 (hardcover)
  ISBN-10: 0-7637-4856-0 (hardcover)
  1. Physicians—Malpractice. 2. Insurance, Physicians' liability. 3. Physician and patient. I. Quinn, Christine J. II. Donohue, Geraldine M. III. Title.
  [DNLM: 1. Malpractice. 2. Liability, Legal. 3. Physician–Patient Relations. 4. Professional Practice. W 44.1 T459p 2009]
  RA1056.5.T48 2009
  610.68—dc22

                                           2008013288

6048

**Production Credits**
Publisher: David Cella
Editorial Assistant: Maro Asadoorian
Production Director: Amy Rose
Senior Production Editor: Renée Sekerak
Associate Marketing Manager: Lisa Gordon
Manufacturing and Inventory Control Supervisor: Amy Bacus
Assistant Print Buyer: Jessica DeMarco
Cover Design: Brian Moore
Composition: Paw Print Media
Printing and Binding: Malloy Incorporated
Cover Printing: Malloy Incorporated

**Printed in the United States of America**
12  11  10  09  08    10 9 8 7 6 5 4 3 2 1

This book is dedicated to
all of the devoted physicians
who strive every day to keep
their patients safe.

# Contents

# About the Authors

**Marjorie O. Thomas, MPA, ARM, RPLU, FASHRM**
Marjorie O. (West) Thomas is Senior Vice President for Risk Management and Underwriting for Administrators for the Professions, Inc. (AFP). Since joining AFP in 1985, she has translated her passion for developing methods for improved patient safety into innovative programming that has energized the field of health care risk management, with an emphasis on the ambulatory care practice. Prior to AFP, Ms. Thomas spent several years in hospital administration and established the risk management department at New York's Bellevue Hospital.

Ms. Thomas holds a BS degree and a Master's degree in Public Administration (Health Care); she has also earned the ARM and RPLU designations. Her work in this field has also earned her the designation of fellow of the American Society for Healthcare Risk Management. After receiving training in their program to prepare facilitators in communication skills, Ms. Thomas became a member of the faculty of the Institute for Healthcare Communication.

**Christine J. Quinn, RN, BSN, MPA, ARM, FASHRM, RPLU**
Christine J. Quinn is Vice President of Risk Management Services for Administrators for the Professions, Inc. (AFP). She began her career as a critical care nurse at New York Hospital–Cornell Medical Center and joined AFP in 1987. At AFP, she is one of the leaders of the team that has pioneered the development of a successful, multi-faceted risk management program for physicians. Drawing on her strong clinical background, Ms. Quinn has a particular desire to help physicians better understand how the application of risk management principles in their practice of medicine can lead to better care. She has lectured extensively on risk management in health care.

Ms. Quinn is a Registered Nurse with a BSN degree and has earned a Master's degree in Public Administration. She has also earned the ARM and RPLU insurance designations and is a fellow in the American Society for Healthcare Risk Management. Ms. Quinn is a member of the faculty of the Institute for Healthcare Communication.

**Geraldine M. Donohue, RN, MSN, ARM**
Geraldine M. Donohue is Associate Director of Risk Management Education for Administrators for the Professions, Inc. (AFP). She joined AFP in 1995, after a long career in behavioral health. Within a multi-disciplinary team, she develops education programs and provides guidance to thousands of physicians in both large and small group settings to help physicians avoid malpractice litigation. As a Clinical Nurse Specialist, with a Master of Science degree in Nursing, Ms. Donohue maintained a private psychotherapy practice, treating individuals and families, for 18 years. Prior to coming to AFP, she held a joint appointment with New York Hospital's Payne Whitney Clinic and The Westchester Psychiatric Division as their Education Coordinator.

She has earned the ARM designation and is a member of the American Society for Healthcare Risk Management and is a faculty member of the Institute for Healthcare Communication. One of her greatest passions has been facilitating over 150 small group communication workshops for physicians on strengthening the physician–patient relationship.

# Contributing Authors

**Anthony J. Bonomo, JD**
Chief Executive Officer
Administrators for the
    Professions, Inc.*
Member of Board of Governors
Physicians' Reciprocal Insurers

**Rita Charon, MD, PhD**
Professor of Clinical Medicine
Director
Program in Narrative Medicine
College of Physicians
    and Surgeons of
    Columbia University

**Stephen Deckoff, MD**
Assistant Professor
Albert Einstein College
    of Medicine

**Gerald Dolman, LLB**
President
Administrators for the
    Professions, Inc.
Member of Board of Governors
Physicians' Reciprocal Insurers

**Mary Jo Fink, MD**
Director
Women's Health in
    Family Medicine
Assistant Clinical Professor
Center for Family and
    Community Medicine
Columbia University

**Seth Goldberg, MD**
Medical Consultant
Physicians' Reciprocal Insurers

**Roy F. Kaufman, JD, MHA**
Director of Claims
Administrators for the
    Professions, Inc.

**Victor R. Klein, MD**
Attending Physician
North Shore University
    Hospital–Manhasset
Clinical Associate Professor
Obstetrics and Gynecology
New York University School
    of Medicine

**Howard D. Kolodny, MD**
Member of Board of Governors
Physicians' Reciprocal Insurers

**Philip A. Robbins, MD**
Attending Physician
New York University Hospital
    for Joint Diseases
Clinical Instructor
New York University School
    of Medicine
Member of Board of Governors
Physicians' Reciprocal Insurers

**Barry F. Schwartz, MD**
Member of Board of Governors
Physicians' Reciprocal Insurers

**James W. Tuffin, JD**
General Counsel
Administrators for the
    Professions, Inc.

*Administrators for the Professions, Inc. is the attorney-in-fact for Physicians'
  Reciprocal Insurers.

# Acknowledgments

We extend our thanks to William Beck, MD, Dwight C. Blum, MD, Joseph Feinberg, MD, Ira Goldman, MD, Joseph Greensheer, MD, Sandra Cicatiello, and Diane Enterlein for their valuable contributions to this book. The tutelage provided to us by Patricia Donohue-Porter, PhD, RN, Patricia O'Brien, PhD, RN, and Michael West, PhD has been essential to the success of this project. Chandra Thomas was unstinting in the advice she imparted. To them we offer our deepest thanks.

We owe a debt of gratitude for the very able assistance of all the creative and gifted individuals who helped this project come to fruition. Among them are Janet Fretto, Astrid Smith, Rosetta Fiorello, Christine Martino, Tanya Oden, Tristan Mueck, Jennifer Pennachio, Zakiya Anderson, and Barbara Palmeri.

David Cella and his most talented team at Jones and Bartlett gave us superb guidance from beginning to end, and for this we are extraordinarily grateful.

Our dear families and friends were particularly patient and supportive throughout the preparation of this work. We are blessed by their encouragement and offer our heartfelt appreciation.

# A Note from the Authors

The cases that are included in this book have been drawn from a variety of sources, including archives of actual lawsuits and claims. Names, locations, and identifying information have been changed to protect privacy.

# Chapter 1

# The Power of Prevention

Anthony J. Bonomo

*An ounce of prevention is worth a pound of cure.*
Benjamin Franklin

A successful physician recently told me about his son, who had chosen to become an investment banker. He explained with both pride and sadness that his son, who was very accomplished, had accurately observed that his parents, both of whom are physicians, no longer seemed to enjoy their work. In discussing his own career choice, the future investment banker explained to his father that if he was going to work the long hours that his parents did, he would rather become an investment banker. In his view, this career would be more financially rewarding and less stressful on his family life. The father sadly commented that he had not encouraged his son to become a physician because medicine had changed so much in the 30 years he had been practicing.

It is a tragedy that many physicians today would not encourage their children to enter the noble profession of medicine. This is a significant change from a generation ago, when many physicians strongly encouraged their children to follow in their footsteps. A variety of economic and social pressures have come together to drive this change. The reasons for the problems in health care are myriad. Low morale among physicians is a contributing factor to physician dissatisfaction. According to the 2006 American College of Physician Executives Survey, almost 60% of 1,198 physicians have considered leaving medicine because they are discouraged over the state of U.S. health care today.[1] The factors contributing to low morale were identified by the survey respondents as low reimbursement, loss of autonomy, bureaucratic red tape, patient overload, loss of respect, and the malpractice environment.[1]

This chapter is not meant to be an exhaustive review of each of those factors, but it does discuss some of the influences that drive this culture change and offers some suggestions for how practicing physicians can find relief for the stresses related to practicing the time-honored and noble profession of medicine. Because of the essential nature of their work, physicians must be able to retain passion for their work, which truly is a gift to their fellow man.

# Overview of Medical Malpractice Crisis: How Did We Get Here?

> A senior physician recalls that when he first entered practice, his malpractice premium was $500 per year. At that time, he thought that was an outrageous sum.

There was a time, a generation or so ago, when the threat of a malpractice suit was far from a physician's mind. It was not an issue when a young physician considered which path he or she might choose as a resident. The decision about his or her specialty choice was based mostly on the aspect of medicine a young physician found to be more interesting or challenging. Sadly, this has changed, as "62% of medical residents reported that liability issues were their top concern in 2003—surpassing any other concern, and representing an enormous increase from 2001, when only 15% of residents said liability was a concern."[2]

Twenty or thirty years ago young physicians did not worry that the malpractice suits they would face during their career might make it hard for them to earn a living. There was no worry that a high-risk patient might be a threat to his or her practice because a large lawsuit resulting from a less than ideal outcome might result in negative publicity that would result in a loss of patient base or the loss of a position at a hospital or clinic. These considerations are very real today: "99% of [American Medical Association] AMA members surveyed are very or somewhat concerned about the current medical liability environment, with 87% being very concerned. One-third of the members surveyed have begun referring complex cases in the last 12 months and 98% reported that medical liability pressures were important in their decision."[2]

At a time when we face a shortage of physicians, many experienced physicians are leaving medicine earlier than they had planned or are restricting their practices to exclude high-risk patients. The AMA reports that "twenty-seven percent of member physicians have stopped providing certain services in the last 12 months and 96% of them indicate that medical liability pressures were important in their decision."[2]

# How Are Insurance Rates Determined?

As with all types of insurance, medical malpractice premiums are primarily based on the frequency and severity of claims reported. Frequency relates to the number of claims reported in a given time period. These terms might be more understandable by thinking of them in terms of homeowner's insurance. In areas where a hurricane has hit, the insurer will experience an increase in claim frequency because many homes in a single area may have been damaged by the same storm. The severity relates to the dollar amount paid per claim. In an area near the impact of a hurricane, an insurer may experience many high-severity claims because homes are destroyed or severely damaged. Further away from the storm area, damage may be less severe, resulting in claims for smaller amounts, such as to repair broken windows or damaged roofs.

In medical malpractice, claim frequency relates to the number of claims reported in a given policy year. This can vary by specialty or location. Physicians in high-risk specialties such as neurosurgery or OB/GYN tend to be sued more often than primary care physicians. Doctors in larger cities, such as Chicago and New York, tend to be sued more often than those in rural areas. Severity is the amount paid per claim. OB/GYNs and neurosurgeons tend to have cases with more severe, permanent injuries that result in higher payments.

# Why Are Medical Malpractice Premiums So High?

Some people think that malpractice premiums are high because insurance companies are making a lot of money. In reality, however, most physicians in the United States are insured outside the commercial market. "Today the primary sellers of physician medical malpractice insurance are the physician-owned and/or operated insurance companies that, according to the Physician

Insurers Association of America, insure approximately 60% of all physicians in private practice in the United States."[3] The reason for this is simple: Insuring medical malpractice is not a money-making operation. If it were, there would be a great deal of competition for your business. Medical malpractice is a unique type of insurance because, unlike other types of insurance in which a claim for damages is usually apparent quite quickly after the incident/accident that results in a claim (a tree falls on your house, you crash your car, a fire or flood damages your office), in medical malpractice, it may be one to three years (or even longer if the case involves an infant) before you and subsequently your insurer know about the claim and even longer before any payments that may be required to defend and resolve the claim are made. Thus, it is very difficult to set rates. Also, in most types of insurance, when a customer makes a claim for damages, the claim is often resolved objectively and quickly—the cost of repairing your roof, your car, and so forth is usually clear cut and easily determined. The complication arises if bodily injury is involved in the claim (e.g., a driver who is hurt in a car accident). In these cases, it may not be clear about how much money is required to settle the claim. Will the injured party be out of work for an extended period of time? Is the injured party a high wage earner? How much lost earnings will the injured party incur if he or she is disabled for an extended period? What will be the cost of the required medical care? Medical malpractice claims are almost exclusively about these types of issues. Sometimes the injuries are clear cut—the wrong leg was amputated or a sponge was left in an abdomen after a surgical procedure; more often, however, the cases are more subtle and complex and involve 20/20 hindsight.

---

Consider a 30-year-old male with no risk factors for cardiac disease who comes to you with symptoms of gastroesophageal reflux disease (GERD) and is experiencing recurrent chest discomfort consistent with the diagnosis. Would you work him up for cardiac disease? If you do not and he has a myocardial infarction (MI) a week later, is that malpractice?

---

Many malpractice cases involve a bad outcome or complication that results in a severe permanent injury or disability to the patient.

---

Consider a child with cerebral palsy (CP) or a patient who undergoes brain aneurysm repair that leaves the patient permanently disabled. It may not be clear that the physician was negligent in his or her care of the patient, yet a lawsuit results.

---

These types of cases are very difficult on many levels. Would a child with CP have had a better outcome if a Cesarean section (C-section) had been performed earlier? The medical issues here can be complex and murky. This connection between the alleged failure of the physician to meet the standard of care and the actual injury is known as *causation*. In malpractice cases, the law requires a *direct* connection between the physician's failure to meet the standard of care and the injury the patient suffered. For example, a surgeon may break sterile technique during a surgical procedure. This is a deviation from the standard of care; however, if the patient does not develop an infection and no injury is sustained as a result of this breach of the standard of care, there are no grounds for a malpractice action against the physician. The law will find that there is no causation or direct connection between the deviation from the standard of care and an injury to the patient. Consider a case that involves a severely handicapped child. Based on a retrospective review of the clinical picture, very experienced physicians may have different opinions on whether a C-section should have been performed earlier or if at all. The first question concerns the standard of care. Was a C-section required in this particular circumstance? The second, which is equally important, concerns causation. If there is an agreement between the experts for both the patient and the doctor that a C-section should have been performed sooner, is there medical evidence that performing the C-section earlier would have made a difference in the patient's outcome? In other words, did the delay or failure to do a C-section actually cause the CP in the infant? Experts may disagree on this point, making it difficult for a jury to decide which expert is correct. When you have a case in which the injury is significant and the expert testimony is unclear or contradictory, the sympathy value of the case often comes into the equation. These types of cases in which the injury to the patient is significant and perhaps even heartbreaking are very difficult to present to a jury of lay people who may not be able to appreciate fully the complex medical judgments involved in such a case. These cases often represent a potentially high financial exposure because jurors may not be able to separate their feelings or emotions from the medicine. Beyond the financial issues, the defense of such a case is difficult for the physician and his or her legal team because he or she is faced with an allegation that something he or she did or did not do might have resulted in a different outcome for this patient.

Now consider the most unpredictable aspect of a malpractice case: how to decide the value of pain and suffering. This is sometimes spoken about as the "lottery" aspect of a malpractice case. If you consider that the legal purpose of a lawsuit is to make the injured party "whole," how can we quantify the economic value of pain and suffering? The questions here are staggering. How would you put a dollar value on someone's pain? Is there a formula to quantify pain over time? What is the value of a minute, an hour, a day, a month, or a lifetime of pain? How can any of this be fairly quantified and expressed in a dollar amount? This aspect of cases/injuries scares defense attorneys and doctors who are defendants in malpractice suits because it often results in the multimillion-dollar verdicts that you hear or read about.

It is possible for these types of high-exposure cases that have sympathy value with jurors to exceed insurance policy limits. This is a real concern to a doctor who may have only $1 or $2 million of insurance coverage for a single claim. In order to address this, some states now have caps on pain and suffering awards, but these continue to be a controversial and contentious issue. Most plaintiffs feel that $250,000 is too low of a cap. Most doctors and medical malpractice insurers think $1 million is too high. Who is right? It is hard to know, and your perspective may depend on your circumstances. If you are the injured party, what is your pain worth?

A final component of malpractice premiums includes the cost of defending the claim. Defense costs, which are almost always paid by the medical malpractice insurer, can be exorbitant. In 2005, the Physician Insurers Association of America reported that the average cost per claim in cases in which the defendant prevailed at trial was $110,346.[4] Remember that every case, whether successful or not, incurs legal costs. The Physician Insurers Association of America (PIAA) reported that in 2005 the average expense to defend a claim was $34,182.[5]

# Why Do Patients Sue Their Physicians and Other Healthcare Providers?

Many changes have influenced the increasing number of lawsuits patients file against their physicians and other healthcare providers. Undoubtedly, medicine has made great strides in curing or curbing many previously debilitating illnesses. This is a double-edged sword that may result in some patients having unrealistic expectations about what medicine can and cannot do. For example, the almost routine nature of successful cardiac surgery and organ transplantation instills in some patients the belief that an unfavorable outcome is synonymous with physician negligence.

Plastic surgeons and other physicians who perform elective surgeries are at particular risk here. Patients who do not have a good outcome after an elective surgery are more likely to sue the doctor, especially if they have paid cash for or taken a loan to finance the procedure.

Some patients have an unrealistic expectation of a good outcome when one is not probable. Physicians should always be cautious not to "oversell" the likelihood of a good outcome with a particular diagnosis or injury.

Trauma and orthopedic surgeons are usually adept at this. Although it is always important to be optimistic with a patient so that he or she does not lose confidence in you, you must also be realistic about the patient's chances of returning to their prior state of health. If a patient will walk with a limp or have pain/arthritis secondary to the injury, he or she must understand that this is due to the injury and not a result of poor treatment.

The legal concept of informed consent is based on the patient's right to choose or refuse a treatment option. This informed consent discussion is designed to benefit both the doctor and the patient. A patient faced with options on how to treat his or her illness or condition has the right to make an informed, educated decision that is based on objective, accurate information about risks, benefits, and alternatives to the offered treatment. These discussions are always important, but they take on greater significance in malpractice cases when the options available to the patient are not clear cut. It is best to document this discussion carefully.

---

Consider a patient who has suffered a life-threatening injury, such as a crush injury in an auto accident. This patient may not have many treatment options available if he or she wants to survive. The decisions made to save a trauma patient are time sensitive and often do not allow the patient the opportunity to consult with other physicians or family members; however, these are not the types of situations in which informed consent plays a big role in malpractice cases. In these cases, a "reasonable person" rule applies. If a reasonable person faced with the same situation would have accepted the treatment to save his or her life, most cases are decided in the doctor's favor.

Now consider a patient with a diagnosis of prostate cancer, who may have several different treatment options from which to choose, each with its own advantages and disadvantages. This patient has time to consider the various treatments available and may even seek other opinions before deciding on a course of treatment. This type of case can present a more challenging question on the issue of informed consent.

---

Patients must understand the risks and potential side effects and complications that may occur with the treatment option they choose so that they are not surprised or disappointed about the outcome. Surprised or disappointed patients often become angry over time and may be more likely to sue their doctor.

---

Consider elective, quality-of-life surgeries (e.g., a patient who has a knee or hip replacement because of pain that limits his or her activity). This patient needs to understand the risks the surgery involves in order to make an informed choice about the available options, which may include doing nothing. For example, a jogger who undergoes a hip replacement will be discouraged from this form of exercise. If this patient has an unrealistic expectation about the outcome of the surgery or the risk of a complication, the informed consent discussion may play a significant role in the case.

---

Preventable adverse events are leading causes of death in the United States. In its landmark report, *To Err Is Human*, the Institute of Medicine estimated that between 44,000 and perhaps as many as 98,000 Americans die in hospitals each year as a result of medical errors.[6]

A great deal of focus exists in the media about medical errors and preventable deaths. This focus on reducing errors is valid and helpful in improving patient safety.

One death caused by a preventable error is one too many. We undoubtedly need to focus effort and resources on improving patient safety in our healthcare system. Many recommendations on how to do this go beyond the scope of this chapter; however, remember that patients are aware that there are problems in our healthcare system that lead to preventable injuries, and they are holding us accountable for these injuries by filing malpractice suits. When viewed from the patient's perspective, one can understand their anger and frustration if they have experienced a negative outcome in their care.

While watching television, especially late at night, you may see or hear commercials in which viewers are asked to call their lawyers if they have suffered an injury as a result of malpractice or negligence. How did we get to the point where patients feel that they must have an attorney to learn the "truth" about their medical care? Do patients feel that there is a code of silence about the problems in health care? No patient seeks to be injured as a way to earn a windfall of money. Much of the remainder of this book focuses on specific items that physicians can and should do to prevent lawsuits.

# Many Things Are Not in Your Control

The issues that we face in health care are complex. Even if we focus on malpractice issues exclusively, there is likely not a single solution that will resolve all of the medical malpractice issues that physicians face. Many different proposed solutions deal with various aspects of the problem. Some of the solutions being debated are political and are supported or opposed by various groups (the AMA, the plaintiffs' bar, etc.), depending on your perspective. Some are far reaching; others are not. Many ideas for reform are state specific, whereas others are national. For example, caps on pain and suffering have been implemented in several states. A 2004 analysis by Thorpe found that malpractice premiums in states with caps on awards are 17.1% lower than premiums in states without caps.[7]

Caps on awards have received significant support from many politicians, physicians, and healthcare executives; however, they should not be seen as the "magic bullet." Although they may be useful in reducing rates in the short term, they probably do not offer the ultimate long-term solution to this very complex problem, and in some states, such as New York, where rates are mandated, rates are kept artificially low to allow access and affordability so that tort reform would probably not result in a diminution of rates.

The concept of mediation panels or arbitration is attractive because this removes the lay jury from the equation. The concept of a jury of your peers is hard to attain in a medical malpractice case. Should the jury be of the patient or the doctor's peers? Can a jury of lay people really understand medical issues? Often malpractice cases become a "battle of the experts," where jurors hear conflicting testimony from medical experts and must then make decisions about very complex medical issues that they are not qualified to evaluate. Although jurors usually make a good-faith effort to decide a case fairly, often they are swayed by nonobjective issues such as sympathy for the plaintiff or the likeability of the witnesses or lawyers. Arbitration and mediation panels were supposed to allow for an objective evaluation of the case by experts who could fairly decide the medical and legal issues in the case. Typical proposals include a panel comprised of medical experts and legal experts who decide causation and compensation. The debate about this type of system often focuses on how the "independent" experts are chosen. It may be difficult for both sides to agree on this. For instance, in the state of New York, this type of system was tried in the form of malpractice panels. A "panel," which consisted of a physician, an attorney, and a judge, was assigned to review each malpractice case. The court assigned a physician and an attorney from a list of volunteers. The attorneys for the parties submitted written contentions and then made oral presentations to the panel. The panel members would then each cast a vote for liability or no liability. If the vote was not unanimous, the panel proceeding was disregarded. A unanimous finding could be presented to the jury if the case was not discontinued or settled. These panels were met with mixed reviews and ultimately were disbanded because it was felt that they slowed cases down.[8]

Other ideas to reduce costs in malpractice cases include proposals to reduce or eliminate plaintiff attorneys' contingency fees. In malpractice cases, the plaintiff attorney's fee is traditionally a percentage of the amount the patient receives (typically 30%). The benefit of this system is that it allows patients who might not be able to afford to hire a lawyer an opportunity to pursue a case without any out-of-pocket legal expenses. The legal principle is that an injured patient should not be blocked from suing someone who has injured them because they cannot afford to hire an attorney. There is a concept of fairness in this tradition that should not be discarded. However, a bias exists in this system.

Attorneys whose fees are a percentage of the awards they recover for their clients have an incentive to take cases with the potential for a large award. (One-third of a multimillion dollar award or settlement is a considerable amount of money.) In malpractice cases, this sometimes means that a patient who has suffered a catastrophic injury is an attractive case for a plaintiff's attorney, regardless of the quality of care provided to the patient. A way to restructure this incentive equitably would be to establish a flat fee with a cap to limit the fee paid to the attorneys in cases in which patients have suffered catastrophic injuries. This compromise would provide a fair incentive for compensating plaintiff's attorneys while safeguarding the patients who are injured. These types of caps and flat-fee arrangements are often resisted by plaintiff's bar for obvious reasons.

Some states have tried implementing a no-fault system similar to Workers' Comp and some automobile claims, whereby a payment is made based on the type of injury regardless of who is at fault. These plans are especially attractive for high-exposure cases, such as cases with neurologically impaired babies. The purpose of these programs was to remove some of the most expensive cases from the tort system. Thus, hopefully, if expensive neurologically injured infant cases were removed from the tort system, rates of claims and levels of awards would stabilize.[9] Therefore, the fund provides compensation to neurologically impaired infants under a "no-fault" system. The issue of how to fund these plans is dicey.

A neurological injury no-fault system has been tried in Florida and Virginia. Under these plans, physicians and hospitals pay a set amount into the fund. For example, in Florida, obstetricians pay $5,000 per year, and hospitals pay $50 per live birth into the fund. All other physicians pay

$250 per year as a condition of licensure.[9] The American College of Obstetricians and Gynecologists supports this type of initiative and also suggests including all insurers (not just medical malpractice insurers) as contributors to the fund.[10] This may be hard to sell politically. Should physicians other than obstetricians bear the cost of these types of claims? Should a neurosurgeon who may also have patients with significant neurological injuries contribute to a fund that benefits only obstetricians in terms of malpractice relief? Should insurers underwrite the cost of these funds? Does this imply that this is more of a global health issue rather than a medical malpractice issue?

One of the concerns is that a no-fault system may actually increase the number of claims because a large number of infants who otherwise would not be compensated for their injury might file claims under a no-fault system.[11] This theory is supported by studies such as the 1990 Harvard Medical Practice Study, which demonstrated that a majority of patients who are injured from negligence do not file a malpractice claim.[12]

Although supported by the American College of Obstetricians and Gynecologists (ACOG), these funds have had mixed success and do not seem to have widespread support among the general population or among legislators.[10] This may be because they are complex and hard for the average person to fully understand. For example, even the definition of how an infant is classified as neurologically impaired is complex. In Virginia, "birth-related neurological injury means injury to the brain or spinal cord of an infant caused by the deprivation of oxygen or mechanical injury occurring in the course of labor, delivery or resuscitation in the immediate post-delivery period in a hospital which renders the infant permanently nonambulatory, aphasic, incontinent, and in need of assistance in all phases of daily living. This definition shall apply to live births only."[10]

Also, should this be an expansive program that includes all neurologically impaired infants, even those who are preterm or with impairments that are the result of genetic or congenital abnormalities? This would likely make establishing such a fund cost prohibitive. An argument can also be made that those types of impairments should be funded on a more widespread basis, not as an alternative to medical malpractice premiums/payments.

In summary, most of these proposals to alter the way malpractice cases are handled would have some advantages to physicians, but they also will continue to face objections from the patients and the plaintiff attorneys' bar. There will probably not be a consensus on how best to proceed in the short term. Nonetheless, it is helpful (and probably necessary) for physicians to continue to educate themselves about these various proposals and how they would impact their practices if they were adopted. Because of its importance to your professional life and future, you should devote some time and effort to being knowledgeable about the impact of various proposals would have on your practice and become involved in lobbying for these issues.

It is also important to realize that these are political issues that will not be resolved in the short term and these issues are not in your or the insurer's direct control. Every practicing physician must have an awareness of the other steps that are in your control to prevent lawsuits in your own practice.

# The Best Lawsuit to Defend Is the One That Never Happens

This is a simple but powerful truth. If you are not sued, no lawsuit exists to defend. Avoiding a lawsuit is often possible if you try to do the right thing for your patient. Many patients will forgive an error if they have a good relationship with their physician. Maintaining effective and therapeutic relationships with your patients can go a long way in reducing your risk of being sued and increasing your satisfaction in your work. Patients can be very tuned in to recognizing how passionate and enthusiastic their physician is about the care of his or her patients. That passion and enthusiasm can build a patient's trust and confidence and can translate to better relationships with patients.

Although it is impossible to make yourself entirely lawsuit proof, you can do many things to reduce the risk of being sued. This goal is worth pursuing because after you are sued, a traumatic event has occurred that will extract a price from you even if you ultimately "win" the case. The emotional toll of being sued for malpractice is high for even those with nerves of steel. (This is discussed in Chapter 14 of this book.) The time it takes to defend a lawsuit is often significant. According to Studdert, "The average length of time between the occurrence of the injury and the closure of the claim was five years."[13] This is a very long time to live with the stress of an unresolved lawsuit on your mind. Also, an award could exceed your insurance coverage. You may face criticism in the media, if the case is media worthy, which may damage your reputation.

---

Think of the many cases that you have heard about in the media in which the sound bite paints a dreadful picture: "wrong leg amputated," "doctor operates on the wrong side of the brain," "transplant gone wrong at major university center."

---

When you hear these stories, as a physician, your reaction might be somewhat different from the general public. You may wonder how that could happen. It sounds reckless. You may think that there must be more to the story, but as you know, the full story is rarely told in sound bites or on the evening news. The lingering negative image the public derives from these types of stories is hard to overcome. For every "medical horror" story reported on the news, hundreds or thousands of patients have been treated successfully—those "ordinary" events, however, are not newsworthy and rarely receive front-page coverage.

At times, it may feel that patients have become your enemy and that you cannot reduce your risk of being sued; however, Mello and Hemenway noted that "a patient who suffers a negligent injury is more than 20 times more likely, on average, to file a claim than a patient who does not."[14]

Consider that there is no lawsuit to defend or even worry about if the patient is not injured, dissatisfied, unhappy, or angry. How do you prevent these types of adversarial outcomes with patients?

The remainder of this book focuses on the steps that an individual practitioner can take to reduce the risk of being sued for malpractice. The goal is to take as many steps as you can to *prevent* the type of injuries to patients that result in lawsuits. This book also includes suggestions to improve your communication with patients, as we know that so many lawsuits are a direct result of communication breakdowns with patients and their families. It will also give you a better understanding of how you can reduce the likelihood that a patient or family will sue you after a complication or untoward outcome.

Although things at times may look grim in the medical malpractice world, all is not lost. By retaining your passion for your patients and your work and keeping your focus on improving the things that you can by promoting positive change in your area of influence, medicine can continue to be a rewarding and satisfying profession for many years.

## REFERENCES

1. Steiger B. Survey results: doctors say morale is hurting. *The Physician Executive.* 2006;32(6):6–12.
2. American Medical Association. *Medical Liability Reform-NOW! A Compendium of Facts Supporting Medical Liability Reform and Debunking Arguments Against Reform.* Chicago, IL: American Medical Association; 2006:4. Available at: http://www.ama-assn.org/go/mlrnow, accessed October 2, 2007.
3. *Medical Malpractice Insurance: Multiple Factors Have Contributed to Increased Premium Rates.* Washington, DC: US General Accounting Office; June 2003:6. GAO-03-702.
4. Physician Insurers Association of America. *2005 Claims Trend Analysis: A Comprehensive Analysis of Medical Malpractice Cases.* Rockville, MD: PIAA; 2006:exhibit 6–v.
5. Physician Insurers Association of America. *2005 Claims Trend Analysis: A Comprehensive Analysis of Medical Malpractice Cases.* Rockville, MD: PIAA; 2006:exhibit 1–ii.

6. Kohn LT, Corrigan JM, Donaldson MS, eds. *To Err Is Human: Building a Safer Health System*. Washington, DC: National Academy Press; 1999.

7. Thorpe KE. The medical malpractice "crisis": recent trends and the impact of state tort reforms. *Health Affairs-Web Exclusive*. 2004;W4:20.

8. McKinney's Judiciary Law § 148-a Repealed. L. 1991, c. 165, § 47, eff. Oct. 1, 1991.

9. Horwitz J, Brennan TA. No-fault compensation for medical injury: a case study. *Health Affairs*. 1995;14(4):165–177.

10. The American College of Obstetricians and Gynecologists. *No-Fault Liability for Birth-Related Neurological Injury*. The American College of Obstetricians and Gynecologists; 2007. Available at: http://www.acog.org/departments/dept_notice.cfm?recno=15& bulletin=1925, accessed February 19, 2008.

11. Studdert DM, Thomas EJ, Zbar BIW, et al. Can the United States afford a "no-fault" system of compensation for medical injury? *Law and Contemporary Problems*. 1997;60(2):2–3.

12. Harvard College. *Patients, Doctors, and Lawyers: Medical Injury, Malpractice Litigation, and Patient Compensation in New York, The Report of the Harvard Medical Practice Study to the State of New York*. Harvard College;1990:6.

13. Studdert DM, Mello MM, Gawande AA, et al. Claims, errors, and compensation payments in the malpractice litigation. *N Engl J Med*. 2006;354:2026.

14. Mello MM, Hemenway D. Medical malpractice as an epidemiological problem. *Soc Sci Med*. 2004;59:39–46.

# Chapter 2

# It's Not Just About Avoiding the Lawsuit

Gerald Dolman and Marjorie O. Thomas

---

*The best interest of the patient is the only interest to be considered.*
William J. Mayo, MD (1910)

---

An obstetrician was soon to go off duty. He had tickets to attend a World Series baseball game with his family in 2 hours. He was thrilled. His patients in labor and delivery were stable, and his partner was soon to relieve him. In the midst of this calm came an urgent request for the OB resident from a head nurse down the hall. A pregnant patient had just collapsed; her obstetrician was on his way to the hospital, but this could not wait. The obstetrician who was preparing to leave shortly, immediately responded and found a woman, at 30-weeks gestation, to be hypotensive, weak, and apparently in crisis. Clearly, she may not have a good outcome and would need a crash Cesarean section. The nurse offered to call the staff obstetrician, but the obstetrician who was now attending to her declined—he would take care of this patient. Upon entering the abdomen, he encountered a significant hemorrhage. The baby, although he had very low Apgar scores, survived—his mother did not.

---

## The Fear of Litigation

Physicians carry many burdens—some related to each of their patients and the care that they need, some related to the business of a medical practice in today's reimbursement arena, and others, professional and personal. Paramount among these burdens is that, despite their diligence and best efforts, patients or their families may consider their care less than optimal and seek redress through a medical malpractice suit. This particular burden looms large because "malpractice suits often threaten the core of a physician's self-esteem."[1]

Many physicians, voicing their frustration at being sued, make statements such as, "I see every patient as a potential lawsuit." When that is the die in which a patient is cast, the interaction between physician and patient is reduced to one in which one of the physician's main goals is to escape being a party to that lawsuit that he or she sees lurking in the heart and mind of each patient. Such a mindset will undoubtedly manifest itself in unhealthy ways. Even though a lawsuit may be far from the patient's mind, the relationship that is now being developed on that premise is "fertile ground"[2] for legal action were the seed of any error or untoward outcome to fall into it. Dr. Bernard Lown, in his book *The Lost Art of Healing*, underscores this point: "Fear of litigation, when uppermost in a physician's mind, sets the stage for it."[3]

The fear that seems to be part of many physicians' daily interactions is never far from their individual and collective thinking. Physicians discuss these worries among themselves whenever and wherever the opportunity arises. Drs. Robert M. Wachter and Kaveh G. Shojania capture this pervasive sentiment well:

> Every physician knows that his or her career can be ruined with a single slip. This ever-present pressure comes to the fore when we must act in an emergency, or make judgment calls based on scanty evidence. Just when our complete concentration should be focused on the patient, we reserve a little bit for self-preservation.[4]

Quoting from a U.S. Department of Health, Education, and Welfare Report issued in 1973, Robyn Shapiro et al. include in their survey report the following statement from a physician:

> I live in an aura of fear—fear of a suit. Fear contributes to hostility and rarely contributes to constructive action.[5]

Placing both Drs. Wachter's and Shojania's and Ms. Shapiro's statements in juxtaposition, one begins to feel a sense of dismay for this state in which "patients and physicians . . . view one another not as partners in a healthcare program, but as potential adversaries."[6]

# What Can We Learn from the Data?

One could consider that the fear that physicians experience is not well founded, based on available data related to the numbers of medical malpractice suits that are brought. Referring to two prior significant studies in his report on malpractice claims in 2000, David Studdert pointed out the great discrepancy between the number of negligent medical events and the number of claims filed against physicians and other healthcare providers.[7] These studies demonstrate that only a small percentage of patients who are injured in the course of their medical care brings suit against their physicians.

As important as they are, however, these statistics do not tell the story of a physician's feelings and suffering when he or she is confronted with a medical malpractice lawsuit. It is not the probability with which the physician lives, but the daily worry that cuts to the core of who he or she is. Many related concerns flood the physician's mind, not the least of which is how an allegation of improper care will affect his or her standing in the community.[8]

In their report concerning a study carried out in New Zealand that explored the types of accountability sought by patients who are injured in the course of medical care, Marie Bismark et al. pointed to earlier work done in the United Kingdom and the United States. These studies "suggest that monetary compensation is frequently not the primary goal." Bismark et al. concluded that although compensation is the goal for some patients turned plaintiffs, particularly when they may have suffered significant economic loss as a result of iatrogenic injury, for others, the goal is not strictly monetary compensation.[9]

Many patients use legal actions to obtain information about what may have gone awry in the course of their care. That a patient would have to go to that length is a cry for physicians to consider the manner in which relationships are built with their patients and whether a foundation is being laid for a healthy therapeutic alliance. This foundation also becomes important for the disclosures and discussions, which become necessary when, to borrow a title from a notable African novelist, "things fall apart."[10]

Patients are also dissatisfied when explanations are not forthcoming, when they perceive dishonesty,[11] and certainly when they do not experience their physicians' empathy.

---

Consider, for example, a case with which we are familiar, in which a pediatric patient undergoes surgery to correct a significant skeletal abnormality. This procedure required sensory monitoring by a technician. He did not inform the surgeon for an extended period of time that the signal was lost, by which time the patient had been irreparably damaged, resulting in paraplegia. This explanation was not given to the parent. She knew only that her son was admitted to the hospital with a deformity that was to be improved through surgery and was returned to her in a condition requiring life-long, total care.

---

In the absence of any explanation from those to whom she had entrusted the care of her child, it is not difficult to see how a combination of lack of information, anger, and myriad other emotions would leave this parent feeling the need to seek the aid of an attorney.

Reliable literature points to the communication and relationship problems that exist in the practices of physicians who are sued frequently.[12,13] Patients emphasize feelings of desertion, particularly around their inability to make contact with their physicians, sometimes having to do with those who may be acting as intermediaries, for example, a nurse or a secretary, between the physician and patient.[14]

---

In another case, a patient is admitted for a laparoscopic cholecystectomy and is advised that he would be discharged after the surgeon sees him the following morning. That evening following the surgery, the nurse gave the patient a regular meal and, after some debate between the patient and the nurse, the patient ate the meal and soon vomited.

---

Although he was in some discomfort the following morning, the patient waited anxiously for the physician to arrive, hoping that he would be discharged. His mother also arrived to accompany him home. After several hours had passed, the mother contacted the physician, as the nurse did not know when he would arrive. The physician advised the mother that he was several miles away and that it had actually slipped his mind that the patient was to be seen. The patient was ultimately discharged home that evening without being seen by his surgeon. At home, the patient continued to experience pain and two days later, went to the emergency department. He was readmitted to determine the cause of his continued difficulty. The patient had to undergo additional procedures but ultimately recovered.

This patient, disappointed not only in his medical care but also in the demeanor of his surgeon, brought a suit against him. This disappointment is certainly understandable. When errors are made or a patient's course does not proceed as expected, more, not less, communication is required between physician and patient. Unfortunately, in many cases, physicians avoid "confrontation" with patients at the very point at which some of the patients' anger could be diffused through better communication.

Dr. Michael Woods, in his book *Healing Words*, describes the case of a 24-year-old patient who sues him. Dr. Woods had planned a laparoscopic appendectomy for this patient; the surgery was converted to an open procedure after it was discovered that a participating resident's umbilical incision had injured an artery. Dr. Woods confesses to being "floored" by the reason the patient offered for suing him. "I sued because he acted like what happened to me was no big deal. One time, when I saw him in the office after this happened, he actually put his feet up on the desk while we talked. He just didn't care." Dr. Woods came to the following realization after hearing this testimony from the patient:

> It wasn't the injury and outcome that led to that miserable day in court—it was her perception that I didn't care. My actions had communicated apathy.[15]

Apparently, the quality of care is not the basis on which most patients make the decision to sue. Rather, it is "the combination of a bad outcome and patient dissatisfaction [that] is a recipe for litigation."[16] Irwin Press quotes an unnamed source as having said, "Incidents don't sue—patients do."[17] By identifying what moves a person from patient to plaintiff, from physician to attorney, we may be able to identify areas where improvement is necessary and ways in which they can be made.

## Let Us Consider the Causes

Whether one gives credence to the numbers offered in the various studies and reports, most recently those published by the Institute of Medicine,[18] it is indisputable that preventable errors occur in the course of providing care to patients and also that there are unplanned outcomes that render patients incapable of returning to the lives they once knew. Unfortunately, after these events, patients are sometimes left without much information and may feel that they can only learn the "truth" if they find an advocate, usually an attorney.[19] Richard Boothman, in his testimony before the U.S. Senate Committee, offered that such a perceived need on the patient's part raises a "difficult question," which he suggests physicians should consider: "Why would my patient feel the need for an advocate?"[20]

The economic pressures that physicians feel, and which precipitate unmanageable workload increases, leave the physician very little time to perform clinical tasks, communicate effectively with the patient, and engage in thinking that results in good medical care. Dr. Jerome Groopman, in his recent book, captures this concern in this dictum: "Haste makes cognitive errors."[21] Often these errors form the basis on which the allegations of the medical malpractice case are built. In his book, Dr. Lown says, "The doctor, constrained by the clock, may have only twenty minutes for a visit."[22] Sadly, in our own work, we encounter many physicians for whom 20 minutes would be a luxury.

In our discussions with these physicians, often in the context of malpractice cases against them, the brevity of office visits clearly negatively influences the patients' care and experience with the physician and may have influenced the patients' decision to sue.

Our observations and communications with a large number of physicians and medical practices in connection with thousands of lawsuits lead us to conclude that most medical malpractice lawsuits are not merely about the medical care. Rather, they are about the relationship of physician and patient and, in some instances, the others who are perceived to be part of the physician's team. We are, of course, not singular in this point of view, which is solidly supported by the work of many.[12–14,23,24] In their conclusion to a study examining whether the severity of clinical outcome made a suit more likely and whether the nature of the physician's relationship with the patient influences those claims, Dr. Moore et al. stated that "although a more serious medical outcome may not make patients more inclined to file a claim against a physician, a less severe outcome may not be sufficient to prevent a claim when the doctor–patient relationship is poor."[25]

Dr. Gerald Hickson and his colleagues attributed patients' dissatisfaction, among other factors, to their perception that their physicians were unavailable and lacked adequate time to spend with their patients. Dr. Hickson and colleagues concluded that "the frequency with which physicians are sued is related in part to patients' satisfaction with interpersonal aspects of medical care."[26] Dr. Edward Hsia, in his letter to the editor of *The Lancet* about Dr. Charles Vincent's study[11] said, "The true motives for litigation are unhappiness and anger; probably much less commonly vengeance and greed."[27]

# Defensive Practices: Do They Help or Hurt?

In an effort at self-protection, many physicians, some even unwittingly, begin to incorporate defensive strategies in the way that they treat their patients. The United States Office of Technology Assessment in its report on *Defensive Medicine and Malpractice* includes in its definition of defensive medicine "tests, procedures, or visits" that are carried out "primarily (but not necessarily solely) to reduce [their] exposure to malpractice liability."[28]

This consideration is troubling from a number of perspectives, including a patient's. Clearly, defensive medicine means that a patient will be subjected to testing that is not medically indicated but that is being performed essentially because the physician believes that the test will improve his defense if the patient's outcome is not satisfactory and a suit is filed. Considering all that undergoing a test implies, from the time and effort one must expend, the risks it poses, particularly if it is invasive, to say nothing of the anxiety that medical investigation produces in most patients, this is a troubling thought.

Several studies point to the widespread nature of these practices among physicians.[24,28] From one such study, David Studdert et al. reported that of their over 800 physician participants, 92% "reported ordering tests unnecessarily and more than 60% of physicians in all specialties except neurosurgery reported performing or requesting invasive diagnostic procedures." The authors pointed to the detrimental effect of defensive medicine on the quality of care and the relationship between physician and patient. They concluded that "the most frequent form of defensive medicine, ordering costly imaging studies, seems merely wasteful, but other defensive behaviors may reduce access to care and even pose risks of physical harm."[29] Because one test often leads to others, the patient is exposed to a greater possibility that their safety will be compromised.[30] The plethora of "defensive" tests that may be ordered also causes other problems where appropriate systems are not in place to track the receipt of pending reports. Once a test is ordered, the physician is responsible to make sure that the results are received, noted in the patient's medical record, and discussed with the patient. If the results are not received, the physician must be aware of this missing data. This "closing of the loop" necessitates that tracking systems are established in the physician's practice.

This notion of defensive medicine is also troubling when one considers the profession of medicine and the sacrifice of its members, in study and practice, for the art and the science of healing. It is disheartening that the day has dawned when a physician considers it necessary or acceptable to subject a patient to a possibly unnecessary procedure or test in order to defend against possible allegations of inadequate care. Dr. Hsia wisely said in his previously described letter to the editor, "A physician who . . . insists on too many self-protecting diagnostic or therapeutic precautions may encourage the very thing he or she is trying to avoid."[27]

The tabulated costs of these defensive practices do not account for the economic price exacted by the overordering of tests and procedures that have dubious medical value. Estimates vary greatly but are enormous by any measure.

# What Are Some Constructive Responses?

In most discussions regarding medical malpractice, the question of tort reform and its value in addressing certain obstacles physicians face are part of the debate. Many opinions exist regarding tort reforms. Emerging among them is the idea that there is much more that can be accomplished in evaluating what the data show as the causes for medical malpractice suits and addressing those reasons rather than putting all of our "eggs" into the tort reform "basket."

In his testimony before the Senate Committee, Dr. Studdert asserted, "Conventional tort reforms such as damages caps . . . will not make health care safer, nor will they grapple seriously with the medical liability system's key problems."[31] Speaking before the same group, Dr. William Sage recommended that malpractice reform should start with patient safety and how healthcare providers respond where injuries occur in the course of care—a greater focus on "the bedside, and less on the courtroom."[32] Many physicians and their professional societies focus on tort reform (caps on damages) as a means of reducing the physician's insurance costs in the face of diminishing reimbursement rates. Although "caps" may afford a quick fix for premium rates, improvements in patient safety and efforts to reduce the numbers of medical errors offer long-term benefits to both physicians and their patients.

Mr. Boothman, also testifying before the Senate Committee, endorsed the patient safety approach. He offered that improved patient safety and communication would have a far more beneficial effect on the malpractice problem than the defensive approach. He described how such an approach has had a salutary effect on their experience at the University of Michigan. He referred to this as focusing on "the primary causes for most patient litigation: a failure to be accountable when warranted and a reluctance to communicate." As part of this approach, the patient safety leaders at Michigan have developed a yardstick against which they measure patient complaints. The following are some of the questions that they pose to themselves:

- Why did this patient complain?
- Could we have done better?
- How can we avoid a future occurrence?
- Are there lessons to be learned?

Anyone involved in patient care should consider these self-reflective questions. We offer as an addition to this list the following question: Is this the health care experience I would want for myself or a loved one?

The result of this changed process at the University of Michigan over a four-year period was a 60% reduction in the number of new cases brought against the institution. Other benchmarks also showed significant improvement.[33]

"True reform," said Dr. William Sage, must include in its goals "to reduce the need for litigation by linking patient safety to risk management" and "communicating effectively with patients."[34] In a later article, Dr. Sage advocated for the early education of medical students and residents in identifying medical errors and caring for patients so affected.[8] That training must also include the prevention of errors primarily through educating aspiring and young physicians in ways to improve communication with patients, families, and others who are part of the healthcare team. "Reforms that fail to harness the intellect and energies of physicians to address the largest problem— patient injury—miss a central cause of claims as well as a central issue for better health care."[35]

Many physicians who are sued tell us that the cases against them are "frivolous," meaning that they have done nothing wrong in the care of the patient, that is, there was no malpractice. This perception affects their interactions with other patients; nevertheless, in almost all of the suits, the patient suffered an injury of some sort and often does not know why. Even efforts to reduce these "frivolous" suits may not have the effect on claims experience that physicians would desire. In a recent study, Studdert et al. found that most of the money paid for malpractice cases is paid for claims in which errors have occurred.[19]

# What Then?

If a physician's work is not simply about avoiding a lawsuit, then what does it concern? It is about the physician honoring the responsibility for helping the patient care for what is very likely one of his or her most prized possessions: his or her body and ultimately his or her life. Honoring that responsibility includes the many areas of a relationship that the physician and patient will have to forge together. The evidence demonstrates that claims do not appear to occur randomly but instead show a strong correlation to communication and rapport with patients.[12] Where then should we direct our attention?

Dr. Steven Cole offers some help in categorizing the failures that lead to malpractice litigation. They are: "inadequate understanding of the patient's problems; poor rapport with the patient or family; inadequate education of the patient or family."[36] The physician and patient must become partners in patient safety. "Patients can play an active part in preventing mistakes and ensuring their own safety if given the correct information and the right tools for the job."[37] These tools are developed and honed through communication and patient education.

When this kind of collaboration is functioning, the groundwork is laid for preventing and addressing those problems that may arise in the course of care. Discussions, if those problems arise, take place in an arena of trust between physician and patient, increasing the likelihood that the patient will be more understanding of the problem that has developed.[38]

Efforts made in building strong teams, including members of the physician's staff in an office practice, help to create strong relationships with patients. A stable, well-trained staff speaks volumes to patients. The consistency of dealing with the staff over an extended period indicates to patients that the physician is one with whom the staff also has good experience. This can be a confidence builder.

Dr. Hickson et al., in another study, examined unsolicited patient complaints to identify physicians at high and low risk for malpractice suits. They found that "physicians' complaint generation was positively associated with risk management outcomes, ranging from file openings to multiple lawsuits."[39] Drawing on some of his earlier work and the work of others, Dr. Hickson observed that "risk appears related to patients' dissatisfaction with their physicians' ability to establish rapport, provide access, administer care and treatment consistent with expectations, and communicate effectively."[40] The process of understanding the patient's perspective must begin long before the patient has any reason or desire to visit an attorney and consider bringing a lawsuit.

"Healing," Dr. Lown said, "begins with listening to the patient."[41] To be effective, listening cannot be "just an exercise in customer relations."[42] The efforts a physician and others involved in patient safety expend must come from a place that is not simply about protecting the physician, the hospital, or the insurer against a lawsuit, but must genuinely emanate from a desire to prevent injury and the harm and suffering that attend the patient who is injured, while he or she is in the hands of the medical profession. The introduction of a method to help identify the errant laboratory or radiology report, the procedure that ensures that the covering doctor knows enough about the patient's care to assume that care, ought not be put in place and followed to make sure the doctor is not served with the dreaded summons announcing his new role as "defendant."[43] Rather, such measures are to be adopted to ensure that that patient, who has entrusted his or her care to a physician, receives the best care that he or she is able to provide. That care, per force, must include ensuring that the administrative infrastructure, which supports the clinical care, is put and kept in place.

In our years of interactions with physicians, we have encountered many physicians who take pains to provide excellent care for their patients and who recognize the importance of and, therefore, integrate into that care, measures that may seem minor and insignificant to others, but show their caring to their patients. Consider, for example, a gastroenterologist, who having received test results that he knew his patient was restless about, took time in the very late evening to call her. He said, "I didn't want you to have to spend an unnecessary minute worrying about this." The thinking and ideas of physicians such as these must be included in the training and discussions around patient safety and improved physician–patient relations. "Among other things, it would be enlightening to examine the zero-complaint physicians as intensively as the high-complaint physicians. It never hurts to figure out what people are doing *right*."[44]

In their well-reasoned piece, Dr. Stephen Schoenbaum and his co-author Mr. Randall Bovbjerg issue a clarion call to physicians to become more involved in the prevention of injuries to patients.[35] Their assertions about the absolute necessity for physician involvement in patient safety efforts are borne out in our experience in attempting to move large medical practices into the development of risk management and patient safety initiatives. Steps to address medical malpractice litigation must take into consideration its root cause, patient injury (or, in some cases, the perception of injury), and steps to prevent patient injury must be viewed as a priority.

In his 1910 address to the Rush Medical College's graduating class, Dr. William J. Mayo is reported to have said:

> The best interest of the patient is the only interest to be considered, and in order that the sick may have the benefit of advancing knowledge, union of forces is necessary. . . . It has become necessary to develop medicine as a cooperative science; the clinician, the specialist, and the laboratory workers uniting for the good of the patient, each assisting in elucidation of the problem at hand, and each dependent on the other for support.[45]

Much has changed in the almost hundred years since Dr. Mayo issued this challenge to a group of newly minted physicians. What has not changed, however, is the need for members of this noble profession to always consider the best interests of their patients and to work with others on their team cooperatively to accomplish what is in the best interest of their patients.

## REFERENCES

1. Anderson RE. Billions for defense. *Arch Intern Med.* 1999;159:2400.
2. Press I. The predisposition to file claims: the patient's perspective. *Law, Medicine & Ethics (Harvard Law Library).* 1984;12(2):53–62.
3. Lown B. *Lost Art of Healing.* Boston, MA, and New York, NY: Houghton Mifflin Company; 1996:150.
4. Wachter RM, Shojania KG. *Internal Bleeding: The Truth Behind America's Terrifying Epidemic of Medical Mistakes.* 1st ed. New York, NY: Rugged Land LLC; 2004:301.
5. Shapiro RS, Simpson DE, Lawrence SL, Talsky AM, Sobocinski KA, Schiedermayer DL. A survey of sued and nonsued physicians and suing patients. *Arch Intern Med.* 1989;149:2190.

6. Shapiro RS, Simpson DE, Lawrence SL, Talsky AM, Sobocinski KA, Schiedermayer DL. A survey of sued and nonsued physicians and suing patients. *Arch Intern Med* 1989;149:2196.

7. Studdert D, Thomas EJ, Burstin HR, Zbar BIW, Orav EJ, Brennan TA. Negligent care and malpractice claiming behavior in Utah and Colorado. *Med Care.* 2000;38(3):250–260.

8. Sage WM. Malpractice liability, patient safety, and the personification of medical injury: opportunities for academic medicine. *Acad Med.* 2006;81(9):823–826.

9. Bismark M, Dauer E, Paterson R, Studdert D. Accountability sought by patients following adverse events from medical care: the New Zealand experience. *Can Med Assoc J.* 2006;175(8):889–894.

10. Achebe C. *Things Fall Apart.* New York, NY: Anchor Books; 1994.

11. Vincent C, Young M, Phillips A. Why do people sue doctors? A study of patients and relatives taking legal action. *Lancet.* 1994;343:1609–1613.

12. Hickson G, Clayton EW, Entman SS, et al. Obstetricians' prior malpractice experience and patients' satisfaction with care. *JAMA.* 1994;272(20):1583–1587.

13. Levinson W, Roter DL, Mulooly JP, Dull V, Frankel R. Physician–patient communication. *JAMA.* 1997;277(7):553–559.

14. Beckman HB, Markakis KM, Suchman AL, Frankel RM. The doctor–patient relationship and malpractice. *Arch Intern Med.* 1994;154:1365–1370.

15. Woods MS. *Healing Words.* 2nd ed. Oak Park, IL: Doctors in Touch; 2004:9.

16. Levinson W, Roter DL, Mulooly JP, Dull V, Frankel R. Physician–patient communication. *JAMA.* 1997;277(7):553.

17. Press I. Notre Dame, IN. The predisposition to file claims: the patient's perspective. *Law, Medicine & Ethics (Harvard Law Library).* 1984;12(2):61.

18. Kohn LT, Corrigan JM, Donaldson MS, eds. Institute of Medicine. *To Err Is Human: Building a Better Health Care System.* Washington, DC: National Academics Press; 1999.

19. Studdert DM, Mello MM, Gawande AA. Claims, errors, and compensation payments in medical malpractice litigation. *N Engl J Med.* 2006;354:2024–2033.

20. *Medical Liability: New Ideas for Making the System Work Better for Patients, 2006: Hearings Before the Senate Committee on Health, Education, Labor, and Pensions.* Testimony of Richard Boothman, chief risk officer, University of Michigan Health System. Washington, DC: Committee on Health, Education, Labor, and Pensions, 2006:7.

21. Groopman J. *How Doctors Think.* Boston, MA: Houghton Mifflin Company; 2007:88.

22. Lown B. *Lost Art of Healing.* Boston, MA, and New York, NY: Houghton Mifflin Company; 1996:140.

23. Hickson GB, Wright Clayton E, Githens PB, Sloan FA. Factors that prompted families to file medical malpractice claims following perinatal injuries. *JAMA.* 1992;267(10):1359–1363.

24. Shapiro RS, Simpson DE, Lawrence SL, Talsky AM, Sobocinski KA, Schiedermayer DL. A survey of sued and nonsued physicians and suing patients. *Arch Intern Med* 1989;149:2190–2196.

25. Moore PJ, Adler NE, Robertson PA. Medical malpractice: the effect of doctor–patient relations on medical patient perceptions and malpractice intentions. *West J Med.* 2000;173:249.

26. Hickson G, Clayton EW, Entman SS, et al. Obstetricians' prior malpractice experience and patients' satisfaction with care. *JAMA.* 1994;272(20):1586.

27. Hsia YE. Why patients do not sue doctors [letter]. *Lancet.* 1994;344:480.
28. Office of Technology Assessment, Congress of the United States. *Defensive Medicine and Medical Malpractice.* Congress of the United States; 1994. OTA-H-602.
29. Studdert DM, Mello MM, Sage WM, et al. Defensive medicine among high-risk specialist physicians in a volatile malpractice environment. *JAMA.* 2005; 293(21):2617.
30. Lown B. *Lost Art of Healing.* Boston, MA, and New York, NY: Houghton Mifflin Company; 1996.
31. *Medical Liability: New Ideas for Making the System Work Better for Patients, 2006: Hearings Before the Senate Committee on Health, Education, Labor, and Pensions.* Testimony of David M. Studdert, LLB, ScD, MPH, associate professor of law & public health, Harvard School of Public Health. Washington, DC: Committee on Health, Education, 2006:2.
32. *Medical Liability: New Ideas for Making the System Work Better for Patients, 2006: Hearings Before the Senate Committee on Health, Education, Labor, and Pensions.* Testimony of William M. Sage, MD, JD, professor, Columbia Law School. Washington, DC: Committee on Health, Education, Labor, and Pensions, 2006.
33. *Medical Liability: New Ideas for Making the System Work Better for Patients, 2006: Hearings Before the Senate Committee on Health, Education, Labor, and Pensions,* Testimony of Richard Boothman, chief risk officer, University of Michigan Health System. Washington, DC: Committee on Health, Education, Labor, and Pensions, 2006.
34. Sage WM. Medical liability and patient safety. *Health Affairs.* 2003;22(4):34.
35. Schoenbaum SC, Bovbjerg RR. Malpractice reform must include steps to prevent medical injury. *Ann Intern Med.* 2004;140(1):51.
36. Cole SA. Reducing malpractice risk through more effective communication. *Am J Manage Care.* 1997;3(4):650.
37. Mattison J. The patient's role in safety: a physician's perspective. In: Spath PL, ed. *Partnering with Patients to Reduce Medical Errors.* Chicago, IL: Health Forum, Inc; 2004:37.
38. Moore PJ, Adler NE, Robertson PA. Medical malpractice: the effect of doctor–patient relations on medical patient perceptions and malpractice intentions. *West J Med.* 2000;173(4):244–250.
39. Hickson GB, Federspiel CF, Pichert JW, Miller CS, Gauld-Jaeger J, Bost P. Patient complaints and malpractice risk. *JAMA.* 2002;287(22):2955.
40. Hickson GB, Federspiel CF, Pichert JW, Miller CS, Gauld-Jaeger J, Bost P. Patient complaints and malpractice risk. *JAMA.* 2002;287(22):2951.
41. Lown B. *Lost Art of Healing.* Boston, MA, and New York, NY: Houghton Mifflin Company; 1996:156.
42. Vincent C, Young M, Phillips A. Why do people sue doctors? A study of patients and relatives taking legal action. *The Lancet.* 1994;343:1613.
43. Charles SC, Kennedy E. *Defendant: A Psychiatrist on Trial for Medical Malpractice.* New York, NY: The Free Press; 1985.
44. Sage WM. Putting the patient in patient safety. *JAMA.* 2007;287(22):3005.
45. The best interest of the patient. Mayo Clinic. Available at: http://mayoclinic.org/tradition-heritage/best-interest-patient.html, accessed August 13, 2007.

# Chapter 3

# Professional Responsibility

Howard D. Kolodny and Marjorie O. Thomas

---

*Medicine is not a trade to be learned but a profession to be entered.*
Francis W. Peabody, MD (1927)

---

The literature concerning physician responsibility is sizable; however, it is largely limited to the experience of physicians working in institutions. In this chapter, we broaden that scope to include concerns related to physician responsibility that we have reviewed in malpractice cases involving physicians in private practice.

One who performs one's duty with dependability and accountability is responsible, according to the *Oxford Dictionary*. Although this broad definition is correct, it lacks the specificity that describes the physician in the physician–patient relationship. The relationship between a physician and his or her patient is much more than the simple, technical practice of medicine. Consider the following case:

---

The patient, a 74-year-old woman, reportedly ate a heavy meal and shortly thereafter began to experience chest pain and epigastric discomfort. She called her physician who instructed her to go to the emergency department for evaluation. The patient arrived at the emergency department at 8:30 p.m. and reported the chest pain to the triage nurse. She also told the nurse that she was to be seen by her primary care physician. The emergency physician performed a physical examination, ordered laboratory studies, and documented the history and physical examination.

---

When the primary care physician arrived, the laboratory values were not yet available; however, she located the EKG in the patient's chart and interpreted it as demonstrating "no changes." Also, the patient was asymptomatic. Satisfied with these findings and without seeing any of the laboratory studies, the primary care physician discharged the patient and instructed her to come to her office the following morning. The physician did not realize that the EKG she had read was not her patient's. It had been mistakenly placed in the chart.

The primary care physician spoke with the nurse who was taking care of the patient and left the hospital without writing any notes in the patient's chart. The emergency physician learned from the nurse that the primary care physician had examined and discharged the patient. The emergency physician expressed relief that that responsibility had been taken care of and did not review the EKG, chest X-ray, or laboratory studies.

---

This patient felt well cared for. She spoke to her physician, who assured her she would meet her in the emergency department and did so, late in the evening. The doctor wanted to personally take care of her long-standing patient. After her arrival in the emergency department, the primary care physician had no communication with the emergency department physician. Among other concerns, this absence of communication produced no clear handoff of this patient from one physician to the other, resulting in a lack of clarity between the physicians about who was responsible for this patient's care. The primary care physician made the decision to discharge the patient without benefit of the results of all of the pending laboratory data and interpreted, in error, another patient's normal EKG for this patient. At the end of that encounter, the physician left no record of her examination, her communication with the patient, or her decision regarding the patient's discharge and follow-up care.

It was a busy night in the emergency department. The emergency physician was relieved that the primary care physician had taken care of the patient and assumed responsibility for the patient's evaluation and discharge. He too fell far short in his understanding of his responsibility of their mutual patient and the management of her care. The emergency physician had ordered tests for this patient. The ordering of the tests obligated him to obtain the results. The patient came to the emergency department; he was the physician who was ultimately responsible for her care, and nothing short of direct communication with the primary care physician concerning this patient, with documentation to support this transfer of responsibility, was acceptable.

Later review showed that the cardiac enzymes were elevated and that the patient's correct EKG showed ischemia. The EKG reports and the reports of the other studies were forwarded by mail to the primary care physician's office. There is no indication in the office chart of the primary care doctor's review of these reports or of any attempt to contact the patient.

The significance of the EKG reading and the laboratory data required the emergency physician to call the primary care physician, as she was the physician who was now responsible for the patient's continuing care. When the primary care physician finally received the reports from the patient's emergency visit, her office procedure did not ensure that the physician reviewed these reports before their being filed in the patient's chart.

The patient continued to experience periodic chest discomfort and returned to the emergency department several days later, complaining of difficulty breathing and sweating profusely. Her condition rapidly deteriorated, and a cardiac arrest code was called. Despite all efforts, the patient was pronounced dead within 60 minutes of her arrival.

What we observe with both of these physicians is that although they each wanted to do what was best for this patient, the seemingly minor skimping on their responsibility here and there contributed to a poor outcome for the patient. Between the physicians, there was confusion about the lines of responsibility that left neither of them taking full charge of her care. Who was in charge of this patient's care: her primary care physician who came to the emergency department to attend to her or the emergency physician who is ultimately responsible for each patient admitted to his department? Did the emergency physician relinquish that responsibility without verifying with the primary care physician that he was handing off the patient to her? Multiple points in this patient's care showed that, with a more thorough understanding of physician responsibility, the physicians could have altered their patient's course.

# The Formation of the Responsible Physician

Referring to the educational and religious literature, Dr. Thomas Inui defined *formation* as a "process by which an individual *becomes* . . . the person who can successfully serve a calling—in the case of medicine to care for those with illness."[1] Another educator, Dr. Katharine Treadway, emphasized the character of the individual. She wrote that "in the practice of medicine, the person you are is as important as what you know."[2]

Students entering medical school are adults who have already developed a whole host of attitudes and varying levels of responsibility. Admissions committees work diligently to select the most appropriate candidates, with grades, MCAT scores, carefully tuned résumés, as well as interviews playing a significant role in a student's ability to gain admission. Many factors, however, which are important in the making of a physician, cannot be completely evaluated by the admissions process. Regarding this area of concern, Dr. Neeli Bendapudi and co-authors suggest that "a profile of ideal physician behaviors could serve as a training platform, an assessment model for healthcare professionals, a prototype for educator role-modeling skills, and even an assessment tool for admission to medical school."[3]

In the past, medical students received their white coats in a ceremony during the clinical years of medical school. In more recent years, this rite of passage has been accelerated to the first year of medical school. This begins the period in which medical students are taught communication skills, techniques in gathering information, details concerning healthcare services, and many other lessons that constitute the fundamentals of their education. All of this information is vital to the practice of medicine, yet the basic behavior and morals of that aspiring physician have already been patterned before entering medical training. Usually the students with the best academic, moral, and ethical qualities will perform best in their medical careers. Sadly, Dr. Inui reported this: "Many observers of the 'natural history' of altruism, social-mindedness, interest in the psychosocial issues embedded in all illness, and the host of strongly other-directed qualities of the maturing medical student, however, suggest that these attributes *decline* during undergraduate medical education."[4]

The Accreditation Council for Graduate Medical Education stated this as its goal: "patient care that is compassionate, appropriate, and effective."[5] Physicians responsible for teaching those who wish to join the ranks of the medical profession must not only instruct their students in these behaviors, but also demonstrate them in their own care of patients. The physician author of this chapter recalls a case from his fourth year of postgraduate training, in which one of the most deeply ingrained lessons of his training was imparted without much in the way of words, but in the *caring* of a senior physician for his patient.

---

The hospital had a homecare service staffed by family physicians and where residents served a rotation. As one such resident, he was asked to make a house call to a patient of a family physician. The young doctor found the patient to be very ill, suffering from a serious cardiac problem requiring highly specialized care, which was not available in her community. This patient's life was complicated by the fact that she lived alone and had no family. Her family physician arranged for her admission to a specific university hospital, and as the patient had no one to accompany her to the hospital, he canceled office hours, went to the patient's home, and drove her to the hospital. The physician remained with his patient overnight. In the morning, after he was able to speak with the surgeon who would be assuming the patient's care, this noble physician returned home. He spoke with the patient almost daily during her hospitalization and, when she was ready for discharge, arranged for her transportation home.

---

In contrast to the opinion of several of his colleagues, this physician held that he had done nothing more than perform what he believed was his duty to his patient.

Biomedical knowledge alone will not suffice in caring for patients. Dr. Treadway describes that in her training of young physicians she uses stories of patient care ("vaccines") to help them appreciate the patient's perspective. She says, "I hope these vaccinations will remind them during the long nights ahead that there is always a person attached to the disease and that giving comfort is one of their fundamental tasks."[6]

Graduating medical students have been taught a language that enables them to communicate with other physicians; they have also attended lectures about ethics, behavior, attitude, and responsibility to the patient. This information must now be applied to the patients in their care. As new resident physicians, they will be under great time constraints and pressure, yet this does not alter their responsibility to each patient. Their mentors will teach these principles to the inexperienced physicians, mostly by example. This teaching by example is variously referred to as the *informal curriculum*[7] or the *hidden curriculum*.[8] Dr. Inui defines this as "the students' exposure to what we *actually* do in our day-to-day work with patients and one another—not what we say *should* be done when we stand behind podiums in lecture halls." Referring to the work of others on this subject, Dr. Inui concludes that teaching by example "constitutes the most powerful influence on students' understanding of professionalism in medicine."[9]

The physician author of this chapter recalls another case from his residency that has helped to guide his practice of medicine for an entire career.

---

An unconscious middle-aged woman was admitted to his service. The patient was hypotensive, cool to the touch, and deteriorating rapidly. He notified his attending, who responded immediately. The attending's physical examination did not add much information to what was an increasingly bleak scenario. He demanded that his resident summon the patient's family immediately so that he might obtain a history. First to arrive was her 30-year-old daughter, who gave a history of a severe upper respiratory infection earlier that week; it had been treated with antibiotics. She related that her mother had developed diarrhea and then became very ill. The attending then inquired concerning the family history and learned that the patient's daughter had been adopted. He immediately theorized that the patient was infertile as a result of a pituitary tumor and was suffering from acute adrenal insufficiency that had been precipitated by her recent illness. He began treatment with steroids and saline. Emergency skull films demonstrated a large pituitary tumor. The treatment was begun, and the radiographic studies were performed within 1 hour. The patient survived.

---

What had this physician taught by example? Several unforgettable lessons have stood the test of time: Follow the classic pattern of history, physical, and differential diagnosis; act quickly to obtain information; and waste no time in providing life-saving treatment.

The physician's responsibility goes beyond earning a medical license in recognition of the completion of a prescribed course of study and training. Its scope is described in a number of documents, which call on the physician to be competent, compassionate, honest, and respectful of the rights of patients, colleagues, and others on the healthcare team and to be committed to professional responsibility.[5,10,11] Unfortunately, knowing what is right can be significantly different from doing what is right. In writing about their work in teaching professionalism at the Indiana University School of Medicine and also drawing on the work of Dr. Inui, Dr. Anthony Suchman and his colleagues offer that "one of the most consequential and enduring aspects of learning to be a doctor is the formation of one's professional identity—the development of a set of personal beliefs, values and role expectations that guide and inform virtually all subsequent behavior."[12]

Medical students and residents cannot learn everything before entering into the practice of medicine. They will experience a markedly different environment after they leave the protected academic setting. Hopefully, the resident has learned most of his or her lessons well; those that have not been well-learned will endanger patients, decrease efficiency, and make it more difficult to implement the lessons learned on the journey to becoming a responsible physician.

The attending physician who skillfully made the pituitary tumor diagnosis also served as a mentor to the physician author of this chapter during his residency training. This teacher and mentor demanded much of his students. His aspiration was to help shape them into the only kind of physician that he believed was worthy of the title of physician: those who were considerate of their patients and compassionate in their dealings with them. He instilled in his students that nothing should be left to chance, and therefore, every aspect of their work required their diligent management and follow-up. His parting advice to his student was to remember a word that he, the teacher, had formulated, to describe the demeanor that physicians should have: *humbility*. His only explanation was that this word was a contraction of two others.

# Out of the Cocoon

The resident completes his or her training and becomes an attending; the institutional support structures are gone. He or she is often alone and fully responsible for his or her clinical decisions. The care of his or her patients will include others outside of his or her own practice. His or her patients will require laboratory work or consultations with other physicians. It is crucial that the physician develops strong professional relationships with facilities, such as laboratories, where his or her patients will have testing performed as well as with other physicians and practices. He or she will be relying on these professionals and entities as team members in the care of his or her patients, and the strength of those relationships will affect the care his or her patients receive. Without these alliances, how will a physician know that the care his or her patient will receive from a consulting physician measures up to what he or she believes is best for the patient? How will he or she understand what his or her patient's experience will be like when the patient is seen in that other practice? To build and nurture these relationships is to help ensure, for example, that a consulting physician will, even before he or she is able to prepare the written report, pick up the phone and call the referring physician when he or she believes that communication is important to the care of the patient. Through these associations, physicians strengthen their own medical knowledge, and through this direct communication, they are even better prepared to carry out the recommendations made by their consultants.

The physician's responsibility for the review of consultation and laboratory and radiology reports received in his or her office is significant. The receipt and review of these reports are usually followed by the need to contact the anxiously waiting patient with the findings and a plan for follow-up. Documentation of all of these steps is important. Then there is the sometimes overlooked responsibility of knowing whether a report for a test or consultation has been received in the time that the physician would have expected.[13] Ensuring timely receipt of these reports requires that the physician establish a system in which his or her staff is trained to help him or her to identify when reports have not been received. In some cases, this may point to nonadherence on the part of the patient; follow-up with the patient is now essential.

Physicians sometimes bristle at the notion that they are responsible for the monitoring of the receipt of these reports, to say nothing of the added responsibility of tracking down a patient who may have been noncompliant with a request for a study or consultation. The necessity for a system in the physician's practice to help head off the problems that arise when a physician is not aware that he or she has not received reports of studies and consultations and, therefore, is not aware that the evaluation of his or her patient is incomplete, is addressed in a separate chapter of this book (see Chapter 7).

Many times, an attempt to understand the reasons behind a patient's failure to comply will lead the physician to consider the patient's financial and social setting, which may require the modification of treatment plans[14] or, in some cases, the physician's advocacy with a specialist, pharmaceutical company, or other agency to ensure the patient's care. Being a responsible physician often means going the extra mile for the benefit of the patient.

The physician entering practice will also find that a significant amount of time is spent in telephone contact with patients and pharmacies over the renewal of prescriptions. Even more time may be required to help patients navigate the troubled waters of their insurance companies. The help that a patient could need may require providing documentation (e.g., so that the patient can obain a wheelchair or so that an important diagnostic study or procedure can be performed in a timely manner). Without appropriate protocols in place, any of these communications have the potential for untoward result.

---

A 45-year-old female complained of sleeping poorly. Her physician prescribed 50 mg of Trazadone to be taken nightly. The patient called the office for a renewal of the prescription and spoke with a member of the staff, who recalls that she consulted with the doctor to obtain his approval to renew the patient's "sleeping medication." The staff member called in the prescription to the pharmacist; however, no entry was made in the patient's chart. The patient was given 50 mg of Prednisone rather than Trazadone, and after taking the new medication for several months, she developed florid iatrogenic Cushing's syndrome.

Each person involved in this scenario was convinced that he or she had delivered the information correctly. Those of us who have played the childhood game "telephone" know how messages change in transmission, whether in a playground game or in a medical office.

This patient's change in medication and the resulting toxicity took the physician completely by surprise; however, from the staff person's perspective, not having been trained or advised differently, she may have seen taking care of this request as one more thing she thought she could do to ease the physician's burden on a busy day. Perhaps he had permitted her to call in prescriptions that he approved in the past, and she broadened that permission to this situation.

Cases such as these remind us that training of staff and establishing guidelines for the practice cannot be left to chance. *The absence of a system is a system.* As Dr. Donald Berwick said, "every system is perfectly designed to achieve exactly the results it gets."[15] This unclear situation for the staff member is what is referred to in the safety literature as a "latent error,"[16] an error that may not be so readily apparent but is part of the way business is done in an organization that, in time, will contribute to failures that could cause harm. The physician in no way meant to introduce error into his practice or injury to his patient; however, this significant part of his responsibility, the delineation of responsibilities for his staff, was inadvertently neglected.

The physician who is new to practice will, sooner rather than later, find himself or herself in the role of employer/supervisor of office personnel. This among his or her other responsibilities will require that he or she establishes guidelines for the responsibilities of these staff persons and the scope of their work. This is an essential consideration in light of many of the cases we see. The following is another such example.

A 5-year-old patient had previously been seen in consultation by an allergist who prepared the allergen, the dilutions to be administered, and a schedule of doses for the referring pediatrician to follow. The child presented to his pediatrician's office for an allergy injection. The pediatrician asked one of his assistants to prepare the injection, which he then administered. Soon after the injection, the child experienced an anaphylactic reaction and died in his mother's arms. It was later discovered that the child had received an excessive dose of the allergen because of a dilutional error.

An exploration of the root causes of this very tragic event leads to a number of weaknesses in the operations of the practice. The physician entrusted the reading of the injection schedule, the selection of the appropriate vial, and the dilution of the allergen to an assistant with no formal training in these areas. This was not an allergist's office with a specifically trained staff. The physician did not examine the vial, nor did he review the allergist's recommended schedule to determine how accurately his assistant had performed these tasks. Permitting a staff member to assume this highly specialized function was fraught with danger.

Efforts to resuscitate the child were also hampered. The emergency kit was not readily available, as it was stored in an area away from where the injection was being administered. A review of the incident demonstrated that several of the emergency medications had passed their expiration date. Although the defibrillator was not used for this patient, there was no evidence that it had ever undergone routine maintenance. The office had no established protocol to review and document how often and when emergency equipment and medications were checked, and the staff had not been trained to assist in a meaningful capacity when an office emergency arose.

When a significant error occurs, where its causes are explored, it is not unusual to discover a cascade of problems that contributed to the disaster. This benefit of error analysis raises a very important consideration that is pivotal to the leadership responsibilities of the physician: the cultivation of a culture in the practice that will encourage the other members of the team to be willing to speak up concerning problems and errors that are identified in the course of their work.[17] To encourage others to speak, one has to be willing to take time to listen. This skill, as well as the importance of honesty in the face of errors, is most effectively taught by the physician leader's example. One cannot fix that which he or she does not know is broken. Openness helps to create a climate in which, as many were admonished as youngsters, we learn from our mistakes.

# Risk Management as Physician Responsibility

Much has been written concerning physician responsibility. Articles on this subject often fail to discuss risk management and patient safety, the area of medical care that focuses on the prevention of errors, a vital part of physician responsibility. Regrettably, this area of physician responsibility also receives very little attention in most graduate training programs; however, it is essential that physicians incorporate into their care of patients methods for avoiding the many injuries patients suffer because of systems failure.[18] Physicians certainly do not set out to have accidents, but they often do not plan to avoid them; yet, by physicians' very nature, they would have avoided them had they been able to foresee them.

Every contact point between a patient, his doctor, the hospital, the staff, the pharmacy, or any other person or site where care is provided is a place where an error could potentially occur. Each step requires analysis and planning to minimize the potential for errors. In the practice of clinical medicine, the physician should not make the same error more than once. This calls for a concerted effort to learn the lessons of each error and to share those lessons with others. A personal experience from a hypertension clinic illustrates this need to learn from errors. Many obese patients were referred to this clinic for uncontrolled hypertension after having been previously treated with antihypertensives over significant periods of time. It would come as a surprise to their referring physicians that normal blood pressure readings would be obtained for these patients at the clinic. These diagnoses of hypertension stemmed from the repeated error of the patients' blood pressure being measured with an incorrectly sized cuff. This problem was not a newly detected error in medicine. The literature regarding this problem is substantial and dates back at least a couple of decades.[19] Because this lesson was not learned, and for the want of the appropriate-sized blood pressure cuff, a large number of patients who came to that clinic were misdiagnosed and unnecessarily treated.

Putting a plan in place to improve safety is essential because, by the very nature of the work and the numbers of people involved, hospitals and medical offices can be dangerous places. Defects in office and hospital organizations are a significant cause of injury and malpractice suits, even though many of these errors that result in injury or death are preventable.[18] Is this effort to prevent errors worth it? To begin to answer this question, it is only necessary to observe the many industrial risk management programs. Many high-risk industries, such as aviation and nuclear power plants, carefully and successfully evaluate even minor problems to determine how to avoid them and to prevent injury and loss of life. They report remarkable successes in their safety programs. Patient care deserves the same kind of error-prevention strategies and root-cause analysis where errors occur, thus allowing us to fulfill our role as responsible physicians and healthcare providers. Good care cannot be provided in a chaotic system. The daunting task of processing the vast amount of information, which is the "stock in trade" of physicians, requires planning and organization.

# The Responsible Physician and the Patient's Safety

The physician is "the captain of the ship" and must provide the leadership that is necessary for a safe practice, yet most medical schools and graduate training programs have not yet begun to teach residents how to organize a safe and efficient practice. The physician entering private practice may have to hire a consultant or attempt to develop his or her own systems. Loopholes in these systems will permit the "what-can-happen-will-happen" effect. Ultimately, system error that results in injury to a patient is a physician error.

Medical education concentrates on disease processes and treatments; the area of patient safety is not usually included. Could it be that efforts to prevent errors may have benefits to the individual patient that far exceed many of our available treatments? The stellar advances in treatment lose their luster when, because of a simple ministerial error, we operate on the wrong patient or the wrong side or write a prescription that, because of its illegibility, results in a patient receiving multiple times the intended dose of an anticoagulant. In medicine, we publish our achievements and often bury our errors. This approach prevents us from learning about and thereby preventing the preventable. When walking down any hospital or clinic hallway, one is likely to see announcements of conferences titled "Case of the Week" or "X-ray of the Week." A conference entitled "Preventable Error of the Week" is unlikely to be among these postings; nevertheless, it is one in which very important lessons could be learned.

A significant number of errors and malpractice suits are not the result of a lack of medical knowledge, but rather are the result of inadequate communication and systems to improve the quality of care and guard against error.

---

A 65-year-old male patient was a heavy smoker and had a family history of coronary artery disease, chronic obstructive pulmonary disease, transient ischemic attacks, and a myocardial infarction. The patient's primary physician referred him to a cardiologist because he was experiencing episodes of chest pain. In his consultation report, the cardiologist recommended cardiac catheterization and also described "a prominent abdominal pulsation . . . which makes me suspicious of an abdominal aortic aneurysm." The cardiologist's plan was to request a sonogram of the patient's abdominal aorta while he was hospitalized for the cardiac catheterization, which was to be performed by an interventional cardiologist.

The patient was hospitalized and underwent the cardiac catheterization. The results of this test showed extensive coronary artery disease, which led to a coronary artery bypass. The patient was not evaluated for the suspected abdominal aortic aneurysm during the transfemoral angiogram or by sonography. He was discharged from the hospital to be followed by his primary physician.

Two months later, the patient presented to his primary physician with severe back pain. The physician did not recall and failed to review the cardiologist's findings and recommendations that were in the chart. His diagnosis was sciatica, and the patient was given a prescription for Tylenol with Codeine. Two weeks later the patient fainted in his bathroom, and his wife called the primary care physician. The physician was on vacation, and his associate instructed them to go to the emergency department, where he would meet them. The patient presented to the emergency department complaining of severe pain in the lower back and right buttock. As part of the physical exam, the associate documented that the "abdomen was soft and nontender." There was no mention of abdominal pulsations in the record. The note indicated a possible reaction to the Tylenol with Codeine; however, the admitting diagnosis was documented as "syncope r/o MI and sciatica." Demerol was administered for the severe back pain. The patient was stabilized and transferred to the coronary care unit under the care of the associate.

The patient continued to complain of severe back pain throughout the night and the following morning and required pain relief frequently. Laboratory results showed decreasing hemoglobin and hematocrit. By noon, the patient was very restless, pale, diaphoretic, and in excruciating pain. Soon thereafter, he coded and expired.

---

Every request for a consultation obligates the referring physician to review and understand the consultant's report. Many times this understanding requires taking time to hear from the consultant, beyond his or her written report, about what his or her thoughts and ideas are concerning the care of the patient. Firming this understanding sometimes calls for a visit to the radiology department or looking on with the hematologist at peripheral smears. In this case, it is not clear whether the cardiologist's finding and plan were appreciated by the primary care physician, as his office notes failed to mention the consultant's report and the suspected aortic aneurysm. There was no follow-up on the part of this physician about this potentially catastrophic finding; the patient and his wife were not informed of it, the symptoms that would require immediate intervention, or the need for the patient to be evaluated for an abdominal aneurysm.

What about the communication between the physicians who were responsible for the care of this patient? No direct communication appears to have occurred between the primary doctor and the cardiologist. Did such a finding on the cardiologist's part warrant a call to the referring physician? Was this a finding that should have first been delivered in a written report that, by its very nature, will be delayed by at least a few days? Surprisingly, the interventional cardiologist was not provided with a copy of the cardiologist's consultation report before performing the angiogram. His being aware of the possible abdominal aneurysm would likely mean that he would have evaluated it during the catheterization, probably even sparing the patient an additional diagnostic test. What about the associate who assumed care of the patient? Did he have access to the primary care physician's chart? If not, why not? His review of that record (particularly the cardiologist's report because we know the concern about the aneurysm not being mentioned elsewhere in the chart) would likely have led to the diagnosis on the day the associate first saw the patient.

This case provides a dismal example of what is, to a large extent, a failure of teamwork, a critical component in the delivery of medical care. These well-trained physicians likely did not lack the knowledge or skill to diagnose and treat an abdominal aneurysm; however, they did not take the time to speak with each other about this patient's care, and as a result, the patient was not helped by that knowledge and skill. The patient was treated for his coronary artery disease and not for his aneurysm because the physicians lost track of the fact that the possibility of an aneurysm had been raised but not pursued. The patient and his wife had no idea that he was carrying this potentially catastrophic problem in his abdomen. This point is highlighted by the statement of Dr. Bendapudi and his colleagues: "The patient is at a considerable knowledge disadvantage and has little choice but to trust the physician to perform the right service in the right way."[20]

# The Responsible Physician and Life-Long Learning

"Physicians *must* be lifelong learners."[21] It is unlikely that any physician would deny this mandate; however, much will impede the physician's desire to commit to this responsibility. Personal and family obligations exist on top of the burdens of building and maintaining a successful medical practice as well as other professional responsibilities. Where among these competing commitments does the physician find time for the reading of journals, attending professional meetings, or even preparing an occasional lecture? In fact, he or she cannot afford not to. Medical information supposedly has a life of three to five years; this makes it easy for one to lose sight of new thought and new diagnostic and therapeutic advances. Drs. Christine Laine and David Weinberg define this responsibility to keep abreast of medical information as needing to both learn new information and revisit that which may have been forgotten.[22]

Physicians describe many different approaches, suited to their own life situations, to keep abreast of the literature. Some set aside early morning hours; for others, time in the evenings or on weekends is a better option. The availability of many medical journals on the Internet increases their accessibility to the physician who has a precious few moments here and there for reading. Indeed, this time for study may be hard to come by, but it is what both the physician and his or her patient deserve.

Another key to learning is teaching. One's students, whether they are residents or patients, will create a need for the physician to research and explore. The teacher will always be faced with questions from his or her students that require reading and, often, consultation and discussion with colleagues. These opportunities should be embraced for the learning that they yield for both student and teacher.

# Moving Forward

Dr. Peabody said it well: "Medicine is not a trade . . ."[23] It is a profession on which much of humanity relies for its health and well-being. Medical malpractice concerns, costly professional liability insurance premiums, and the ever-changing healthcare insurance marketplace have added a previously unanticipated complexity to the practice of medicine. The concerns related to these and other areas sap the time and energy of many physicians who often speak of the "good old days" when, free of many of these concerns, one could be fully devoted to the care of patients. There may not be much that physicians can do to effect change in these areas of concern; however, what every physician can do is to be mindful of the professionalism to which they committed themselves and guard against its erosion.

Patients entrust much to their physicians, and medicine offers a multitude of medical advances and hope to suffering patients. Sadly, in many instances, care is not delivered effectively because of our long-standing inattention to errors and the development of systems to avoid them. In a recent interview, Dr. Lucian Leape referred to the science as one half of medicine and added that "the other half of the practice of medicine, which is how you apply that knowledge to the care of a human being, gets short shrift."[24]

Dr. Jerome Lowenstein wrote, "I have come to believe that the time and place to teach compassion are the time and place in which all of the rest of medicine is taught."[25] We submit that this is also the time and place for the teaching of methods and practices to help prevent the many preventable injuries that patients experience in medical care. Just as the scientific principles are upheld by the majority of physicians, if taught the safety principles, they too will become interwoven into the fabric of medicine to the benefit of both patient and physician. The physician's professional responsibility includes patient safety; patient safety is the physician's professional responsibility.

## REFERENCES

1. Inui TS. *A Flag in the Wind: Educating for Professionalism in Medicine.* Washington, DC: Association of American Medical Colleges; February 2003:27.
2. Treadway K. Notes to the class—first day. *N Engl J Med.* 2005;352(19):1944.
3. Bendapudi NM, Berry LL, Frey KA, Turner Parish J, Rayburn WL. Patients' perspectives on ideal physician behaviors. *Mayo Clin Proc.* 2006;81(3):338.
4. Inui TS. *A Flag in the Wind: Educating for Professionalism in Medicine.* Washington, DC: Association of American Medical Colleges; February 2003:15.
5. Accreditation Counsel for Graduate Medical Education. ACGME General Competences. *ACGME.* 2003. Available at: http://www.acgme.org/outcome/comp/compMin.asp, accessed February 20, 2008.
6. Treadway K. Notes to the class–first day. *N Engl J Med.* 2005;352(19):1943.
7. Suchman AL, Williamson PR, Litzelman DK, et al. Toward an informal curriculum that teaches professionalism: transforming the social environment of a medical school. *J Gen Intern Med.* 2004;19:501–504.
8. Inui TS. *A Flag in the Wind: Educating for Professionalism in Medicine.* Washington, DC: Association of American Medical Colleges; February 2003: 16.
9. Inui TS. *A Flag in the Wind: Educating for Professionalism in Medicine.* Washington, DC: Association of American Medical Colleges; February 2003: 16.
10. American Medical Association. *Principles of Medical Ethics.* AMA; 2006. Available at: http://www.ama-assn.org/ama/pub/category/print/2512.html, accessed February 20, 2008.
11. Medical Professionalism Project: ABIM Foundation. Medical professionalism in the new millennium: a physician charter. *Ann Intern Med.* 2002;136:243–246.
12. Suchman AL, Williamson PR, Litzelman DK, et al. Toward an informal curriculum that teaches professionalism: transforming the social environment of a medical school. *J Gen Intern Med.* 2004;19:501.
13. Poon EG, Gandhi TK, Sequist TD, et al. "I wish I had seen this test result earlier!": dissatisfaction with test result management systems in primary care. *Arch Intern Med.* 2004;164:2223–2228.
14. Piette JD, Heisler M, Wagner T. Cost-related medication underuse: do patients with chronic illnesses tell their doctors? *Arch Intern Med.* 2004;164:1749–1755.
15. Phillips DF. "New look" reflects changing style of patient safety enhancement. *JAMA.* 1999;281(3):217.
16. Reason J. *Human Error.* Cambridge, UK: Cambridge University Press; 1990.

17. Marx D. *Patient Safety and the "Just Culture": A Primer for Health Care Executives.* New York, NY: Trustees of Columbia University; 2001. Available at: http://www. mers-tm.net/support/marx_primer.pdf, accessed October 23, 2007.
18. Institute of Medicine. *To Err Is Human: Building a Better Health Care System.* Washington, DC: National Academics Press; 1999.
19. Maxwell MH, Waks AU, Schroth PC, Karam M, Dornfeld LP. Error in blood-pressure measurement due to incorrect cuff size in obese patients. *Lancet.* 1982;2(8288):33–36.
20. Bendapudi NM, Berry LL, Frey KA, Turner Parish J, Rayburn WL. Patients' perspectives on ideal physician behaviors. *Mayo Clin Proc.* 2006;81(3):340.
21. Greenberger NJ. Reading: finding the time and place. In: Manning PR, DeBakey L, eds. *Medicine: Preserving the Passion in the 21st Century.* 2nd ed. New York, NY: Springer-Verlag New York, Inc; 2004:109.
22. Laine C, Weinberg DS. How can physicians keep up-to-date? *Annu Rev Med.* 1999;50:99–110.
23. Peabody FW. The care of the patient. *JAMA.* 1984;252:813–818.
24. Buerhaus PI. Is hospital patient care becoming safer? A conversation with Lucian Leape. *Health Affairs.* 2007;26(6):w687–w696.
25. Coles R, Testa R, eds. *A Life in Medicine: A Literary Anthology.* New York, NY: The New Press; 2002.

# Chapter 4

# Communication Is Crucial

Barry F. Schwartz and Geraldine M. Donohue

*The most basic and powerful way to connect to another person is to listen. Just listen. Perhaps the most important thing we ever give each other is our attention.*

Rachel Naomi Remen, MD

Until last fall, I had spent a considerable part of my career as a healthcare lawyer. I came to know a lot about healthcare policy and management, government regulations and contracts; but I knew little about the delivery of care. All that changed on November 7, 1994, when, at age 40, I was diagnosed with advanced lung cancer. In the months that followed, I was subjected to chemotherapy, radiation, surgery, and news of all kinds, most of it bad. It has been a harrowing experience for me and for my family. And yet, the ordeal has been punctuated by moments of exquisite compassion. I have been the recipient of an extraordinary array of human and humane responses to my plight. These acts of kindness—the simple human touch from my caregivers—have made the unbearable bearable.

In my new role as patient, I have learned that medicine is not merely about performing tests or surgeries or administering drugs. These functions, important as they are, are just the beginning. For as skilled and knowledgeable as my caregivers are, what matters most is that they have empathized with me in a way that gives me hope and makes me feel like a human being, not just an illness. Again and again, I have been touched by the smallest kind gestures—a squeeze of my hand, a gentle touch, a reassuring word. In some ways, these quiet acts of humanity have felt more healing than the high-dose radiation and chemotherapy that hold the hope of a cure.

If I have learned anything, it is that we never know when, how, or whom a serious illness will strike. If and when it does, each one of us wants not simply the best possible care for our body but for our whole being. I still am bound upon King Lear's wheel of fire, but the love and devotion of my family and friends and the deep caring and engagement of my caregivers has been a tonic for my soul and have helped to take some of the sting from my scalding tears.

Kenneth B. Schwartz died of lung cancer in September 1995. Shortly before his death he founded the Kenneth B. Schwartz Center housed at Massachusetts General Hospital, which is dedicated to strengthening the relationships between patients and caregivers.[1]

---

Kenneth Schwartz described with eloquence how vital the humane treatment was that he received when facing an overwhelming cancer that ultimately took his life. Cared about and understood, he felt that the compassion offered to him was equal to, if not more important than, the chemotherapy running through his veins. His words define that communication as crucial, as he poignantly writes that the manner in which he was treated "made the unbearable bearable."

Some physicians are not confident about their abilities to communicate in an effective way with their patients. Physicians often view learning as a life-long process, and the information offered here may help doctors to discover hidden strengths within or further develop those already strong.

## The Influence of the Healthcare Crisis

Strengthening communication within the physician–patient relationship is crucial. Alarmingly, Riess and Marci[2] reported this:

> Breakdowns in communication between patients and physicians and patient dissatisfaction are key factors in more than 80% of

malpractice claims, far exceeding medical negligence and quality of care as reasons leading patients to pursue litigation.

The healthcare state is spiraling out of control—that is a crisis. The relationship between the doctor and the patient is being caught in the crossfire—that is a tragedy. After closer examination, the physician and patient are sharing an experience that is more similar than disparate.

Physicians never thought that they would see the practice of medicine undergo such drastic changes. Managed care—once thought to be a "phase"—is not only surviving but also flourishing as reimbursement for physicians dwindles. Insurance premiums are skyrocketing while doctors are consumed with pervasive fears of malpractice litigation. Physicians never imagined that patients of long term would be leaving because their insurance plans changed. Physicians never expected to spend endless hours battling to get approvals for the care their patients need. Physicians never imagined that when a diagnosis was made, the patient may return with an exhaustive, yet poorly documented, Internet review of the literature in hand. Physicians never thought the hospital would pressure them to release patients well before they belong home.

Patients never thought they would have to say good-bye to physicians that they had a sacred trust in for years. Patients never contemplated feeling forced to bring premature closure to relationships with their beloved physicians because their doctors were not participating in their new plans. Patients never thought that there would be an explosion of medical information available to them at the click of a mouse, often resulting only in escalating, unfounded worry. Patients never thought they would have a baby one day and be discharged the next. Patients never thought that doctors would perform surgery on them in the morning and discharge them in the evening, leaving them without the safety and protection of the hospital's care.

Physicians and patients alike never thought that hospitals might lose their reputation for safety, never picturing that the hospital environment could become a place of apprehension, dread, and alarm. Physicians and patients need each other in this healthcare crisis state more than ever before. Nevertheless, it seems that the very issues of concern to both physician and patient are the very issues that are at risk for parting them.

All the while, in the backdrop, medicine has never known such sophisticated technology, has never learned more about the inner workings of organs vital to survival, and has never conquered more diseases and extended human life further. With such advances, the healing elements in the physician–patient relationship must be also be preserved, valued, and held in the highest esteem.

# The Power of the Therapeutic Relationship

Michael Balint describes the potency of the physician's healing influence on the patient:[3]

> By far the most frequently used drug in general practice was the doctor himself. No pharmacology of this important drug exists. No guidance is contained in any textbook as to the dosage the doctor should prescribe himself.

The essential ingredients in the therapeutic relationship are conveying empathy, being supportive, building trust, listening, providing guidance, encouraging emotional expression, and encouraging self-forgiveness.[4] "It is the first of these, conveying empathy that lies at the heart of a physician's supportiveness" according to Branch.[5]

In empathy, the patient feels unconditionally understood without feeling judged or shamed. How might this occur? The focus of the interaction must be exclusively on the patient's experience. The doctor's emotions and values are put aside with full attention given to the patient's experience and feelings. There is no need to inquire, "How do you feel?" because the answer has been revealed while *listening* to the patient's story.

Listening carefully, encouraging the patient to "go on" as an unfolding of the events of his or her life is expressed while conveying an understanding for the patient's emotional experience from joy to suffering—that is empathy. According to Riess and Marci[6]

> Empathy in the patient–doctor relationship is among the most powerful factors in the medical profession.

Empathy is often confused with sympathy, and many think the two words are synonymous. Why is it so important to discern the difference between sympathy and empathy in the practice of medicine? Both approaches do represent kindness and compassion in the physician's approach to his or her patients. When a physician is sympathetic in his or her communication style with his or her patients, he or she is offering his or her own emotions and sorrow for what the patient is experiencing. This brings the risk that the physician will become overburdened and emotionally exhausted. This is what occurred to family physician David Hilfiker, who says in his brave and honest disclosure:[7]

> The blessing and the curse of medicine is that we physicians are privileged to share the most intense moments of life with our patients: birth, death, fear, sorrow, anxiety, disability, healing, joy. These moments are shared without the usual social barriers; thus, we are privy to the deepest of humanity's experiences. But with this

privilege comes the burden of availability, of openness to the needs revealed at those intense times. I could not sustain the degree of openness required to go from the deepest need to the deepest need and consequently found myself refusing the very service that a major part of me was committed to giving.

The sympathetic physician gives so much of himself or herself in the care of patients that he or she can cause himself or herself, for a time, to be unable to give any further. Contrast this with the physician who stays with the patient in his or her experience, understanding the range of emotions felt, but does not deplete his or her own emotional self. Empathy has classically been described as an attempt to temporarily "walk in the shoes of another." The patient feels understood; the physician has a healing effect on the patient, and yet the physician is left with energy to continue to minister to his or her other patients.

Empathy is a process in which two people become connected in the moment. This is a skill that can be mastered. The physician "steps in the shoes" of the patient, gives careful attention to the patient's feelings and perspective, relays understanding, and then gently and near seamlessly "steps out of the shoes" and is emotionally available again to continue to care for those also in need. This is a learned skill stemming from observation of one's clinical supervisor and enhanced by one's own professional experience. To be empathic in the rendering of care to patients will leave the physician healthier, less encumbered, and less drained, according to Aring, in his 1958 classic article "Sympathy and Empathy."[8]

Aring writes, "It is hardly possible to overstate the importance of the uses of empathy in the practice of medicine." "The ultimate test of any medical endeavor is what it does for the patient. The doctor proceeding bravely and courageously, to say nothing of good-humoredly, continuing to learn about himself and his own problem will be good for the patient."[9]

Consider the following account of a young, married, pregnant woman from the patient's perspective. The second trimester brought concerns of the baby's ability to thrive. The patient and husband went for specialized testing and learned of an extremely rare condition that the unborn child was suffering from in utero. It was a fatal, genetic disease that usually does not evidence itself until adulthood (Huntington's disease). In the same moment, the patient learned that both the baby and her husband had an incurable illness. The patient related the following:[10]

That unbearable evening that we got the news—the phone rang. It was my doctor. To this day, I do not know how he learned about the results of the test. It wasn't as if I was in his office that day.

> They either called him or he got a report faxed to him . . . I don't
> know. I never would have expected that he would call, but I know
> that it meant everything to me that he did. And I remember
> exactly his words. "Hi . . . I heard the . . . news." That was all he
> had to say. He knew, and I knew. It was the best call I ever had,
> and all these years later I could not be more grateful to him.

Often, when faced with such human tragedy, physicians can easily feel at
a loss for words. Although some consideration needs to be given to the words
selected, it is the "being there" for the patient/family that is long remem-
bered. Medical doctors can at times think "let's leave the psychological talk
to the psychotherapists." This thinking can often be used to shield oneself
from getting too close to a situation that is becoming too painful. Physicians
need to recognize that they are not expected to assume the role of therapist
during times of heightened emotions but that patients need to know that their
doctors will not abandon them emotionally.

According to Hilfiker, learning how to communicate well with patients and
families is important because they have needs "that I could not refer to a
counselor or psychiatrist, for they are an integral part of daily practice."[11] At
the same time, he writes of regret in failing to understand better the lives of
his patients during training. "The diagnosis was everything! We were so busy
trying to figure out what was wrong and what should be done that there was
no time or energy left to understand how an acute medical problem fit into
the life of the patient. Even those professors that tried to focus in on the inner
lives of the patient could not keep the attention of the medical students
because its relevance paled in comparison to medical pathology."[12]

# The Impact of Medical Training

The benefits of empathy in the care of patients are immeasurable. Interestingly, the communication experts have difficulty coming to consensus on just
how to define it; however, after the concept is grasped, it is never lost but,
sadly, may become buried under the demands and stresses the physician
faces in the practice of medicine.

Many years ago we participated in an extensive faculty training program
devoted to developing excellence in communication with patients. As part of
that training, "standardized patients," actors trained in simulating patients
possessing particular personalities and bearers of specific diseases typically
encountered in daily medical practice, were brought before us. Physicians pos-

sessing a wealth of clinical expertise and experience expressed great confidence in interviewing these "patients." That was until the interviewing began.

Basics such as saying hello, calling the patient by name, introducing oneself, maintaining eye contact, and *listening* to the person were ignored. The mission was to ask the right questions efficiently to make the diagnosis that, although necessary, left the patient encounter as a secondary concern. This painful occurrence was from a self-selected group of physicians motivated to improve doctor–patient communication yet failing to do so.

Empathy may begin to become eradicated from the emotional world of the young doctor in training right from the onset of his or her education:[13]

> Medical students begin their education with the dead body and the living cell; they learn that the patient is passive and that the cells are alive. Dissection of a cadaver in medical school teaches primacy of the eye over the ear, for cadavers do not complain, and no one has to listen. It is then that students first learn to harden themselves against empathy.

The statement "and no one has to listen" is both true and tragic. That cadaver was once a person who gave the gift of his or her body for students of medicine to examine in order to develop into expert physicians of tomorrow. Spiro brings forth an interesting, albeit controversial, observation where the young medical student, early on, is indoctrinated into a world in which listening to the patient is secondary. The generosity of the donor could result in providing medical students with a rite of passage that limits learning only to the physical and not the indispensable emotional needs of their patients. Spiro addresses the critically important "ears" for the physician to listen beyond what is visually present. Spiro describes the essential element of listening:[14]

> Listening goes straight to the heart and helps create empathy. Empathy opens our eyes to let us see what the CT scan had missed. The ear is as important as the eye in medical practice. Is it too much to claim that the physician must be the mediator between the images and the patient?

Drastic change, increased responsibility, and great stress occur as the medical student transitions into the role of intern. As the internship year proceeds, anger and depression increase along with a decrease in empathy for the patient.[15] The next transition of the young doctor to that of resident increases susceptibility to stress, burnout, and a continuing loss of empathy.[16] Spiro gives the following example:[17]

> A medical student told how he and a group of residents were laughing and joking through "work-rounds" one morning; they expressed

amused resentment toward their next patient, a comatose old man awaiting his PEG (percutaneous endoscopic gastrostomy) ticket to a "nursing warehouse." After the ritual chest examination and a few shouts in his ear, they turned to go, when their attention was caught by a new card on the wall, colored by a child's hand. "Get well soon, Grandpa," it read. The troupe fell silent as they left the room, and for a moment, the joking ceased. That was empathy, with the child if not with the old man.

Doctors in training are proud and ambitious; however, they are also young and may lack the maturation to cope with the human indignities and sufferings surrounding them. Respect, kindness, and the demonstration of empathy must come from the role models of these physicians of the future. The seasoned physician–teachers may be in such difficult positions themselves given the complexities and extraordinary demands placed on them; they are unable to recognize the example that needs to be unfailingly set for the next generation.

In *Teaching the Human Dimensions of Care in Clinical Settings*, the authors discovered that role modeling was the most frequent method used by physician faculty to teach medical students in the clinical setting.[18] In their review of the literature, the authors raise concerns that informal and hidden curricula are obstacles to the provision and modeling of humanistic care.[18] An example of hidden curricula would be the sharp contrast of a senior physician's lecturing on the significance of addressing the emotional needs of patients while students observe an absence of such humanistic care displayed at the bedside by that very same physician. This can create confusion as well as cynicism in the young doctor.[18]

Parker Palmer, in his book *The Courage to Teach*, captures the concerns of teachers finding themselves in a world in which intent may not match their principled desires:[19]

> Academics often suffer the pain of dismemberment. On the surface, this is the pain of people who thought they were joining a community of scholars but find themselves in distant, competitive, and uncaring relationships with colleagues and students. Deeper down, this pain is more spiritual than sociological: it comes from being disconnected from our own truth, from the passions that took us into teaching, from the heart that is the source of all good work. If we have lost the heart to teach, how can we take heart again? How can we remember who we are, for our own sake and the sake of those we serve?

Medicine has never been more innovative. Ground-breaking discoveries have become expected. Physicians can scarcely respond to rapid changes happening across specialties while fiscal crises of grand proportions simultaneously create fear that hospitals may close. The physician–teacher cannot help but become entangled in the repercussions of directing medical education within a healthcare system in such distress. In Parker's words[20]

> To reduce our vulnerability, we disconnect from students, from subjects, and even from ourselves. We build a wall between inner truth and outer performance, and we play act the teacher's part. Our words, spoken at remove from our hearts, become the "balloon speech in cartoons," and we become caricatures of ourselves. We distance ourselves from students and subject to minimize the danger—forgetting that distance makes life more dangerous still by isolating the self.

A parallel process could be at play: between physician and patient and physician and student—both using distancing when the relationship becomes too uncomfortable. Teaching takes place in the public arena and such exposure can bring vulnerability, resulting in the physician–teacher reflecting, "Am I being true to myself?"[20] As the medical profession strives for new advances in the face of financial hardship, burdensome politics, and fragmentation of healthcare delivery, this question emerges: Can attention to the patient's humanity become lost?

Medical education addresses the significance of communication and teaches the importance of developing and strengthening one's interpersonal skills. Role modeling effective communication skills by senior physicians, in the clinical environment, will help to close the gap that leaves the young doctor with barriers to facilitating communication with his or her patients.[18]

Attending physicians need to begin the process of increasing an open display of caring behaviors toward patients in front of residents, residents in turn in front of interns, and interns before medical students.[18] It is a difficult task for some but one that must be conquered. The sacredness of the relationship between physician and patient is at stake and must be protected.

# When the Patient Becomes Routine

Physicians will often see patients with similar conditions repeatedly in their practices. While conditions can become routine, can patients remain distinctive?

Consider the following case from the patient's perspective. A 42-year-old healthy and physically fit female patient sought the help of an orthopedist for hip pain of four months duration, precipitated by a fall. The pain had been tolerable, but recently, a pattern of increased pain after any new or strenuous activity was noted. She prepared a brief list, consisting of four bullet points, identifying what actions increase the pain. The patient arrived at the physician's office in a timely way and was seen nearly immediately:[21]

---

He came in the exam room and while still looking at my file asked, "What seems to be the problem." I began to say that I have had a pain in my hip when he interrupted me and said, "Show me where the pain is?" I pointed to my right hip. He said, "That's not your hip." I suddenly felt foolish and stupid. The next thing I know he sent me for an X-ray, and then I was back in the exam room. He came back in with the X-ray and said, "There is no fracture. If there was a hair line fracture, this X-ray would not be able to show it anyway. You have a muscle pull."

He proceeded to advise Advil daily, along with icing the painful area and said, "Call me in three weeks if you are not better." I asked him if he would want me to call him even if I was better so that he would know that the treatment worked, and he said in a condescending tone, "No, that's not necessary." I didn't even get to show him the list. It did not matter. He was not interested.

---

The patient wanted engagement—what she received was detachment. She wanted information—what she received was silence. She wanted comfort—what she received was remoteness.

This orthopedist, prominent in his field and highly recommended, never took a history. Had he, he would have learned that her work required her to be on her feet 10 hours a day. He would have also discovered that she had concerns about taking NSAIDS and would be reluctant to begin them now. He would have learned that she needed education regarding where the hip is, as many lay people mistake the pelvic bone for the hip. A dangling curiosity was left with her as well: "The X-ray would not show a hair line fracture," she wondered. "So did I possibly break a bone or not?" The orthopedist also missed finding out that the patient is stoic and does not disturb physicians easily.

How did the physician's poor communication skills impact this encounter? Communication was minimal as was any display of understanding. This seasoned physician developed a clinical impression rapidly and moved efficiently in his care of the patient; however, he completely left the patient out of his thinking.

Bernard Lown, in his book *The Lost Art of Healing: Practicing Compassion in Medicine*, reflects on the changes that he has witnessed in 45 years of medical practice:[22]

> A three-thousand year tradition, which bonded doctor and patient in a special affinity of trust, is being traded for a new type of relationship. Healing is being replaced with treating, caring is supplanted by managing, and the art of listening is taken over by technological procedures. Doctors no longer minister to a distinctive person but concern themselves with fragmented, malfunctioning biologic parts. The driistressed human being is frequently absent from the transaction.

In this orthopedic clinical case, the patient was left to feel alone, uncertain, misunderstood, and disillusioned about the care she received. The physician, having immediately interrupted her, never got to see the note she prepared providing clues to what triggered the pain. A medication was offered to her with no dosing schedule. She thought, "Do I just take the Advil according to the directions on the bottle for three weeks," but was too intimidated to ask.

Empathy is not something reserved only for some patients and not others. All patients need understanding from their physicians and all will benefit from it, regardless of the specialty of the physician and the nature of the visit. What becomes routine for the doctor is never routine for the patient.

If the physician used more effective communication skills, what might this patient's perspective be?

---

> The doctor entered the exam room, shook my hand, and asked what he should call me. I thought that was very respectful and I liked him already. I told him about the hip pain, and it turns out I don't even know where my hip is. He clarified the difference between the hip and pelvic bones. When he heard I am on my feet all day long, it concerned him. He thought I should slow down because I might be fighting the healing process. Although I hate pills, I will go on Advil—if it works, then we will know it was a muscle pull, and if it doesn't work, I will need more X-rays.
>
> He was amazed that I took so long to see a doctor and said, "You sure don't ask for help easily, do you?" This made me feel pretty good. He read the notes that I jotted down and thought it

> was still likely my muscle and wanted me to call him either way in a few weeks so we could know for sure.

In this second scenario, with the physician's use of essential communication skills such as greeting the patient, attentive listening, and showing respect would not, in reality, have extended the office visit beyond a few minutes. The patient would have been left comforted, reassured, educated, willing to comply with the treatment plan, and satisfied with her experience. This would be in sharp contrast to her expressing that she would neither return to him nor refer others to him. The physician would have gained the trust of his patient and would have been left with a sense of satisfaction from the encounter. The physician, as well as the patient, would have had a far more gratifying experience instead of leaving the patient with unanswered questions through this demoralizing experience. This physician would have listened to her, treating the person, not the "routine" condition.

# The Challenges of Nonverbal Communication

It would seem reasonable to deduce that the relationship between physician and patient, driven by physicians wanting to help patients and patients in need of help from their doctors, would facilitate good communication. The synergistic nature of the relationship would be sufficient to support a successful encounter; however, powerful factors at play make the physician–patient encounter complex. These factors are often nonverbal and often at times not within the conscious control of either physician or patient.

In *The Expression of Emotions Through Nonverbal Behavior in Medical Visits* (2006), the authors describe three interconnected ways in which emotions shape and influence the nature of the physician–patient relationship. The first is that physicians and patients both have emotions that they bring to the encounter based on their past and present experiences, as well as emotions they anticipate having in the future.[23] Although the emotions of patients have received far greater study, the emotions of physicians are significant in the establishment of the relationship.[23]

How is this evidenced? If a patient is agreeable and friendly, some physicians' emotional states can be affected and similar feelings can emerge in them. Confronted with the hostile or belligerent patient, feelings of anger can be triggered in some physicians.[23]

The second element addressed is that both physicians and patients show emotions.[23] Both doctors and patients can be unaware of the nonverbal messages sent, which can either kindle the development of an excellent union or ignite an eruption of a troubled relationship. It is essential that the physician become self-reflective as to his or her nonverbal communication style. The patient is in need of care, perhaps suffering. The patient should not have to incur the additional burden of showing positive emotions to gratify the physician.

The third interconnected way in which emotions influence the doctor–patient relationship is in judgment. The authors write, "The evidence that emotions are shown in the medical visit implies that both physicians and patients judge each other's emotions."[23] Judging another's emotions can be dangerous. Wrong assumptions can be made. Patients are watchful and judging can occur rapidly. For instance, a common question patients pose to physicians is this: "Would you recommend this for a member of your family?" The physician may momentarily ponder the question. The patient is expecting that the physician would immediately say, "I sure would," and the patient may mistakenly judge his or her hesitation as an unspoken negative response.

Physicians need to be acutely aware of the power of the nonverbal messages sent when communicating with patients. Nonverbal communication can help foster or can significantly hinder the doctor–patient relationship. "Perhaps related to nonverbal sensitivity, physicians who appear to exhibit more emotionally expressive nonverbal behaviors—including facial expressiveness, eye contact, head nods, body posture, and voice tone—are generally viewed more favorably by patients. These behaviors, in turn, are linked to a variety of patient outcomes, including patient satisfaction, health services utilization and appointment keeping, and functional status."[24]

# Follow the Patient Home

Patients today are yearning for the "old-time" physician that brought trust and comfort into a world filled with worry and fear for their health. They are searching for physicians that see beyond the illness and into their very hearts and souls. Hippocrates, 2,500 years ago, said this:[25]

> For some patients, though conscious that their position is perilous, recover their health simply through their contentment with the physician.

Communication is crucial with the words the physician uses as well as how the words are expressed. When the physician must tell patients information that may be difficult for them to hear, what kind of process does he or she use to select his words? Does he or she consider this: are these the words that I would want to have told to me if I was in this patient's predicament? Would I want these words to be told to the people in my world that I care about and love? Are there other words that could have been selected that would make the information less difficult to process? Is my tone calming and soothing? Is the patient put at ease? Is the communication leading to a healing process?

When a physician needs to inform a patient about a diagnosis, treatment, medication, instructions, imagine following the patient home. Imagine how this news will penetrate and anticipate what questions and concerns might likely emerge. It is well known that patients can become anxious from "white coat syndrome" and now what was once a fear of an illness has become a reality. While in the presence of the physician, the patient can become disconnected from the impact the news will have on his or her life. The literature has well established that the patient has already forgotten 50% of what the physician has said upon leaving the office.[26]

It might be a situation in which the patient, who has learned to control diabetes through diet, now requires daily administration of insulin. *Follow the patient home.* Perhaps the patient has been given a diagnosis in which treatment is available but no known cure (i.e., rheumatoid arthritis). *Follow the patient home.* What could he or she be experiencing? What is going on in his or her mind and body as he or she leaves the physician's office? *Follow the patient home.* Perhaps the patient has a diagnosis that will now require life-long treatment with a potentially fatal medication (e.g., warfarin) that will significantly alter activity. *Follow the patient home.* What is the experience going to be like for that patient after he or she leaves your office? Foreseeing what is ahead for the patient will increase the physician's ability to ask more astute questions and learn more relevant information from the patient.

Ask the patient such probing questions as these: "Who will you speak to when you get home?" "What will you tell them about our visit today?" "What can we discuss further now so it will be clearer for you later?" Taking a few moments in your mind to imagine *following the patient home* while the patient is actually still present in the office may provide the opportunity for a more productive dialogue and a deepening of an understanding of the patient's journey ahead. Imagining what the patient's experience is by "trying to walk in his or her shoes" will establish a bond with the patient that remains even when physician and patient are apart.

Empathy in relationships with patients is not limited to one conversation or one meaningful response. It is the creation of an empathic bond that becomes a continuous process, a bond that will make the patient feel less alone as extraordinary challenges ahead are faced. In the empathic physician–patient relationship, two people are connected in a healing way, and that healing truly follows the patient home. When home, the patient will feel an attachment to the physician, feel an understanding and a caring, feel that the burden of the illness is being shouldered with another, another for whom the patient has great admiration, and both doctor and patient will benefit from an increased satisfaction in the relationship.

# Dispelling the Myth of the "Uncaring" Physician

Caring and compassion are needed to develop an empathic doctor–patient relationship. There is some belief that certain physicians are not caring. Has anyone ever heard a physician report that he or she is absolutely devoid of caring? If so, the number must be miniscule. If, however, the question "have you ever seen an uncaring physician?" was posed, then a response of "yes" may emerge. Because some compassionate physicians are not able to demonstrate their caring, they display behaviors that can be taken for callousness, coldness, and insensitivity. What do these behaviors look like? Avoidant, abrupt, silent, and busy are just a few of the words commonly used.

Patients view their physicians from two perspectives: competence and caring. When an individual is recommending a physician who is deemed as "the best," he or she will do so in an extroverted, nearly bragging manner, and all too often, then with a whisper, say, "But the bedside manner isn't great." This can often mean that the doctor has successfully treated a challenging clinical course of the individual or a loved one. In such cases the interpersonal communication may be overlooked. However, what about the circumstance when the outcome is not favorable and the physician–patient relationship is weak?

Breakthroughs are being made that link biology with difficulties in displaying empathy. Research has demonstrated that the apparently uncaring physician is caring but does not have the behaviors available to him or her to be able to demonstrate a caring response.[2]

What follows is an interview with a family member whose brother was dying of lung cancer, and the treating oncologist, although caring, lacked the ability to show such feeling:[27]

---

My brother was 48 and a father of 4 when he was diagnosed with lung cancer. I went with him for an MRI of the brain to see if the cancer had spread. After the test, they called both of us in to see the doctor. We were in a tiny room, and his films were up on the wall. The doctor took his pen and simultaneously pointed to, while he said quietly, 1, 2, 3, 4, and 5. . . There are 5 lesions in your brain. Very somberly, he said "That is not good," and then he just got up and left the room, perhaps too difficult for him to bear.

---

A greater understanding has now been discovered that explains the need for bridges to connect the physicians' behavior to the physicians' compassion.[2] The physicians are suffering along with their patients; however, their autonomic systems have been triggered, permitting neurobiological processes to block the demonstration of caring behaviors. As Riess and Marci report[2]

> Physicians find themselves in the unique role of sharing bad news with patients who they care for whom may be very anxious and fearful. This presents an important challenge to physicians, who through autonomic neurobiological empathy processes may feel the patient's pain so acutely that sharing the bad news creates autonomic arousal in physicians, stimulating their own fear and anxiety about "hurting" the patient with the bad news. These kinds of states of heightened physiological arousal can lead to awkwardness, abruptness, or avoidance that interferes with the empathy the clinician wants to convey.

Often such physicians are quite aware of their limitations but lack the resources to change their behaviors. A critical, small first step will give birth to a giant leap of success when the physician recognizes the feelings being experienced are entirely normal. This in itself will be masterful in reducing the physician's anxiety. This more comfortable emotional state for the physician will allow his or her focus and energy be turned back toward the patient and family.[2] Some physicians may benefit from communication skills training; there are many such programs available today that will strengthen and deepen the doctor's ability to understand and establish increasingly therapeutic bonds with his or her patients.

# The Bad News Must Be Told, But How?

A difficult and emotionally strenuous responsibility of the physician is to deliver news to a patient that may be life altering. Harking back to the days of Hippocrates, deeply rooted in medical training, was the belief that the less said to patients about the gravity of their health the better it would be for them.[28] The American Medical Association's first code of medical ethics in 1847 read, "The life of a sick person can be shortened not only by the acts, but also by the words or the manner of a physician. It is therefore a sacred duty to guard himself carefully in this respect, and to avoid all things which have a tendency to discourage the patient and to depress his spirits."[29]

Times have changed. Emotions and fears have not. Patients are more educated and more empowered, and most wish to take an active role in their illness; nevertheless, the news of a catastrophic illness may weaken the strongest person. The physician's first task is to establish how much the patient wants to know and how much the patient can handle.

As a public service, a television news anchor maintained a video diary of her battle with breast cancer. The video begins with anchor Hoda Kotb telling of how the news of the cancer came to her at work. She was at the television station, working with an intern, when the phone call came:[30]

> It was the hospital, and then he said "It's cancer, you have breast cancer." Everything else he said I didn't hear. I didn't hear what he said. That was it. That was it.

The majority of physicians do not have a consistent plan for informing their patients of bad news, according to a recent survey.[31] Physicians do have a wealth of experience to rely on to help guide them through difficult encounters; however, they cannot escape their own human frailties and emotions when faced with tragedy. Learning to recognize areas of vulnerability will strengthen the physician suddenly placed in a situation in which, at a loss for words, he or she resorts to avoidance. This occurs in the following case:

---

This patient, a physician in his early 70s, was diagnosed with a high-grade carcinoma of the prostate. An appointment was made to see a radiotherapist with particular expertise in treating such a lesion. When the patient went into the physician's office, only a resident was there. Offhandedly, he asked the resident, "How am I doing?" The resident replied, "Not so good." Taken aback, he said, "Why, what's the matter?" and the resident replied, "It's more extensive than we thought, and it's probably outside the capsule."

Then the radiologist walked in and spent a few minutes explaining that the patient would be given greater than usual amounts of radiotherapy because of the nature of the patient's disease. When he arrived home, the patient was quite upset and thought of a number of questions that he wanted to discuss with the radiologist. He called for an appointment in which he and his wife could speak to the radiologist about their concerns. When he arrived at the office, with his wife, the radiologist said, "I hope you can understand that I'm having a bad day. I'm very busy." Looking at his watch, he said, "I'll give you five minutes."

---

In this situation, a resident informed the patient about the spread of the disease. This should not have occurred. Such news must be delivered by the attending physician and, for his medical experience, perhaps with the resident in attendance.

Returning back to the study of the neurobiology of empathy,[2] as in this example, the physician had to give devastating news to a patient, difficult enough under ordinary circumstances and more so as he was a physician. This may support the belief that the physician was using busyness and avoidance to shield himself from his own pain in identifying with the suffering of his patient.

If the news to be delivered involves the patient undergoing surgery, this may cause a feeling of a loss of control for the patient, and tremendous faith in the surgeon is required. The patient wants to know that the physician will do his or her best to prevent any harm from coming to him or her. The necessary informed consent must be adhered to, but the words that a patient longs to hear from the surgeon are these: "I will take care of you." Television anchor Hoda Kotb, in her search for a breast surgeon, heard those words come from the doctor who she ultimately decided to have perform her surgery. When interviewed, she voiced that it was those words that made the difference for her in selecting her physician.[30]

The breaking of bad news is, at once, a change in the world of the patient as he or she once knew it. It serves as an opportunity for the physician to be instrumental in having the patient face a monumental challenge of life. Robert Buckman, author of *How to Break Bad News*,[31] offers a multistep program for the patient and physician.

Recognize that each patient deserves an individualized approach to learning of life-altering news; thus, the following six steps, as developed by Buckman, may prove useful in providing structure and direction to a painful conversation.

1. *Start off well.* Immediate considerations would include determining whether the physical setting is right and who should be there; this should be followed by asking the patient this: "Are you feeling well enough to talk a bit?"

2. *Find out how much the patient knows.* Ask this: "Have you been very worried about these symptoms you have been having?"

3. *Find out how much the patient wants to know.* Ask this: "If this condition turns out to be something serious, are you the kind of person who likes to know exactly what's going on?"

4. *Share the information.* Asking these questions: "Am I making sense?" "Do you understand what I am saying?" "Does this all seem sensible to you?" "This must be bewildering, but do you follow roughly what I'm saying?" "Do you see what I mean?" Encourage feedback from the patient.

5. *Respond to the patient's reaction.* The success of the breaking of bad news conversation is dependent on how the physician responds to the patient's reaction and feelings. When a patient receives bad news, the range of normal reactions is wide. If, in the physician's experience, the patient's reaction seems beyond the scope of normal, a referral to an expert in such matters may be indicated.

6. *Organize a plan and follow-through.* Provide an overview of the plan of care going forward. To support a patient, you do not have to agree with the patient's point of view, but you need to listen to it and identify what the patient is saying and feeling.

# Overcoming Barriers to Effective Communication

## Health Literacy Recognition

Breakdowns in communication in doctor–patient relationships can often be understood as a failure on the part of patients to have comprehended their illnesses and treatments. What is the responsibility of the physicians? Nearly all patients want to be given information in the easiest and simplest way to enable them to understand their illness.[32] There is a silent healthcare crisis, and any individual can be affected by it regardless of age, racial or ethnic group, education, or employment. It is believed that less than one in every six patients is fluent in health literacy.[33] Health literacy is defined as this: "The ability to obtain, process, and understand basic health information and services needed to make the appropriate decisions."[33]

The highly regarded Ask Me 3 Program, now under the auspices of the National Patient Safety Foundation,[33] recommends that the patient answers three simple questions before leaving the encounter with the physician:

- What is my main problem?
- What do I need to do about it?
- Why is it important for me to do this?

Physicians and patients alike are being educated to address these three questions at each visit to combat the devastating impact on an individual's health status related to a lack of understanding. Patients with low healthcare literacy should not be overloaded with more information than can be processed. The doctor's responsibility is to ensure that the information provided to the patient regarding his or her health care is adequate and well understood.[34]

For example, when a patient is readmitted for an exacerbation of heart failure, the assessment could include a determination of the patient's ability to understand complex medication instructions and any recent changes to the regimen. Rather than simply prescribing new medications, a complete plan would include a discussion of how additional help may be provided by using a pill box, providing more extensive counseling, or involving family members.

Because of the patient's need to work harder to comprehend his or her medical situation, a respectful and compassionate approach is essential from the physician, as he or she assists the patient to navigate the easily overpowering healthcare system.

## Valuing the Multicultural Milieu of Medicine

A dangerous obstacle in the delivery of medical care today is that of language barriers. Patients cannot be successfully treated if they tragically and frustratingly cannot communicate with the physician. Every measure that can reasonably be taken to open the lines of communication must be sought. In the absence of translators, there are an increasing amount of venues today that are offering translation services in a multitude of languages via the telephone. An interview with a physician revealed his memory from his medical training:[35]

> While an intern, I witnessed a very poignant episode between a physician and his patient. There was an elderly patient lying in her bed and looking sad and speaking to no one. She could not converse with the staff because she only spoke Yiddish. When we made rounds, the internist in question recognized that, sat down on her bed, and spoke to her in Yiddish. She told him that she was a cigar roller in Poland and came to the lower East Side to work as a cigar roller. The thing I remember from this episode was the tears coming down her eyes as she spoke.

With the introduction of such a vast amount of cultures to American society, physicians have little preparation about assimilating cultural differences into their practices.[36] Medical educators as well as other healthcare professionals must actively incorporate the value of the cross-cultural experience into their programs today. "Becoming culturally competent is a complex, life-long process."[37] To quote Sir William Osler, "It is much more important to know what sort of patient has a disease, than what sort of disease a patient has."[36]

When cultural differences go unrecognized or unexamined, the health status of patients can be placed at risk. For example, for some Latina women, the discussion of reproductive organs is considered taboo.[38] As a result, in some cases, Latina women are hesitant to provide an accurate history of the presence of abnormal bleeding to their physicians, left to be ultimately diagnosed with late-stage cervical cancer.[38]

In *Cross-Cultural Primary Care: A Patient-Based Approach*, the authors present a thorough and intensive curriculum, divided into five modules, to help physicians improve the care delivered to patients in the multicultural environment of medicine today.[36] The program's intention is to bridge the cultural divide that can exist between physicians and patients and allow for a progressive, deepening appreciation of the relationship and to "lift the veil of social and cultural misunderstanding."[39]

The curriculum as set forth "can facilitate all medical encounters but is particularly important in the setting of cultural and social differences. These tools help physicians to do what 'good doctoring' is all about—listening, asking the right questions, and meeting the patients where they are."[39]

# Communication and Litigation

Physicians want to deliver excellence in patient care and do not wish to be burdened by threats of litigation. Physicians want to communicate with their patients openly and freely, in partnership together, always making the decision that is in the best interest of the patient. Physicians are informed that research continuously shows that poor communication and malpractice litigation are intertwined. Nevertheless, physicians are still skeptical that effective interpersonal skills will prevent a lawsuit. They believe that they are powerless and helpless over malpractice litigation.

Patients want to have good communication with their doctors. They want to be listened to and to feel understood. Patients can at once have astoundingly unrealistic expectations of their physicians' abilities while skeptical as to whom within the healthcare team can truly be trusted. Patients may not be aware that research has shown that good communication and the risk of litigation are intertwined; however, they do know that if they are disappointed with their care, if they feel that their physicians have not treated them with respect and honesty, if they believe too many questions have gone unanswered, the legal system is an available recourse.

Is a lawsuit an indicator that a physician was a poor communicator? To answer that, a look back in time is required.

Medical malpractice litigation has a long history. In the 1800s, well-trained physicians welcomed lawyers to bring suits against those who were perceived to be charlatans.[40] It was a time when the professions of both medicine and law were working together to keep the public safe.

The 19th century brought advances in medical treatment but not without the risk of disappointed outcomes. Stunningly, the best trained and most successful physicians of the 1840s and 1850s were faced with their own lawsuits.[40] Many of the first lawsuits were orthopedic in nature. In the mid-1800s, after surgery for a compound fracture, a shortened lower extremity that gave way to a slight limp found the physician with a lawsuit in hand. The irony is that before the discovery of the orthopedic procedure, the limb would have just been amputated.[40]

One hundred and fifty years ago, when medical practice standards began to be established, lawyers were then able to demonstrate deviations from acceptable practice.[40] Presently, in the 21st century, as written by Charles and Frisch:[41]

> In tort law, errors are judged as significant if they violate the prevailing standard of care, which is defined as a standard of practice adhered to by reasonably competent physicians in the same or similar circumstances, either in their own locality, termed the community standard; or in their medical specialty, termed the national standard.

Standards of care are essential to the rendering of consistent, careful, and safe treatment to society. The legal profession remains confident that it has an important role in protecting the public if there is a deviation from medical standards. As long as the profession of medicine continues to push forward to conquer disease and extend life, as it must in this millennium, adverse outcomes will occur and litigation may indeed result.

Ambitious and well-regarded research studies were undertaken, beginning in the 1970s, with one of the missions being to investigate the relationship between negligent acts and malpractice litigation.[42] The findings were remarkably the same (California, 1973; New York, 1984; Utah/Colorado, 1990s): Negligent acts far surpassed claims of medical malpractice.[42] This raises the question of why one person decides to pursue legal recourse against a physician and another person does not.

Often, the nature of the bad outcome determines whether a patient will pursue legal action, having nothing to do with the strength of the doctor–patient relationship. These can be the most devastating of suits for physicians to face.

What also is apparent, however, is that two seemingly equally competent physicians, practicing in the same area, find that a great disparity exists in their lawsuit history. Why do some patients sue doctors when there is no bad outcome and other patients who have been significantly injured would never consider legal action against a caring physician? Although multifactorial in analysis, it is widely believed that poor communication is an outstanding determining factor that provides an individual with the impetus to go from "patient" to "plaintiff."[43–45]

If patients are not satisfied with an outcome and are not satisfied with the physician's manner, the doctor is placed at a greater risk for medical malpractice litigation.[45] Levinson and associates found a statistically significant difference in the communication skills used by physicians without a malpractice litigation history from physicians who had been sued.[45]

What are the explicit interpersonal skills used by the physicians who had never been sued? These physicians spent a slightly longer time with patients (18.3 minutes vs. 15.0 minutes).[45] They oriented the patient to the visit. This was done by using statements such as, "First I will examine you, and then we will talk the problem over" or "I will leave time for your questions." Additionally, facilitative comments were used, such as, "Go on; tell me more about that." The patients' opinions were asked for, such as, "What do you think caused that to happen?" or "What do you think about taking these pills?" These physicians also displayed warmth and friendliness by the use of humor with the patient during the visits.[45]

# The Bond That Sustains

In the *A Piece of My Mind* section of the *Journal of the American Medical Association*, a physician wrote about his experience of facing retirement after 40 years of practice. He wrote that many of his patients had been with him since his first years in practice. Some were patients of his original partner and as a result had been with the practice longer than he. This physician was guided in his care of patients by the words of Michael Balint that "the most powerful therapy I have to offer my patients is me, and I have tried that prescription as much as possible. The patient–physician relationship has sustained me and my patients, and I hope contributed to our health and quality of life."[46]

Now, at the close of his medical career, as he is faced with beloved patients asking him what they will do without him, his response is this:[46]

No, my dear patients, when I retire, what will I do without you?

# REFERENCES

1. The Kenneth B. Schwartz Center. Available at: http://www.theschwartzcenter.org, accessed December 13, 2007.
2. Riess H, Marci C. Behavioral science: the role of neurobiology and physiology of empathy in enhancing the patient doctor relationship. *Med Encount.* 2007; 21(3):38–39.
3. Balint M. *The Doctor, His Patient, and the Illness.* 2nd ed. New York, NY: International Universities Press; 1972:1.
4. Branch WT Jr. Is the therapeutic nature of the patient–physician relationship being undermined? A primary care physician's perspective [commentary]. *Arch Intern Med.* 2000;160(15):2257.
5. Branch WT Jr. Is the therapeutic nature of the patient–physician relationship being undermined? A primary care physician's perspective [commentary]. *Arch Intern Med.* 2000;160(15):2258.
6. Riess H, Marci C. Behavioral science—The role of neurobiology and physiology of empathy in enhancing the patient doctor relationship. *Med Encount.* 2007;21(3):38.
7. Hilfiker D. *Healing the Wounds: A Physician Looks at His Work.* New York, NY: Pantheon Books; 1985:37.
8. Aring CD. Sympathy and empathy. *JAMA.* 1958;167(4):448–452.
9. Aring CD. Sympathy and empathy. *JAMA.* 1958;167(4):449.
10. Anonymous Patient Interview. Interview with the author (GMD). October 28, 2007.
11. Hilfiker D. *Healing the Wounds: A Physician Looks at His Work.* New York, NY: Pantheon Books; 1985:52.
12. Hilfiker D. *Healing the Wounds: A Physician Looks at His Work.* New York, NY: Pantheon Books; 1985:53.
13. Spiro HM. *Empathy and the Practice of Medicine: Beyond Pills and the Scalpel.* New Haven, CT: Yale University Press; 1993:9.
14. Spiro HM. *Empathy and the Practice of Medicine: Beyond Pills and the Scalpel.* New Haven, CT: Yale University Press; 1993:4.
15. Bellini LM, Baime M, Shea JA. On call: issues in graduate medical education: variation of mood and empathy during internship. *JAMA.* 2002;287(23):3143.
16. West CP, Huschka MM, Novotny PJ, et al. Association of perceived medical errors with resident distress and empathy: a prospective longitudinal study. *JAMA.* 2006;296(9):1071.
17. Spiro H. What is empathy and can it be taught? *Ann Intern Med.* 1992;116(10):843.
18. Branch WT Jr, Kern D, Haidet P, et al. Teaching the human dimensions of care in clinical settings. *JAMA.* 2001;286(9):1067–1073.
19. Palmer PJ. *The Courage to Teach: Exploring the Inner Landscape of a Teacher's Life.* San Francisco, CA: Jossey-Bass; 1998:20.
20. Palmer PJ. The heart of a teacher: identity and integrity in teaching. *Change.* 1997;29(6):15–21.
21. Anonymous Patient Interview. Interview with the author (GMD). October 21, 2007.
22. Lown B. *The Lost Art of Healing.* Boston, MA: Houghton Mifflin; 1996:xiv.
23. Roter DL, Frankel RM, Hall JA, Sluyter D. The expression of emotion through non-verbal behavior in medical visits: mechanisms and outcomes. *J Gen Intern Med.* 2006;21:S28–S34.

24. Roter DL, Frankel RM, Hall JA, Sluyter D. The expression of emotion through non-verbal behavior in medical visits. Mechanisms and outcomes. *J Gen Intern Med.* 2006;21:S32.

25. Lown, B. *The Lost Art of Healing.* Boston, MA: Houghton Mifflin; 1996:3.

26. Kessels RPC. Patients' memory for medical information. *J Roy Soc Med.* 2003;(96):219–222.

27. Anonymous Family Interview. Interview with the author (BFS). November 19, 2007.

28. VandeKieft GK. Breaking bad news. *Am Fam Physician.* 2001;64(12):1975–1978.

29. VandeKieft GK. Breaking bad news. *Am Fam Physician.* 2001;64(12):1975.

30. NBC Today Show. Excerpt from *Battling Breast Cancer: Hoda's Personal Story.* Televised Interview; October 19, 2007.

31. Buckman, R, Kason Y. *How to Break Bad News: A Guide for Health Care Professionals.* Baltimore, MD: Johns Hopkins University Press; 1992.

32. Council Report Health Literacy: Report of the Council on Scientific Affairs: Ad Hoc Committee on Health Literacy for the Council on Scientific Affairs. *JAMA.* 1999;281(6):552–557.

33. National Patient Safety Foundation. Available at: http://NPSF.org, accessed March 3, 2008.

34. Kripalani S, Weiss BD. Teaching about health literacy and clear communication. *J Gen Inter Med.* 2006;21(8):889.

35. Anonymous Physician Interview. Interview with the author (GMD). October 24, 2007.

36. Carrillo JE, Green, AR, Betancourt JR. Cross-cultural primary care: a patient-based approach. *Ann of Intern Med.* 1999;130(10):829.

37. Kripalani S, Bussey-Jones J, Katz MG, Genao I. A prescription for cultural competence in medical education. *J Gen Intern Med.* 2006;21(10):1117.

38. Nápoles-Springer AM, Santoyo J, Houston K, Pérez-Stable EJ, Stewart AL. Patients' perceptions of cultural factors affecting the quality of their medical encounters. *Health Expect: Int J Public Participation Health Care Health Policy.* 2005;8(1):4–17.

39. Carrillo JE, Green AR, Betancourt JR. Cross-cultural primary care: a patient-based approach [Academia and Clinic]. *Ann of Intern Med.* 1999;130(10)833.

40. Mohr JC. American medical malpractice litigation in historical perspective. *JAMA.* 2000;283(13):1731.

41. Charles SC, Frisch PR. *Adverse Events, Stress, and Litigation: A Physician's Guide.* New York, NY: Oxford University Press; 2005:11.

42. Studdert DM, Mello MM, Brennan TA. Medical malpractice. *N Engl J Med.* 2004;350(3):283.

43. Beckman HB, Markakis KM, Suchman AL, Frankel RM. The doctor–patient relationship and malpractice. Lessons from plaintiff depositions. *Arch Intern Med.* 1994;154(12):1365–1370.

44. Hickson GB, Clayton EW, Githens PB, Sloan FA. Factors that prompted families to file medical malpractice claims following perinatal injuries. *JAMA.* 1992;267(10):1359–1363.

45. Levinson W, Roter DL, Mullooly JP, Dull VT, Frankel RM. Physician–patient communication: the relationship with malpractice claims among primary care physicians and surgeons. *JAMA.* 1997;277(7):553.

46. Merenstein JH. What will I do without you? *JAMA.* 2002;288(15):1823.

# Chapter 5

# The Difficult Physician–Patient Relationship

Mary Jo Fink

*If you listen carefully to what patients say, they will often tell you not only what is wrong with them but also what is wrong with you.*
Walker Percy

Two years ago, Maria was diagnosed with diabetes and high cholesterol. She attempted many times to lose weight, and exercising proved inadequate. At the time, the doctor expressed disappointment at the "failure" and ordered oral medications. He assured her that they should take care of the sugar problem. For her part, Maria only knew how difficult it was to follow strict dietary and exercise regimens and hoped that the pills would help. As always, however, her demand was this: "no generics." She came in for her regular follow-up visit armed with new information from the newspaper about the side effects of medications. She sat nervously as she awaited Dr. James. Before entering the room, Dr. James confirmed that the current medications were not controlling the levels; therefore, a new prescription, possibly even insulin, would need to be added.

After warmly greeting her, he initiated the conversation: "Maria, your labs are really out of whack; I think we're looking at adding a medication or even insulin." Maria uncovered the newspaper headlines about the patient deaths and started to express her concerns when Dr. James admonished: "Let me worry about the medication side effects. You just have to take them. Do you want to end up with a stroke or be in a coma?" He gave her a prescription for another oral medication and asked her to have her blood checked that day. She walked out without ever telling him that she had stopped one of the medications weeks before the visit and thought there would be no point in checking labs that day.

# The Practice of Medicine in the 21st Century

Maria represents a patient of the 21st century: She has a chronic condition that is very common and not amenable to improvement by the doctor's prescription alone; she has superficial familiarity with her diagnosis and wishes to make decisions about her care. She expresses entitlement about which medications she will take. Dr. James is a doctor of this century: He is a graduate of a primary care residency program, young but experienced and very busy. Dr. James takes many insurance plans that emphasize cost containment and clinical practice guidelines as part of regular CME; therefore, he is acutely aware of patient benchmarks for diabetes that are recorded in the form of "report cards," and although he is not cynical, like some of his senior colleagues about increased regulation and oversight eroding the autonomy of doctors, he is concerned about more recent talk of pay for performance.

What happened in the dynamic between Dr. James and Maria that hindered the collaborative trust? In personalizing the sense of failure, the doctor may be responding to an idealized portrait of the successful doctor, the one who meets the benchmarks for his patients and is able to motivate them to change behavior. He may be feeling the strain of the onerous insurance report that makes him responsible for this patient's outcome in a more public way, or he may be dismayed that Maria is passive and does not show perseverance and strength. Maria is investing her hope in the medication, a message that has been promoted in the media through direct-to-consumer advertising on television that may result in rising expectations for a quick fix or cure all. She may not even be aware of the continued importance of diet and exercise and instead has delegated responsibility to the medications alone.

This chronicle highlights changes in medicine that can best be understood in the context of a cultural shift that has evolved over the past 60 years. Expectations about power in the relationship itself were changed irrevocably by the civil and women's rights struggles. Additionally, data from the now famous Framingham study pointed to the importance of chronic conditions and their relationship to lifestyle, shifting the clinical treatment emphasis from hospital and office to the home and workplace. Advances in medical and surgical treatments for other conditions such as malignancies and acute coronary syndrome highlight the central role of the patient in the continuing success of the treatment. Resource-intensive and expensive treatment modalities for HIV and tuberculosis further underscore the patients' role in resistance or recurrence in the face of nonadherence. Maria and Dr. James must become partners for his medical expertise to be understood and translated into the particular context of her life outside of the office visit. Thus, chronic conditions make clear that power must be shared, for the doctor alone is impotent if he or she cannot form a collaborative relationship with the patient.

The collaboration is often complicated by discordant patient and physician backgrounds in terms of gender, class, race, and language. With increasing numbers of immigrants in particular, communication challenges have highlighted broader issues best clarified in the studies on health literacy[1] and racial disparities.[2] In our case, both parties speak the same language and may even share the same ethnic heritage. Maria can read and has brought a copy of the newspaper to the office visit to share her concerns with the doctor. In other cases, patients may present with an article from a major medical journal or after having completed a literature search on their own medical condition to suggest a treatment plan. Why did Dr. James not include Maria's concerns in the therapeutic plan? Is he responding to her passive, yet demanding manner? Does outside information present a threat to his authority or knowledge? Is he allowing office pressures to limit his time to query patients as well as reflect on the dynamic of discussions? Perhaps he too is struggling with a chronic condition in his own life or a family member's life and feels powerless in dealing with the challenge?

There is a rich and extensive literature on the dynamics present in the doctor–patient encounter that informs on approaches to promote effective communication. Connection is the sine qua non if the doctor and patient are to form a partnership to discover the healing process for the particular patient with a particular illness.

# Communication and the Art of Medicine

Within this sociohistorical context, a new role for patients and physicians has emerged. In the ideal setting between patient and doctor, there is a dialogue of trust and openness that allows the dyad to explore aspects of both the disease and the illness.[3] There is time to explore and enlighten the patient's signs and symptoms that may indicate a clear diagnosis or condition. In eliciting the patient's description and understanding of a complaint, the doctor employs open-ended inquiries, pauses, and silence to open the space. There is an appreciation for the nuances of verbal and nonverbal expression of the experience of illness. This internal processing of a symptom or feeling experienced by the patient may not be conscious. It includes the fears and fantasies, social supports, as well as the meaning that is attached to the symptom. If the doctor is able to connect with the patient in her or his life context, empathy is established. Empathy, as the foundation in the relationship that helps to maintain the professional role, allows the doctor to step back before responding positively, negatively, or indifferently to the patient. It is especially important in dynamics involving difficult attitudes and behavior.

Studies have shown that mutual satisfaction is increased, patient safety is better assured, malpractice claims are reduced, and patient outcomes and adherence are improved if effective communication exists.[4–7] A comparison of audio tapes of primary care doctors who did not have malpractice claims with those who had two or more claims showed that effective communicators employ a patient-centered style, facilitating discussions with the patient to solicit opinions, checking understanding, and encouraging patients to speak. This increased the visit time by an average of 3.3 minutes.[6] Equally important in this process is the art of empowering patients to express their agenda. A 1984 study investigating the clinical interview showed that it took only 18 seconds before the patient was interrupted;[8] a follow-up in 1999 indicated that this had changed only minimally to 26 seconds. Those patients who were allowed to speak without redirection took only 6 seconds longer and expressed fewer late-arising concerns,[9] the so-called door knob diagnoses. The importance of the therapeutic "preproblem relationship" with the doctor is underscored by the finding that trauma patients had significantly higher malpractice claims when compared with other high-risk groups in women's health and cardiothoracic surgery.[10]

The paramount importance of the patient's life context to the doctor–patient dialogue found expression in the ground-breaking work of Dr. George Engel wherein he challenged the "dogma" of biomedicine to broaden its vision in the biopsychosocial model.[11] This shift from a reductionist model of Cartesian mind-body dualism includes the patient's social context and emotional life that impact the disease process and its very meaning. The patient-centered clinical method offers an interactive framework to include the patient's understanding of the illness and its impact on daily life, the physician's understanding of the entire person, and the need to find "common ground" in the management of the illness. This shared search, negotiated through verbal and nonverbal communication, includes three areas: defining the problem, establishing the goals of treatment, and identifying the roles for the doctor and the patient.[12] Sensitivity and flexibility on the part of the doctor are crucial, for some patients may need the assurance of an authoritative voice and expect a paternalistic doctor. Others seek assurance through collaboration and expect a partner relationship. Still others may need a listening observer as they recount a traumatic experience that may be resurfacing in the form of symptoms. Through the very telling to the witness, the power of the trauma is attenuated. This process of finding common ground can become more complicated if a patient's usual manner of responding changes dramatically when faced with the diagnosis of a chronic or life-threatening condition. This is the art of medicine that can be hard to employ in the difficult doctor–patient encounter.

# Difficult Encounters for Patients and Doctors

Fifteen percent of primary care encounters are considered difficult[13,14] or variably described as "frustrating,"[15] "problem,"[16] "disliked,"[17] and even "hateful."[18] Important patient and physician factors that result in difficult encounters have been noted: Difficult patients are more likely to somatize symptoms with multiple physical complaints and greater severity on the pain scale or express concern that the symptoms represent a threatening illness; these patients are also found more often to have an underlying mood or anxiety disorder. Of the physician factors, including age, gender, ethnicity, and number of years in practice, only poorer attitude scores toward psychosocial problems independently increased the likelihood of difficulty in the encounter.[19] Physicians may lack experience impacting self-confidence or feel overwhelmed when called on to address psychosocial problems that they consider outside of their expertise as physicians.[13]

In the sentinel article on "hateful patients," four patient stereotypes that engender feelings of dread in physicians are described: dependent clingers, entitled demanders, manipulative help rejecters, and self-destructive deniers.[18] These are patients that every doctor knows and whose neediness and dependence, manipulation and threats, pessimism and depression, or self-destructive behaviors threaten the very establishment of the empathy that is so necessary for insight and effective therapeutic intervention.

The needs expressed by the helpless and dependent patient may not always be clear. Cloaked in conscious and unconscious expressions of need, the patient implores the doctor to become the hero or caretaker. The doctor can respond with the prescription pad, cynicism, or even an invitation to a dependent relationship, or the doctor can appreciate the message embedded in the behavior and present open questions about the emotions as assurance of a caring listener. Once interpreted and understood, it is possible to set appropriate limits in the relationship.

---

Marla, a recently separated mother of three young children with headaches, returns to the doctor; she wants to assure him that he is the open communicator she never had in her husband. She was a patient of one of his older colleagues and only recently met him during urgent visits. Since that time, she has called the answering service innumerable times to describe in more detail the headaches and express her gratitude to him. In returning the calls to emphasize the course of therapy and offer encouragement, he feels flattered and occasionally overwhelmed with the responsibility.

---

Had the doctor in the scenario been aware of his own feelings as clues to the subtext in the conversation, he may have noted that the patient, through her charm and calls, was inviting a dependent relationship. Is this the first time he has experienced such an invitation in the professional relationship, or is he bereft of social contacts in his own life and is fulfilling this need through the office visits? Does the helper role make him feel stronger? In responding with concerned calls and visits, he becomes an enabler. The stage is set for unmet patient expectations and physician fatigue. Perpetuation of the dynamic may compromise the very therapeutic connection that she needs. The insightful doctor is invited to view his or her own feelings as a window to the clinical diagnosis and necessary intervention. The doctor would be aware of the feelings that are evoked in the meeting instead of merely reacting to the patient's attitude and behavior.[18,20] In this case, the doctor should consciously note the feelings produced by the charm and flattery as well as the weight of the responsibility. He may interpret these as signs showing the need for clear boundaries between himself and the patient as part of the treatment. He may see a connection between the headaches and the patient's relationship to her husband. Then he may choose to have the nurse return the patient's calls or schedule the patient with her regular doctor and avoid the consequences of greater dependence.

The importance of acknowledging one's own response cannot be overemphasized. This is particularly important in treating patients with a chronic illness or condition. Life's daily rhythms may be interrupted by symptoms of illness to include changes in sleep, work, exercise, or sexual function. The difficulties that threaten the patient's independence are a constant reminder that there has been a change in the old self. The fear of loss or even treatment may delay the visit to the doctor, where the patient may express conflicted feelings or subconscious fears and fantasies with suspicion, anger, listlessness, or a need for control. There is a loss of confidence and with it self-esteem. Progression or recurrence of the condition is often accompanied by feelings of shame, especially if related to personal behaviors, such as smoking or eating.

---

Barbara, a 48-year-old nurse, returns to the office for her monthly check-up. She's been more careful over the past year after having been diagnosed with diabetes. It wasn't a total surprise; her doctor had predicted this over four years ago with a warning about the weight gain. Barbara has tried everything to no avail. The doctor enters the room with the results of her labs and says: "Well, we're inching closer to insulin; I see it didn't help to speak to the nutritionist!"

---

The doctor's frustration with the lack of progress and success in the treatment plan is articulated in sarcasm. At other times, it may be expressed as blame, anger, or resignation. Why is the doctor frustrated or angry? Is it fear of acknowledging defeat? Is it disappointment that the patient is not disciplined enough to carry out the plan, or is the doctor also challenged by the personal experience of a chronic condition that has either been controlled or not? Whatever the background feelings, they are brought into the encounter. They impact the detail of the interaction, the words that are chosen, the stance of the body, and the look in the eye. Understanding them in this context can inform on potential inroads into the life of the patient. In the case of chronic illness, collaboration with other disciplines can greatly enhance the options for effective treatment. In this process, the doctor does not abdicate power and give up, but rather engages with the patient in a process that leads to an agreed-on management plan.[12] At times, the doctor may note feelings of disgust or dislike for the patient or the behavior that may point to a serious underlying psychiatric disorder[15] or organic brain disease with suicidal intentions,[17] which could explain the patient's behaviors and considerably modify the physician's response. Indeed, if the physician is able to hear what the patient is saying about him, he himself becomes part of the patient's therapy to affect change.[21]

Tuning in to feelings elicited by patients' attitudes and behaviors is not as easy as it would seem. The very act of "tuning in" presupposes an ability to reflect on the dynamic between the self and the other. In observing how a patient's whining, drug seeking, beauty, or sweetness is impacting thoughts and feelings, the doctor shows an appreciation of the dynamic role that feelings and personal biases have in doctor–patient communication. Acknowledging one's emotions and responses has been found to be central to coping effectively with patients' reactions.[22] Without this sense of self and ability to stand outside the communication, the doctor's reaction or overreaction represents a risk to the therapeutic encounter.

---

"I had to stop the medication; the nausea was awful, and although I didn't vomit, I constantly felt like it. Can't you find a drug without side effects?" This was the plea of the young man who had been diagnosed with HIV some years ago. The doctor was perplexed and frustrated because he had "failed" so many other drugs and nothing seemed to help. She also recalled that he had written a complaint letter to the medical board about his former doctor. The patient feels betrayed by the doctors and a medical system that cannot provide the right therapy for him. In addressing his accusations, the doctor defends her medical management in response to her feelings of rejection and vulnerability.

---

The doctor is on the defensive with this patient, who is entitled and demanding. To date, neither she nor others have been able to help the patient feel better. Indeed, another physician has already been publicly targeted by the patient. This may hamper her appreciation of her own feelings of vulnerability, which if understood could be a tip-off to the patient's fears and sense of loss that the diagnosis of HIV may imply. If, on the other hand, the doctor interprets her feelings within the context of the empathic dyad, she may be able to address the patient's fears through an invitation to collaborate more actively in the treatment plan while acknowledging his right to high-quality, excellent medical care. It may be enough to say this: "I am sure this is more frustrating for you than it is for me. Together, let us look at the medication possibilities and see if there is anything we can do to minimize the side effects." These words may assure the patient that it is their mutual concern and that together there is hope in finding the acceptable medication. On the other hand, if such an invitation is not reciprocated, this may indicate a need for additional help to address the patient's personality or judgment barriers.

Vague complaints that are often expressed in an unfocused, rambling manner can present challenges to the effective therapeutic relationship. The doctor may feel overwhelmed by the sheer number of concerns that may not fit into one unifying diagnosis or disease, or there could be the thought that the patient is somatizing or malingering to get attention or be difficult. The headache may respond to the therapeutic regimen, only to be followed by "funny feelings" in the abdomen or nervous anxiety. These patients usually have extensive medical records reflecting a multitude of tests, many with normal findings.

During the initial introduction, a 43-year-old patient confided in the doctor that she had been seen by many doctors but has never been satisfied with any of them. Her problems are still the same, and all of the treatments cannot help her. Indeed, as the doctor reviews the voluminous medical record, she notes that the patient has had multiple tests and abdominal surgeries to address her diffuse and "wandering" pain. The doctor feels overwhelmed and defeated.

At this point, the doctor can respond to the challenge to include herself on the list of doctors who have failed to understand and decode the patient's symptoms of pain. On the other hand, she can reassure the patient that there may be hope and ask for time and patience. For this to work, the doctor must engage the patient in her own healing process. The plan may include concrete aspects such as a pain or food diary, regular exercise, or journaling to assess feelings and associations connected with the symptoms. Short, focused visits at weekly intervals at first may assure the patient that her concerns are being addressed and taken seriously. In this initial period, the physical exam is important as a sign of human touch and connection. Equally important, the exam serves as a means to reassure both the doctor and the patient that there is no sign of an acute medical condition. With time and effort, the symptoms may be understood and dissipate, or they may become declarative, calling for adjunct psychotherapy. Indeed, the doctor's own intuition may point in this direction. Hearing and heeding this sense is part of medicine's art.

The patient with chronic pain represents an especially challenging problem for patients and doctors. Even minor, acute pain may change the individual's ability to focus on tasks, cope with unanticipated life events, or relate effectively with others. Whether dull and throbbing, gnawing and constant, or sharp and focused, pain begs for relief. Society has entrusted diagnosis and treatment of pain to the physician with the implicit expectation that treatment for pain will be effective and not result in harm. Ironically, powerful medications have not only the potential to treat pain but also to create dependence. The doctor's fear alone can create a barrier to diagnosis and treatment.

John's cane-assisted gait is not the only reminder of the day he fell from the 20-foot ladder, disabling him from working as a master carpenter. Initially, the pain was not adequately treated in the ambulance; thus, by the time they reached the emergency room, he was writhing in excruciating pain, alleviated by only morphine. Studies excluded severe pathology necessitating surgery, and he was treated for a few days with ever-decreasing amounts of opiates and muscle relaxants. Thereafter, he was discharged in moderate pain on oral medications and given an appointment for rehabilitation. Within days, he was seeing his family doctor to request more pain medications.

If the doctor knows John well, she may know his family and the role that work plays in his life and self-identity. She may know how he copes with pain, stress, or failure. If she ever attended him during a minor or major illness that included pain, she may have clues about his reactions and expectations. Is John someone who tends to exaggerate or minimize? Is he someone who enjoys his work, or would he prefer a change? Has he ever experienced the sick role? How is this accepted in his family and community?

Many people, young men in particular, may not have a regular family doctor who knows them in this sense. They may have only been seen for minor, acute-care visits that offer few clues about the answers to these questions. This creates a powerful dynamic between doctor and patient. The doctor's perspective may be colored by her own experience of pain and the response to pain. In one family or community, a histrionic response is acceptable, whereas in another a more stoic one is the norm, or she may know addiction first hand in herself or in a beloved family member or friend and regard his presentation as a threat. How she has processed these life experiences will impact her reaction to enable the patient in pain, to become hardened to the plight that pain presents, or to use the depth of insight to guide the care of the patient. Her mentors in medical education may have presented the paradox of treating pain in full understanding of the responsibility that physicians bear to relieve suffering without causing harm, or they may have given her messages of cynicism—that pain patients are all drug seekers. Finally, she may be relatively inexperienced and feel manipulated in the course of dealing with the problem. This will all impact her response to this patient. The true healer of pain will be able to establish the trust relationship, remain mindful of the impact that the dynamic is having on her, and step back to reflect with the patient on the meaning and potential resolution. For the plan to be effective, there must be a commitment to the "common ground" that they find. In certain circumstances, it is important to assure the patient that he is welcome to return without the symptoms of pain.

Dealing with the angry patient is one of the most taxing and demanding realities that faces a doctor in the professional encounter. At times, the anger is directed toward the doctor after a perceived mistake or omission. At others, it is based on prior experience with another professional or the "medical system" where the doctor is the visible surrogate for the inefficient registration process or insurance company denial. For some patients, the expression of anger is in response to the diagnosis that has been confirmed. Whatever the source of the patient's anger, it is important to acknowledge it and explore the basic feelings within the context. If it is directed at the doctor, a simple statement of apology may suffice to diffuse the situation and turn attention to the present expectations and future course. If it is more diffuse in its target, it can be helpful to guide the patient in dealing with annoying and frustrating situations that provoke his or her anger. The very act of listening demonstrates professional humility that has power to calm the patient and the dialogue. Admittedly this is not easy: The natural reaction to attack is defense. In the doctor–patient encounter, however, following what seems natural can backfire to escalate the negative emotions and result in a nontherapeutic encounter for the patient and in some cases an unsafe situation for the doctor.

# The Making of a Doctor

Much in the physician's background and training runs counter to the appeal for introspection and reflection. Doctors' training focuses on "doing" something to achieve assurance in the diagnosis and to fix or cure what is broken or diseased. Disease and death are defined as the "enemy" to be eradicated and not meditated. Cartesian influence in education and training emphasizes the reduction of problems into constituent parts and often neglects the whole. Additionally, instruction in decoding the patient's symptoms encourages the search for this broken part or abnormal finding without attention to the *meaning* of patient symptoms. What fears or associations does the symptom or the treatment unleash? Has the patient seen a friend or family member suffering the same? What does the patient expect of the doctor? Has the doctor failed to recognize similar symptoms in another patient that resulted in an adverse outcome and now is overreacting? Exploration of these kinds of questions is often delegated to psychiatry or psychology after the medical workup or therapy has failed, when in fact they are so central to the medical care of the patient.

Indeed, the traditional technique employed to understand the patient's symptom or problem emphasizes facts and objective findings. The maxim to remain objective in diagnosis and treatment may result in the patient's story being selectively recorded so that signs or symptoms fit neatly into a diagnostic package ready for treatment. The very way that physicians interview patients may suppress the patient's complex and rich narrative. This struggle between the voice of medicine and the voice of the lifeworld[23] can end in dissonance and potentially ineffective care. There is unspoken skepticism that an attempt to integrate meaning into the analysis could confuse the picture and add a level of complexity that defies definition. The result is overliteral interpretation of accounts best understood metaphorically.[24] Two serious moral dilemmas are the consequence of this training approach: insensitivity to suffering, as a result of distancing through abstractions, and abuse of power, enhanced by prognostic and therapeutic advances.[12]

In medical school and residency, there is an emphasis on "success" in identifying and treating the right problem. Indeed, patient case reviews in morbidity and mortality conferences focus on the problem that was missed or not properly addressed. This confidential internal case review emphasizes learning and improving knowledge, whereas a more public, "external" review of the case through litigation represents a different threat to the doctor's "success." In this regard, it is important to note a significant study on primary care physicians with and without malpractice claims. Those who did not have claims used more effective communication skills with statements about what to expect at the office visit. Compared with their counterparts, these physicians were also able to employ laughter and solicit patients' opinions.[6] Success then implies more than treating the right problem; it must also include an ability to connect with the patient.

The need to succeed and do things right is served well by the physicians' single-minded dedication to medicine; indeed, few other professions inculcate compulsiveness as a positive trait; however, the limitations were even clear to Sir William Osler: "Engrossed late and soon in professional cares—you may so lay waste that you may find, too late, with hearts given way, that there is no place in your habit-stricken souls for those gentler influences which make life worth living."[25] A compulsive triad of doubt, guilt feelings, and an exaggerated sense of responsibility,[26] all part of medical and residency training, serves the physician in adaptive and maladaptive ways. When maladaptive, the sense of responsibility is not balanced with relaxation, vacation, and time for friends and family. As demands increase, the physician may develop symptoms and signs of burnout, including emotional exhaustion and clinical ineffectiveness.[27] These symptoms may result in medical mistakes and malpractice claims,[28] further eroding "success" and underscoring guilt feelings and the tendency to feel responsible for things beyond one's control.[26] Burnout as "erosion of the soul"[29] represents a vicious cycle, leaving the physician with a poor sense of self and inability to reflect. Without change, the obsessive-compulsive tendencies may even end in addictions beyond work to alcohol and drugs.[30] In 2001, the *Western Journal of Medicine* devoted an entire issue to the timely subject of physician well-being. Not only is there an immense human cost to burnout, but a realization that the cost to health care is enormous when a physician must be replaced; one study estimated the replacement value of a primary care doctor to be around \$250,000.[27]

There has been recognition that the education and training of doctors must change and include life-long learning. The importance of communication in the doctor–patient relationship found its voice in the ground-breaking work of Dr. Barbara Korsch in the late 1960s. Her studies showed how important communication is to patient satisfaction and follow-through with medical advice.[31] Her work continues to inform doctors and patients on the skills and attitudes so necessary to finding "common ground." Although communication in the doctor–patient relationship was integral to family medicine curricula since its inception and central to many primary care medicine and pediatric residencies, there had been a marginal role to this subject until the late 1990s. At that time, the regulating bodies for medical education and residency training showed renewed interest in the role of communication in teaching the art of medicine. Both curricula and evaluation criteria were broadened to include core competencies, including communication and professionalism.[32,33] For physicians in practice, there was a parallel movement from the Institute of Medicine[34] and Joint Commission on Accreditation of Healthcare Organizations[7] that emphasized the importance of communication on patient care. There is an acknowledgment that communication affects patient safety, collegial collaboration, hospital organization, and professional development.

# Toward a Transformative Doctor–Patient Relationship

The ancient implore *know thyself* is central to the physician's ability to listen, be present, and respond empathetically to the patient. If the physician is distracted, unhappy, overworked, sleep deprived, or otherwise unable to pursue interests outside of work, she may not be focused or may become disenchanted and cynical. The first step is recognition and acknowledgment of the need for self-care. For some, adequate time with family and friends, exercise, meditation, or spiritual practice may provide this necessary space.[35,36] For others, it may be a Balint group, a conference, or a conversation with a trusted colleague that enables one to understand and respond to difficult encounters.[22] This work is challenging yet rewarding. The call to reclaim meaning in physicians' working lives begins with a commitment to service.[37] Service offers connection, the physician's very raison d'être. For transformation in the doctor–patient encounter to occur, attention must be given to the work environment as well. Physicians report that control over clinical issues sustains and enhances job satisfaction. Additionally, participation in decision making and resource allocation in the workplace decreases job stress.[36]

Physicians cannot commit to serve if they are not able to function effectively in their places of work.

When respected family doctors were asked about coping skills in the difficult encounter, management strategies were classified into three categories: collaboration, empathy, and the appropriate use of power. This includes establishing teamwork and coaching, agreeing to the same priorities, setting boundaries and rules, and showing compassion.[22] Admittedly, it is not always easy; the tendency to take over the conversation may be ever present. One preceptor, while working with a doctor who was having difficulty being understood, suggested that he just listen and use continuers: "say 'uh huh' three times."[8] There was a perceptible change in a short time! A personable style is appealing; however, chatty, personal stories can take over the conversation and silence the patient.[38] If the doctor can remember that the patient is at the center of the encounter, this pitfall can be avoided, and there can be true dialogue. Most effective communicators report that a nondirective style with open questions such as "what is it like?" or "can you tell me more?" allow for uninterrupted flow of information. While listening, the doctor observes and acknowledges clues about emotions that accompany the information but may not be directly expressed.[39]

The context of care as well as the patient's motivation in seeking care influences the level of communication. In the emergency room visit for minor trauma, a simple inquiry into the mechanism of injury suffices, as does the quick throat culture for a primary care patient who presents with a sore throat in the ambulatory setting; however, if these same patients present with major trauma and threatened limb amputation or a large suspicious mass in the oral cavity, the content of the conversation, the tone of the voice, the pose of one body to the other all change to indicate presence, and attention to the seriousness of the patient's condition and suffering. Indeed, there are certain patient complaints and conditions that call for a deeper level of interpersonal communion: complaints associated with life-threatening disease or unusual, bizarre, nonphysiologic symptoms; complaints arising from life change or conflict; and those that require risky procedures. Additionally, conditions that are incurable, relate to habits and lifestyle, or involve ethical decisions require that the encounter be one of deep understanding and trust.[40] To engage with the patient during these encounters and accompany them through the difficult course invites exchange about the very meaning of life and death. Here, the patient needs to connect with the doctor and present concerns in his or her particular life context; the doctor needs to be open to the entire person as listener and witness. For the patient and doctor who enter into this dialogue built on trust, the level of communication between them will assume meaning that has transforming potential. Life's meaning is realized in this I–Thou relationship.[41] This is the privilege of *being* a doctor.

# REFERENCES

1. Rudd R, Moeynkens BA, Colton TC. *Health and Literacy: A Review of Medical and Public Health Literature.* New York, NY: Jossey-Bass; 1999. Available at: http://www.hsph.harvard.edu/healthliteracy/litreview_final.pdf, accessed November 7, 2007.
2. Betancourt JR, King RK. Unequal treatment: the Institute of Medicine report and its public health implications. *Public Health Rep.* 2003;118(4):287–292.
3. McWhinney IR. Are we on the brink of a major transformation of clinical method? *CMAJ.* 1986;135(8):873–878.
4. Stewart M, Brown JB, Donner A, et al. The impact of patient-centered care on outcomes. *J Fam Pract.* 2000;49(9):796–804.
5. Huntington B, Kuhn N. Communication gaffes: a root cause of malpractice claims. *Proc Bayl Univ Med Cent.* 2003;16(2):157–161.
6. Levinson W, Roter DL, Mullooly JP, Dull VT, Frankel RM. Physician–patient communication: the relationship with malpractice claims among primary care physicians and surgeons. *JAMA.* 1997;277(7):553–559.
7. Joint Commission Resources. *The Joint Commission Guide to Improving Staff Communication.* Available at: http://books.google.com/books, accessed October 1, 2007.
8. Beckman HB, Frankel RM. The effect of physician behavior on the collection of data. *Ann Intern Med.* 1984;101(5):692–696.
9. Marvel MK, Epstein RM, Flowers K, Beckman HB. Soliciting the patient's agenda: have we improved? *JAMA.* 1999;281(3):283–287.
10. Morris JA Jr, Carrillo Y, Jenkins JM, et al. Surgical adverse events, risk management, and malpractice outcome: morbidity and mortality review is not enough. *Ann Surg.* 2003;237(6):844–851.
11. Engel GL. The need for a new medical model: a challenge for biomedicine. *Science.* 1977;196(4286):129–136.
12. Stewart M, Brown JB, Weston WW, et al. *Patient-Centered Medicine: Transforming the Clinical Method.* London: Sage; 1995.
13. Crutcher JE, Bass MJ. The difficult patient and the troubled physician. *J Fam Pract.* 1980;11(6):933–938.
14. Hahn SR, Kroenke K, Spitzer RL, et al. The difficult patient: prevalence, psychopathology, and functional impairment. *J Gen Intern Med.* 1996;11:1–8.
15. Lin EH, Katon W, Von KM, et al. Frustrating patients: physician and patient perspectives among distressed high users of medical services. *J Gen Intern Med.* 1991;6(3):241–246.
16. Drossman DA. The problem patient: evaluation and care of medical patients with psychosocial disturbances. *Ann Intern Med.* 1978;88(3):366–372.
17. Goodwin JM, Goodwin JS, Kellner R. Psychiatric symptoms in disliked medical patients. *JAMA.* 1979;241(11):1117–1120.
18. Groves JE. Taking care of the hateful patient. *N Engl J Med.* 1978;298(16):883–887.
19. Jackson JL, Kroenke K. Difficult patient encounters in the ambulatory clinic: clinical predictors and outcomes. *Arch Intern Med.* 1999;159(10):1069–1075.
20. Goldberg PE. The physician–patient relationship: three psychodynamic concepts that can be applied to primary care. *Arch Fam Med.* 2000;9(10):1164–1168.
21. Balint M. *The Doctor, His Patient, and the Illness.* American ed. New York, NY: International Universities Press; 1957.

22. Elder N, Ricer R, Tobias B. How respected family physicians manage difficult patient encounters. *J Am Board Fam Med.* 2006;19(6):533–541.

23. Mishler E. *The Discourse of Medicine: The Dialectics of Medical Interviews.* Norwood, NJ: Ablex; 1985.

24. Kleinman A. *The Illness Narratives.* New York, NY: Basic Books; 1998.

25. Osler W. *Counsels and Ideals from the Writings of William Osler.* 2007;196. Available at: http://books.google.com/books, accessed August 25, 2007.

26. Gabbard GO. The role of compulsiveness in the normal physician. *JAMA.* 1985; 254(20):2926–2929.

27. Spickard A, Gabbe S, Christensen JF. Mid-career burnout in generalist and specialist physicians. *JAMA.* 2002;288(12):1447–1450.

28. Crane M. Why burned-out doctors get sued more often. *Med Econ.* 1998;75(10): 210–218.

29. Maslach C, Leither MP. *The Truth About Burnout.* San Francisco, CA: Josey-Bass; 1997.

30. Dodd DT. Center for Professional Health, Vanderbilt Medical Center. Available at: http://www.mc.vanderbilt.edu/root/vumc.php?=cph&doc=683, accessed October 25, 2007.

31. Korsch BM, Gozzi EK, Francis V. Gaps in doctor–patient communication. 1. Doctor–patient interaction and patient satisfaction. *Pediatrics.* 1968;42(5):855–871.

32. Markakis KM, Beckman HB, Suchman AL, Frankel RM. The path to professionalism: cultivating humanistic values and attitudes in residency training. *Acad Med.* 2000;75:141–150.

33. AAMC Report III. Contemporary Issues in Medicine: Communication in Medicine. Available at: http://www.aamc.org/meded/msop, accessed October 25, 2007.

34. Washburn ER. Fast forward: a blueprint for the future from the Institute of Medicine. *Physician Exec.* 2001;27(3):8–14.

35. Epstein RM. Mindful practice. *JAMA.* 1999;282(9):833–839.

36. Williams ES, Konrad TR, Scheckler WE, et al. Understanding physicians' intentions to withdraw from practice: the role of job satisfaction, job stress, mental and physical health. *Health Care Manage Rev.* 2001;26(1):7–19.

37. Remen R. Recapturing the soul of medicine. *West J Med.* 2007;174(1):1–4.

38. McDaniel SH, Beckman HB, Morse DS, Silberman J, Seaburn DB, Epstein RM. Physician self-disclosure in primary care visits: enough about you, what about me? *Arch Intern Med.* 2007;167(12):1321–1326.

39. Suchman AL, Markakis K, Beckman HB, Frankel R. A model of empathic communication in the medical interview. *JAMA.* 1997;277(8):678-682.

40. Stephens G. *The Intellectual Basis of Family Practice.* Tucson, AZ: Society of Teachers of Family Medicine (STFM) Foundation; 1982.

41. Buber M. *I and Thou.* New York, NY: Scribner; 1955.

# Chapter 6

# Hallmarks of a Successful Practice

Victor R. Klein

*True success in medicine is not easy.*
*It requires will, attention to detail, and creativity.*
Atul Gawande, MD

A 36-year-old woman with heavy vaginal bleeding saw her gynecologist, who diagnosed dysfunctional uterine bleeding and advised iron and expectant management. The next day the patient called the office and reported that she had heavy bleeding. The gynecologist's associate advised her to make an emergency appointment for that day and promised the patient that she would be seen whenever she arrived at the office. The patient left work but went home instead. She presented to the emergency department the following day with heavy vaginal bleeding and in hypovolemic shock. She received several units of blood but suffered a stroke.

The patient subsequently sued her physician and his associate. The plaintiff's attorney argued in his opening statement that there was a delay in appropriate treatment in a bleeding patient. The defense expert argued that the associate never saw the patient but was willing to see the patient; however, she never showed up. A verdict was returned for several million dollars against the treating physician for failure to assess and treat the patient properly. The jury found no negligence by the second physician, as he was available and willing to see the patient who failed to show up. Imagine if the doctor was too busy to see her and told her to come a few days later.

How often does your staff say to a patient when they call your office for an emergency appointment, "Sorry we are busy today, but next week we can fit you in"?

After hearing the medical facts of the case, jurors serving in malpractice trials often look for certain attributes in the defendant doctor. The jurors consider how that physician conducts his or her practice to help them form an opinion about whether the doctor has committed malpractice. Is the defendant doctor caring and well trained? Was the doctor rushed during an appointment? Was the doctor talking on the phone, or was he or she otherwise preoccupied when making decisions about the patient's care? Was the care that was rendered well documented in the medical record, or is there a lingering question that is not readily answered because the medical record is incomplete? In this chapter, the fundamental aspects of a successful practice are explored, drawing on my experience in a large obstetrical/gynecological practice.

During my obstetrics and gynecology residency at the Johns Hopkins Hospital over 20 years ago, one of my teachers impressed on me the importance of the four A's of being a successful doctor:

Able
Affable
Available
Affordable

I have come to consider these attributes as the basis of a successful practice.

# Ability

An *able* physician is one who is well trained in his or her area of expertise. He or she keeps up to date in the field by learning the newest technology and applying the newest principles to improving patient care. He or she ensures continuing medical education through conferences, journals, grand rounds, and web casts.

An able physician is aware of the limitations of his or her skills and fund of knowledge and, furthermore, is able to guide patients in obtaining the best medical care possible by networking with other physicians in whose ability he or she has developed confidence. An example of changes in practice and skills in obstetrics is the use of forceps and laparoscopy. Physicians who have been in practice for a long time may be skilled in the use of forceps but may not be able to perform newer laparoscopic surgery. Younger physicians and physicians in training are learning advanced laparoscopic surgery but may not be intensively trained in operative vaginal deliveries. This difference in training is not right or wrong. It is an example of the progression in the field of medicine over time.

## Effective Communication

A patient who was expecting triplets was at 26-weeks gestation. The home care company that was assisting in monitoring the pregnancy called the doctor's office on a Friday afternoon to report a problem. The secretary took the message but failed to relay the concern of possible preterm labor to the doctor on call. The triplets delivered prematurely, and their parents subsequently sued the physician for failure to act on preterm labor. The home care company's position was that it fulfilled its duty by alerting the physician's office to the problem.

Central to the physician's ability to provide good patient care is communication, not only with patients but also with other physicians and the staff in the office. In this case, the breach of the standard of care was that the doctor was not told of critical information by the staff, resulting in an adverse outcome.

In order for a practice to function efficiently, there must be effective communication among the physicians in the practice and between the physicians and the staff. Not only must staff be schooled as to how to identify urgent matters that must be brought to the physician's attention urgently, but the practice must also maintain a standardized method of taking and delivering messages to guard against lapses such as those that occurred in this case.

Meetings with the office staff and physicians are an important way of encouraging the desired communication with staff. This is also an excellent forum to introduce new policies and procedures and clarify existing ones. Meetings among the physicians themselves are an important way of helping to ensure that information about their common patients and concerns related to the care of patients and the practice overall are shared with all of the physicians.

It is also important for meetings to be held between the administrative personnel in the practice and staff members at all levels. This provides an opportunity for them to strengthen their own communication concerning the support that they provide in the practice. Often, the people on the front lines, such as your receptionist (more so than the managers who may be insulated from the day-to-day patient flow and contact), can help to identify concerns that should be addressed. We look to the people who answer the telephones for ideas on how to improve the functioning of this very important aspect of the practice.

## Medical Records

"There is evidence to suggest that documentation itself is an important element of quality care."[1] In any facility where medical care is provided, it is important to recognize the critical role of the medical record. The chart is an important vehicle of communication between providers of the patient's care and is also where the care and treatment of the patient is memorialized for future care, reimbursement purposes, and legal reasons.

It is well known that a significant percentage of malpractice cases are lost because of poor documentation. One should be able to read the chart in the office or the progress note in the hospital and understand the patient's course without ever speaking with the persons who wrote the notes. Complete and thorough medical records are particularly important to group practices in which several physicians care for a patient during an illness or, in my specialty, a pregnancy. Handwriting must be legible, and treatment plans must be outlined so that the next physician who sees the patient can indeed ensure the continuity of the patient's care.

It can be very embarrassing in court to try to read your own notes and not be able to understand what you wrote years after they were written, to say nothing of the errors that could result when others who are providing care for the patient are unable to read the chart entries. When I was a Fellow in Maternal Fetal Medicine at Parkland Memorial Hospital in Dallas, there were over 60 residents who worked in the clinic. The chief of obstetrics stressed that the "chart is the patient's doctor." He meant that careful documentation of findings and clinical plans was essential, especially because a large number of physicians and staff provided care for the patients. He wanted us to prepare notes, bearing in mind that there would be no one to interpret what was meant by a note, however, a note written with its true purpose in mind would make the clinical care being rendered clear to any succeeding provider.

Even before HIPAA existed, physicians had a responsibility to ensure the confidentiality of patient information. This is another concern regarding medical records as well as the verbal transmission of medical information. When we consider the kind of information that patients entrust into our safekeeping, it is of utmost importance that patient information is only shared on a need-to-know basis and only with those for whom the patient has issued his or her express authorization.

Caution must be exercised to maintain patient confidentiality. Protocols to prevent medical information from being improperly released must be implemented in each office. All staff should be educated in and familiar with these requirements. For example, in obstetrics, where husbands or significant others are closely involved with the medical care rendered to the pregnant patient, our staff is trained to know that consent must be obtained from the patient if she wants to allow her partner to have access to her medical information. Genetic information must be even more carefully protected.

## Staff and Their Role in the Practice

Doctors are doctors, nurses are nurses, secretaries are secretaries, and receptionists are receptionists. All have specific duties, functions, and limitations. Receptionists should not be permitted to put on a white coat and take a patient's blood pressure. Nurses should not be permitted to perform minor surgical procedures in the office. The professionals who work in your office must work within their scope of practice.

---

A doctor was sued in a medical malpractice action by a patient who had a complication following a surgical procedure in her office. During the discovery portion of the case, it was determined that the "nurse" was really the receptionist who wore a white coat, obtained vital signs, and took care of the patient postoperatively after a dilatation and curettage in the office.

---

The receptionist was considered to be practicing medicine without a license. Not only was there a malpractice action against the physician, but the state also commenced disciplinary proceedings against the physician. From a malpractice point of view, physicians are vicariously responsible for their employees' actions. Staff must not be permitted to function above their level of training nor even be permitted to give the impression that they work in a capacity in which they do not. The staff is to be trained to support your practice of medicine.

## Plans for Patient Safety

In obstetrics and gynecology, Pap smears are the most fundamental tests that we perform. A system must be in place to ensure the careful labeling, logging, and tracking of these and all other specimens. No part of this "operation" should be left to chance. Each and every specimen that leaves the office must be logged in. Careful documentation of the patient's name, the laboratory, and type of specimen is important to ensure that each result is returned. Educating the patient about the timing of the results and asking him or her to call the office is also another safety net to help ensure that the results are received. The same mechanism must be in place for all tests for which patients are referred.

In our practice, patients who have a history of abnormal Pap smears are asked to call in 7 to 10 days if no one from our office has called them with results. This acts as an added safety net to ensure that a Pap smear or the incoming report is not lost without the physician being aware of it. It is critical to keep track of pending test results to make sure that they are received and that the patient is notified.

---

A 25-year-old woman with irregular menstrual cycles went to her gynecologist for mild cramping. A pelvic exam was normal and a serum pregnancy test was ordered to rule out the possibility of an ectopic pregnancy. A week later the patient presented to the emergency department of a local hospital with an acute abdomen, secondary to a ruptured ectopic pregnancy.

---

You have likely guessed correctly that her doctor never received and was thus unaware of the positive pregnancy test result. The patient sued. Two important points were raised in the course of this litigation. First, if it is important for the physician to order a test, it is equally important that he or she ensures receipt of the results. Dr. Eric Poon and his colleagues assert that a "lack of timely action on test results jeopardizes patients' safety and satisfaction." They refer to this area of poor tracking and management of pending test results as a "quality gap."[2]

The second important point that emerged from this case is that (even though the patient may be asked to call the office concerning test results) it is the responsibility of the physician, not the patient, to ensure that test results are received. Do you think anyone could convince a jury that the delay in diagnosing the ectopic pregnancy and the subsequent rupture of the patient's Fallopian tube could not have been prevented? To prevent this type of occurrence, each practice that sends patients for any testing or consultation must maintain a system for ensuring that for each request a report is received in an appropriate time frame. Guidance on developing such systems is provided in Chapter 7.

In the field of gynecology, the failure to diagnose breast cancer in a timely fashion is the basis for many malpractice cases. The physician must be aware of the standard of care with regard to the age at which a woman is to begin getting mammograms. When a gynecologist palpates a breast mass, has a patient who complains of having palpated a breast mass herself, or receives a report of an abnormal mammogram, appropriate follow-up must occur. Interestingly, Dr. Leah Karliner et al. report that in their study almost 50% of women with suspicious mammograms did not understand that their results were abnormal.[3] This communication gap would inevitably lead to poor adherence with the plan for follow-up on these abnormalities.[3,4]

Particular care must be taken to prevent the patient from being "lost" among radiologist, breast surgeon, and gynecologist. We have found that in order to effectively manage patients whose care requires their referral to these other specialists, it is necessary to personally track the referrals. In our practice, we keep log books at our desks for this purpose and regularly follow up on the status of these patients.

---

The patient was a 46-year-old woman who saw her physician with complaints of pain in her right breast. After a normal examination, the patient was given a referral for a mammogram. The patient went for the mammogram, which was read as "BIRADS 4—suspicious for cancer." The report was sent by standard mail from the radiologist to the gynecologist. After receipt in the office, this report was filed in the chart by the secretary and was never seen by the physician. Six months later, the patient returned to the gynecologist complaining of a right breast mass. At this visit, the physician saw the mammogram report for the first time. The patient was referred to a breast surgeon who performed a biopsy, resulting in a diagnosis of breast cancer.

---

The doctor was sued for failure to diagnose breast cancer in a timely fashion. His defense was that he never saw the report. At the time when this case occurred, the standards did not require that the radiologist notify the patient concerning mammography results. Therefore, the radiologist held the position that the abnormal mammogram report was transmitted to the referring physician, and it was not his (the radiologist's) responsibility to contact the patient. This case was settled before trial for a large sum of money because of the lack of follow-up by the gynecologist to ensure that he had received the results of a test that he ordered.

Advances in technology have allowed my office, among many others, to become paperless. We have an electronic medical record that allows for reports of laboratory tests to be sent to the patients' charts automatically. Technology, when wisely used, can enhance the patient safety aspects of a medical practice.

An often overlooked aspect of helping to ensure quality care in the private practice is the importance of providing a period of orientation not only for new staff, but also for physicians joining the practice. Even when the physicians and staff are experienced and may have worked in other practices, they need to be schooled in the operations of their new practice. Much will be different—from the physical location of items that they will need to the culture of the practice. The time spent in acclimating new members of the team will pay dividends in patient safety and error prevention.

When a new physician is brought into our group, he or she is assimilated into the practice over several months. We would not ask a new physician who joins the practice on July 1 to take call the first day. It is also very important for the new physician to have one of the more senior physicians in the practice serve in the role of his or her mentor to help in the transition from residency to private practice. Many lessons are to be learned in this change, and having someone coach the new physician is important to the care of your patients. This mentorship is also important when an established physician joins the group. Procedures in the new office and hospital may be different from those in the physician's prior practice.

Continuing education is a must for the physician who wishes to maintain a level of excellence in clinical practice. It is essential to be aware of and practice up-to-date medicine and to keep abreast of changes in the practice of medicine. The Internet and networking with other physicians in and out of your specialty can be effective tools for continued learning.

Quality assurance and patient safety are central principles to patient care in both the office and hospital. Every aspect of caring for your patient in a medical practice must emphasize safety. Whether it is about how phone calls are managed, how prescriptions are handled, or how patients with emergencies are accommodated in the day's schedule, patient safety must be the first and last consideration.

## Strong Networks

Referrals to other physicians for consultation or second opinions are an important part of a medical practice. The failure to send the patient for a consultation, the failure of a patient to go to a consultation, or the failure to act on the consultant's recommendation are the bases of many legal actions against physicians.

A 36-year-old woman went to see her primary care physician complaining of a breast lump. Her doctor examined her and found a small mass in her right breast and referred her to a breast surgeon for a possible biopsy. The patient called the surgeon's office for an appointment but was told that he did not participate in her insurance plan. The patient was disappointed and frustrated that she could not see the consultant to whom her physician had referred her; however, she did not alert the referring physician about this difficulty.

Ten months later, the patient returned to her primary care physician with a now larger breast mass. This physician called the breast surgeon and sent the patient for consultation. Advanced breast cancer was diagnosed after a breast biopsy.

The patient sued the primary care physician for delay in the diagnosis of breast cancer. The case was settled after jury selection for a large sum of money. This case represents several important factors in risk management. Of great concern is the failure of the referring physician to follow up on an abnormal examination. The physician had no idea that the patient did not see the consultant, even though he was concerned that cancer could be present.

In the modern insurance era, the referring practice must facilitate the patient being seen by a consultant who participates in that patient's insurance plan. On their own, patients often face the roadblock of not being able to get an appointment for several weeks or months or that the doctor to whom they were referred is not in their plan. It is preferable, particularly in the face of an urgent referral, that the referring physician or someone in his or her practice obtains the consultation appointment for the patient. At a minimum, it is critical to advise the patient that if he is unable to get an appointment or if the physician to whom he was referred is unable to accommodate them for some other reason, he must inform the referring doctor so that she can help to get the appointment.

I personally select physicians in several specialties who I feel do an excellent job. I rely on my consultants to be available and communicate with both the patient and me, preferring to use consultants in my hospital to increase the likelihood that I will see those physicians in the hospital on a regular basis. The opportunities for continuity of care and communication that this access to these physicians provides are immeasurable. Poor communication between the referring physician and the consultant predisposes the patient to a lesser quality of care and increases the chances that he or she will be lost to follow-up. We are reminded that with regard to follow-up, "accountability begins—and most often remains—with the referring physician."[5] With that in mind, it is of utmost importance that our tracking systems include patients who are referred to consultants, including radiological consultations for mammography.

As a specialist in Maternal Fetal Medicine, I often see very challenging and rare cases. Sometimes these are patients referred for second opinions by other physicians. I have found that, on occasion, it is better to recommend that patients obtain a second opinion in order to ensure that they obtain the best medical care in a team approach, instead of being left with the uncertainty of whether a fresh mind, a fresh pair of eyes, and a fresh pair of hands might lend new insight for the benefit of the patient's care. Referring a patient to a physician in another specialty or even one's own specialty should be viewed as a sign of good medical care and strength, not weakness. Dr. James Li admonishes that "an underappreciated skill that a physician should master is the ability to recognize one's own limitations."[6]

At times, it is uncomfortable for the physician when patients seek second opinions without their physician's knowledge and, as a result, second guess the physician's management plan. Thus, it is important that physicians manage those emotions well and allow the patient to feel their openness and objectivity and, most importantly, the utmost concern for their care.

## Proper Clinical Protocols

Practice protocols are an important part of a medical practice, particularly where multiple physicians are involved. Patient management protocols or clinical pathways are an integral part of patient care. It is often said that medicine is an art, not an exact science; however, there are standards of care that must be met to ensure quality medicine. In my practice, among other protocols, we follow the established standards for how often pregnant patients are seen and how often sonograms and routine antepartum tests are performed. A similar approach is taken with gynecologic patients with respect to Pap smears and follow-up for abnormal results.

---

A 26-year-old woman had undergone a Cesarean section for a breech presentation in her first pregnancy two years earlier. She desired to have a VBAC (vaginal birth after Cesarean) during her current pregnancy. The obstetrician advised her that there was a 1% to 2% risk of uterine rupture during labor. After his review of the prior operative report, the patient was approved to have a trial of labor. The patient subsequently went into labor at term and had fetal distress, and an emergency repeat Cesarean section was performed. A uterine rupture was diagnosed at the time of the laparotomy.

---

The patient sued for lack of informed consent. She stated that she was unaware that such an adverse outcome could occur. The case, which I was asked to review, was eventually settled for a significant amount of money.

Several issues must be addressed when an obstetrical patient had a previous Cesarean section and expresses a desire for a vaginal delivery. First, we obtain the operative note for the previous Cesarean section to determine whether a VBAC may even be considered. Second, the patient is counseled in detail concerning the risks of a VBAC versus the risks of a repeat Cesarean section. On the basis of this discussion, if the patient wishes to proceed with a VBAC, she is asked to sign a consent form. If the patient's status changes such that we no longer consider a VBAC to be a safe option, the patient is advised. The safety of both the patient and the fetus must be taken into consideration during the counseling session and the decision-making process.

Vaginal births after Cesarean sections are a significant area of litigation against obstetricians. Although patients are usually made aware of the risks of uterine rupture, it is often the poor documentation that the patient was aware of the risk that leads to poor legal outcome. Simply writing "OK for VBAC" is not evidence of informed consent. It is important for the obstetrician to write a note detailing the discussion with the patient, spouse, or whomever else the patient may have in attendance. As previously noted, we also ask the patient to sign a consent form, further documenting that the discussion, including the risks of a trial of labor and of Cesarean delivery, occurred.

# Affability

An affable physician is able to make his or her patients feel comfortable. In gynecology, this is a particularly important attribute—to make patients feel comfortable at visits and in discussions that are themselves often uncomfortable situations. It is important for physicians to have a pleasant manner and be able to spend time with patients. Patients should be comfortable asking questions and not feel belittled or that they are being patronized. Dr. Gerald Hickson and his colleagues found in their study of frequently sued obstetricians that, even among their patients who had not brought suit against them, there was a high incidence of complaints regarding the physicians' interpersonal aspects of care. Patients experienced feeling rushed, being ignored by their physicians, and other communication failures.[7] A patient who experiences the physician's caring is less likely to have a desire to sue that physician.

Patients must be involved in the decision-making process concerning their care. The age of the old-fashioned, paternalistic practice of medicine is long gone. Largely because of access to the Internet, patients have become more knowledgeable regarding different medical conditions and are more aware of options that are available.

If a patient has a good relationship with his or her physician, she may feel comfortable calling with concerns that may be outside his or her field of medicine. Where you receive such a call, are you helpful to the patient, or is he or she simply advised that this problem is not handled in your practice? Such a call should be viewed by the physician as a compliment. I usually find that it is an expression of the patient's confidence in me and in our relationship and will help the patient identify a physician who will be able to take care of her.

## Strong Patient Relationships

"Hello, Doctors' office. How may I help you?" Sounds great, but who is the person "helping" the patient? If your office has a large number of employees, how can you know with whom the patient spoke? The key is accountability. Everyone who answers the phone should state their name. A better formulation is this: "Hello, Doctors' office. This is _____. How may I help you?" This puts a name with the call and makes even a big practice more personable.

Where a patient's call becomes disconnected, having a name is also helpful to the patient. Knowing the staff member's name is also more efficient for follow-up if the patient is satisfied or dissatisfied and wants to have a further discussion with the office manager or the doctor. Knowing who was on the phone with the patient better allows the physician to respond to the patient, recognize staff members for doing a good job, or provide remediation where that becomes necessary.

The phones and staff are a reflection of how you want to be perceived by your patients. It is said that one cannot judge a book by its cover, but patients certainly judge your practice by the way phone calls are handled. The people who answer the phones are the entree to your practice. When a patient calls, he or she wants someone to answer the phones quickly. Placing a call on hold requires that the caller is asked permission, and staff must be careful not to leave calls on hold for an extended period of time. If it is necessary to keep someone holding, he or she should be given the option to be called back or continue holding.

The proper handling of phone messages is imperative. Patients must be directed to the appropriate person in the practice in order to meet their needs. If you have an automated telephone system in place, you need to ensure that patients are given easy prompts to direct them to the area that will best serve their needs. Professionalism, courtesy, empathy, and understanding of patients' problems are all attributes essential for your staff to possess, to handle phone calls in your office.

Secretaries, receptionists, and other personnel who do not have the medical background to answer patients' questions and properly advise them should not be permitted to give medical advice. Either nurses, nurse practitioners, physician assistants, or the physicians themselves should be responsible for handling test results and discussing them with patients. The policy in my office is that abnormal results are reported to the patient only by the doctor. For normal results, patients may be called by the nurses at the physicians' direction.

Most practices have an office manager or practice administrator. This is the person who should have the skills and abilities to manage and resolve nonmedical problems for patients if other staff is not being successful. In every office, there needs to be a "go to person" to whom physicians or staff can go for help in addressing difficult administrative problems. There must be one responsible person who is familiar with all of the operations of the office and is able to solve problems or resolve issues on a day-to-day basis.

The office manager or practice administrator should work closely with a physician in the practice, such as a medical director, who bears the overall responsibility for the practice. The administrative personnel can be most effective where they are able to work in concert with a physician in making decisions and developing policies and procedures, most of which will have medical implications.

Prolonged waits by patients in the office must also be considered as a patient relations issue. Most patients understand that the nature of medical practice does not lend itself to absolute precision in terms of time. Dr. Clarence Braddock and Ms. Lois Snyder, in their work on the ethical significance of time, suggest that if a physician is late for a patient's appointment he or she could respectfully offer "an apology such as, 'I may be late but I will give you my full attention and interest now.'"[8] Just as we expect patients to be respectful of our time, they deserve our respect of theirs.

Clean and pleasant surroundings are a minimum requirement for the waiting area in a practice. Also, where a prolonged wait is inevitable, it is much more tolerable if patients are provided with adequate reading material and other ways of passing the time. With computer and Internet capabilities, monitors in your office may be used in a more educational manner than simply for entertainment. Cleanliness of the office as well as the bathroom facilities reflect for patients how the physician views and cares for his or her patients. The same may be said for the appearance of office staff. We recently instituted a dress code in our practice to ensure that we maintain a professional appearance to our patients.

Several years ago, the staff at the hospital where I practice underwent training in "guest relations." The concept of patients and visitors being treated as customers or guests of the hospital replaced the patient as patient concept. The goal was to improve patient (customer) satisfaction. In medical practice, one of our goals should be that the patient's experience with us is a positive one that leaves him or her feeling that he or she was indeed a guest in our office.

# Availability

An available physician is fundamental to a successful practice. Whether in a solo practice or a large group, the practice of medicine mandates that the patient has access to a physician at all times. Availability entails that the patient is able to get appointments and have access to a doctor after hours. For the physician in a solo practice, if the physician is not available, it is imperative that he or she arranges for a covering physician. A patient must always be able to contact his or her physician or designated covering physician at all times.

Often patients complain that they are unable to see their doctor for an emergency appointment. As an obstetrician, I get numerous phone calls, usually on weekends, from nonpregnant patients who have medical conditions that require attention; however, they are unable to reach their physicians. Whether it is the renewal of a thyroid medication or treatment of an upper respiratory infection, patients need to have access to the physician when the office is closed.

New patients often tell me that they are coming to my practice because they are unhappy with the care that they received from their previous doctor. It may simply be that the doctor has no appointments available for weeks. This kind of delay is unacceptable to most patients who wish to be seen for a medical complaint. Recognizing this, in my office, when appointments are not available for nonemergency patients, we open new slots and extend hours. Even a new patient who cannot get an appointment may decide that his or her inability to schedule a visit is indicative of the difficulty that he or she may experience in the future as a patient in the practice. That thought may be enough to cause the patient to find another physician who has more time to take care of him or her.

---

A patient had an uneventful pregnancy and primary Cesarean section without incident. She was discharged home on postoperative day number four without complications. Approximately one week later she had vaginal bleeding. She was unable to reach her treating obstetrician and went to a local emergency department, where she was seen by an on-call obstetrician. It was determined that she had a retained placenta and she was taken to the operating room for a dilatation and curettage. Heavy bleeding occurred, necessitating a hysterectomy.

---

The patient sued her primary obstetrician for retained placenta even though the dilatation and curettage caused the perforation and the eventual hysterectomy. The case went to trial and the patient was awarded a significant judgment. Jurors do not like it when doctors do not respond to their patients' needs.

If you are going to treat patients and operate on them, you or a covering physician must always be available to attend to complications or other care the patient may need. To leave your patients without your care, or that of someone whom you know and trust, may place you in a situation in which you are held responsible for the actions of others who may not treat your patient as you would. In this particular case, the patient stated that she called the answering service; however, according to the physician, he never received the page. The subsequent treating physician, who perforated the uterus, blamed the treating obstetrician for improper care.

Your ability to be in contact with your patients is a critical part of your practice. Answering services and pagers are important factors. In my practice, the office manager receives a printed report daily of all calls from the answering service for her review to ensure that all messages were transmitted to the physicians. Our answering service has also established internal protocols that help them ensure that where patients' calls are not returned promptly, appropriate follow-up is instituted. Often malpractice cases involve claims of phone calls (real or imagined) to the doctor with complaints that the patient claims were ignored or not addressed.

# Affordability

An affordable physician is one who charges reasonable fees for the services rendered. Affordability has evolved over the years with managed care companies setting fees for medical care, except in a few specialties. Affordability can now be partially defined as accommodating patients by participating in many plans. With the rising costs of health care, many patients are unable to go out of network and must choose a physician who participates in their plan. Physicians who complain that their waiting rooms are empty may consider whether the lack of patients is a function of the number of plans in which they have chosen to participate.

*True success in medicine is not easy. Every effort must be expended to optimize outcomes and reduce risk for the patients who come under your care. A well-trained physician who develops good communication skills and is willing and available to provide the best medical care in a safe manner to all of his or her patients is the foundation for a successful practice.*

## REFERENCES

1. Poon EG, Hass JS, Puopolo AL, et al. Communication factors in the follow-up of abnormal mammograms. *J Gen Intern Med.* 2004;19:321.
2. Poon EG, Gandhi TK, Sequist TD, et al. "I wish I had seen this test result earlier!": dissatisfaction with test result management systems in primary care. *Arch Inter Med.* 2004;164:2223.

3. Karliner LS, Kaplan CP, Juarbe T. Poor patient comprehension of abnormal mammography results. *J Gen Intern Med.* 2005;20:432–437.

4. Poon EG, Hass JS, Puopolo AL, et al. Communication factors in the follow-up of abnormal mammograms. *J Gen Intern Med.* 2004;19:316–323.

5. Pearson SD. Principle of generalist-specialist relationships. *J Gen Intern Med.* 1999;14(suppl 1):15.

6. Li JTC. Humility and the practice of medicine. *Mayo Clin Proc.* 1999;74:529.

7. Hickson GB, Clayton EW, Entman SS, et al. Obstetricians' prior malpractice experience and patients' satisfaction with care. *JAMA.* 1994;272:1583–1587.

8. Braddock CH III, Snyder L. The doctor will see you shortly: the ethical significance of time for the patient-physician relationship. *J Gen Intern Med.* 2005;20:1060.

# Chapter 7

# Things You Didn't Learn in Medical School

Christine J. Quinn

*If you only learn methods, you'll be tied to your methods, but if you learn principles you can devise your own methods.*
Ralph Waldo Emerson

A patient with a history of pulmonary arterial venous malformations (AVMs) that were successfully embolized six years previously began to develop shortness of breath after an episode of bronchitis. After being treated for asthma with no improvement, the patient was referred to a pulmonologist for evaluation.

The patient called the pulmonologist who her primary doctor recommended and was told that the first available appointment for a new patient was in three months. Many physicians may see this as a sign of a successful and thriving practice; however, the patient wondered how a specialist could expect a patient who was experiencing shortness of breath to wait three months to be seen. As a marketing executive, she also wondered why a doctor would not be interested in seeing new patients.

Education in medical school and training in residency focuses almost exclusively on scientific knowledge, standards of care, and clinical protocols. These skills are essential for physicians to provide safe and appropriate care to patients. This chapter focuses on the nonclinical aspects of medical practice that become an integral part of the day-to-day practice of medicine. These "softer" skills of managing a medical practice usually receive very little attention during a physician's medical training. Unfortunately, many medical malpractice cases arise from administrative errors and oversights that have very little to do with a physician's clinical knowledge, training, or experience.[1-3] The goals of this chapter are to provide a roadmap of some of the fertile grounds in which the seeds for a malpractice case are sown, to provide some insights into how preventable malpractice cases arise, and to offer some suggestions of proactive steps you can take to prevent these types of claims from arising in your own practice.

## First Impressions Are Important

After a visit with a physician, a patient comments that he receives more courteous treatment in Starbucks or McDonald's than he experienced in a physician's office. He observes that when you arrive at Starbucks or McDonald's you are greeted. The person who is taking your order makes eye contact with you and appears to be happy that you are there. In contrast, when you arrive in a physician's office, you frequently feel unwelcome and intimidated. Often, you stand before a window or a high counter trying to get the attention of a receptionist to report your arrival for your appointment. Rather than seeming happy to see you, that person often either ignores or treats you brusquely.

These two patient narratives provide a window into patients' experiences. They also provide an opportunity to consider how these experiences influence a patient's image and expectations of the physician they are about to see. In these two accounts, the patient's experience may have been tainted with a negative hue before the physician even meets him or her.

Would a patient's first impression of you as a physician be favorable if he or she is told that he or she cannot get an appointment with you for several weeks or months? Consider the subtle message that this sends to a patient. Are you too busy to see them? Is this the impression that you want your patient to have about you and your availability? Might he or she wonder whether he or she will be able to get an appointment with you if he or she has an urgent problem? Is this what you would want a new patient to wonder about you?

As a benchmark for evaluating your practice, you might recall some of your own experiences as a patient or your experience as a family member of a patient. How were you greeted when you arrived for your appointment? If the person responsible for greeting you remained on the phone and avoided eye contact with you, did that influence your impression of the doctor?

What types of positive things did you experience that you would want to incorporate in your own practice? What types of things did you experience that you would not want to emulate in your practice?

Have you ever considered how a patient experiences your practice? If you view the experience through the patient's eyes, you may see some areas where you might consider making some improvements. A suggestion offered by the Harvard Risk Management Foundation is to walk through your practice with the goal of seeing it as a patient would see it. Give yourself a diagnosis and "go through the experience just as the patient and family would."[4] Attempt to experience what the patient would experience. The goal here is to observe your practice as if you have not been there before. For most patients, their first contact with your practice is via the phone; therefore, listen to your automated phone system as if you were a patient. Is the system easy for a patient to navigate?

The risk management principle is that you must deliberately define the culture of your practice. For example, is it your philosophy that the patient and his or her needs are the priority of the practice and the reason that the practice exists? How is that message communicated to your staff and your patients? Your staff must have clear guidelines for interactions with patients. Details must be considered and evaluated. Without deliberate attention to and ongoing evaluation of details, your practice may not reflect your own values and priorities. Some bristle at the notion of thinking of a patient as a "customer" or "client." That is understandable; patients are really not customers or clients in the traditional sense; however, you are providing a service in a fairly competitive marketplace, and customer service skills may be essential to strengthen your staff's relationships with patients.[5] It is indisputable that improving patient relationships in your practice can only be beneficial because your staff are the gateway into your practice. It is better to accept and address this than to lament it.

# Delegate Responsibilities with Care, Thought, and Confidence

A patient who has an arthroscopy of the right knee under spinal anesthesia calls her surgeon's office 1 week postoperatively with complaints of numbness in her right heel. The orthopedist's secretary

advises the patient that pain and numbness are normal postoperatively and suggests that she should remove the bandage from her
knee. Two days later the patient expired at home from a pulmonary
embolus. The surgeon later stated that he was unaware that this
patient had called his office. He also recounted his surprise when he
learned that his secretary (who had no clinical training) frequently
gave medical advice to patients over the phone without his knowledge. Her explanation was that she frequently received calls from
patients and felt comfortable reassuring patients who asked routine
questions after surgery.

---

It is reassuring for a physician to be able to rely on and trust his or her staff
to handle the day-to-day operations of the office. This allows the physician to
concentrate on caring for patients. Unfortunately, some malpractice cases
arise from situations where loyal staff members who are trying to be helpful to
the physician overstep their bounds. In the previously mentioned case, the
orthopedist's secretary had worked with him for many years. She had observed
him giving reassuring advice to postoperative patients on many occasions and
began to offer similar reassuring comments to patients herself. In this case,
when the patient called with complaints of pain and numbness, she did not
recognize that the patient's complaint should have been relayed to the surgeon
for evaluation. Despite her good intentions, the secretary did a disservice to
both the patient and the surgeon.

These types of cases also arise in pediatric practices where many phone
calls are received from new and sometimes anxious mothers. Staff who are
experienced with common childhood issues may try to "spare" a busy pediatrician from having to respond to routine questions from nervous new mothers by answering parents' questions and offering the advice themselves.

Over time, well-intentioned staff may blur the line between answering a
question and offering medical advice. These imperfect exchanges can result in
allegations of a delayed or missed diagnosis of a medical problem because the
physician did not speak directly with the patient/parent about the problem.

It is important to be cognizant of advice your staff is offering to patients. A
risk management strategy is to have a system for handling phone calls and
ensuring that your staff is not giving advice to patients without your knowledge and consent. A corollary to this is that staff has to feel that you are
approachable with questions or concerns from patients. It is also critical to
ensure that staff members who handle phone calls understand how to triage
calls. Some practices have set times when patient calls are returned. If this
is the policy in your practice, communicate this to patients so that they have
a realistic expectation of when their call will be returned. Staff must also

have flexibility to bring an urgent matter to the physician's attention when necessary. In any event, advice given to a patient over the phone should always be documented.

---

A 35-year-old patient is seen for a routine visit by her gynecologist. During this visit, they decide that the patient should no longer take oral contraceptives, and alternate forms of birth control are discussed. Four months later, the patient calls the office requesting a refill of the oral contraceptives. In accordance with office policy, the receptionist advises the patient that she can phone in a 1-month renewal of the oral contraceptive if the patient agrees to come in for an appointment with the doctor. The patient agrees and schedules an appointment three weeks from the date of the phone call. Two weeks after restarting the birth control pill, the patient suffered a CVA. She has significant, permanent deficits. The patient later sued the gynecologist, alleging that she had been given a contraindicated prescription.

---

In this case, the gynecologist had a system in his practice to prevent patients from receiving multiple renewals of prescriptions without an evaluation by the physician. The weakness in the system was that there was an assumption that a patient would not ask for a renewal of a medication the doctor had discontinued. The receptionist was unable to appreciate this information and following the office policy inadvertently renewed a "routine" medication the doctor had discontinued. In a busy practice, there is a temptation to delegate routine matters such as calling in a prescription to a pharmacy to a reliable staff member. In this case, the lack of the physician's involvement in the process proved to be ill advised. It is critical to ensure tasks delegated to staff are within their training and licensure. In this case, it could appear that a secretary was practicing medicine without a license. In fact, in this case, an unlicensed staff member overrode the doctor's decision to discontinue the medication when she renewed the prescription.

In some practices, staff may be trained to perform tasks such as administering vaccines or allergy injections. These types of clinical responsibilities should be delegated with care. For example, in New York State, unlicensed medical assistants are prohibited from administering injections to patients.[6]

An effective risk management strategy is to be very deliberate and circumspect when delegating tasks to staff. Ensure that staff members perform tasks that they are properly trained to perform and, where appropriate, credentialed and licensed to perform. Maintain and update personnel files to include documentation of your staff's training and copies of licenses and certifications. If a question about your staff's training or licensure arises in the defense of a claim, it can be very burdensome to have to locate a former staff member who provided care to a patient to obtain this documentation after the fact.

# Effective Tracking Systems for Tests and Consults Are Essential for Every Practice

"According to data from the National Ambulatory Medical Care Survey (NAMCS) of 2002 the average family physician and general internist order lab testing in 29%–38% of patient encounters respectively and they order imaging studies in 10%–12% of encounters."[7] This is an extremely large volume of pending information for a physician to manage. Consider the following scenarios:

---

A physician evaluates a middle-aged patient who has anemia and recommends that he have a colonoscopy. The patient, who has a family history of colon cancer, becomes frightened by the possibility of this diagnosis and is a bit intimidated by the thought of what he perceives as a very unpleasant test and puts off scheduling the test.

A physician performs an annual physical on a patient and orders a number of laboratory studies and a chest X-ray. How will the physician know whether the studies are obtained?

A patient follows her doctor's advice and obtains a screening mammogram at a local radiology facility. The result is abnormal, but because of a clerical error, the report is sent to a physician with a similar name as her physician. That physician is out of town for several weeks, and thus, the error is not identified and reported to the radiologist's office until the office of the second physician reopens after the extended vacation.

---

Fortunately, most patients are motivated to follow their physician's advice; however, in some situations, patients are reluctant to follow medical advice. These situations require careful evaluation and management. Because our healthcare system is complex, even patients who intend to follow their physician's recommendations usually have to navigate a variety of barriers and obstacles to obtain a test or consultation. Additionally, our healthcare system is prone to errors that may result in a test result or consultation report being delayed or lost. The malpractice cases that arise in this area are usually a failure to diagnose or a delayed diagnosis of a cancer. These cases are not a result of a gap in the physician's knowledge or a failure of the physician to be well informed about current guidelines or standards of care. The delays are typically a result of a missing report or study that was not identified because of a failure to give adequate attention to the administrative details of how an office is organized.[1] These errors and oversights can be costly for both the patient and the physician. A way to reduce these types of cases is to identify and correct for the variety of things that can go wrong when a patient is referred for a test or a consultation and to have a mechanism to identify outstanding reports. Ensure that safety nets are in place to catch errors.

A general principle is that if a test or consultation was important enough for a physician to order, it is important enough to learn the result. The premise is that the test result is meaningful to the patient's care or else the physician would not have ordered the test. A risk management principle is that if a test or consultation was important enough to order, it is important enough to track.

Many methods can be devised to track pending test results and consult reports. The format used is a matter of personal choice and can run the gamut from a simple three-ring binder to an integrated component of an electronic medical record (EMR). The effectiveness of the system is based on the ability of the system to accomplish its intended goals. In order to be a useful risk management tool the system must accomplish the following objectives:

Record all pending/ordered tests

Monitor the receipt of pending tests

Be used as a tool to identify and follow up on outstanding reports

In order to safeguard against malpractice cases resulting from the mismanagement of pending laboratory and consult reports in your practice, examine the procedures followed in your office for monitoring and tracking of pending test results and consultation reports. A review of the various steps of this complex process can help uncover areas where the process can break down and expose the physician to an increased risk of a malpractice suit. Look for gaps in your process, opportunities for improvement, and loopholes that should be closed.

A referral coordinator for a primary care practice is given the responsibility to track the practice's outstanding test and consultation reports. As she completes the referral authorizations, the referral coordinator makes a list of the patients' names and the tests that they are referred for in a log book. She does not handle or review incoming mail in the practice. Approximately three months after the system was implemented, one of the physicians in the practice asks the referral coordinator how the system is working. She replies

> that it is working well and shows him a list of patients who were referred for consultation. At this point, the physician realizes that the receipt of reports is not being monitored, and therefore, there is no way to identify reports that are outstanding.

The breakdown that causes the failure of most tracking systems is the failure to "close the loop" on the outstanding report. In the case described above, the practice had an effective system to record pending consultation requests, but the referral coordinator was not responsible for processing incoming reports; therefore, she had no way to identify whether an outstanding report was received. This resulted in a log that in reality functioned as a simple listing of ordered tests and consultations. In order for a log to be useful in tracking outstanding reports, all incoming reports must be entered into the log as they are received. The final step, which is the essence of this risk management tool, is that after a specified period of time, the reports that are still outstanding must be actively identified and followed up on.

A critical concept in the successful implementation of a tracking system for pending reports is ensuring that everyone involved in the process understands that the goal of the system is to identify reports that are not returned to the practice in a timely way. Everyone must understand the objective of the system. If the staff members responsible for the system do not fully understand its purpose and goal, they often see the task as busywork and become frustrated by the effort that it requires. If staff members understand that this is a crucial patient safety responsibility that impacts on patient care, they will be committed to ensuring it is carried out effectively.

# Ensure All Incoming Reports Are Reviewed

> Imagine that you are seeing a patient who you have cared for over many years for a follow-up visit. As you review the chart before you enter the exam room, you notice a preoperative chest X-ray report that was filed several months earlier; it includes an abnormal finding that was not addressed. The patient is now presenting with a persistent cough and weight loss.

Countless malpractice claims arise from a delay in diagnosis after the premature filing of a laboratory report or X-ray study into a patient's medical record without review by the clinician caring for the patient.[8–10]

Common examples include blood work from a physical, which reveals an anemia, a screening mammogram with an unexpected finding, a preoperative chest X-ray that identifies a lesion, an abnormal PSA result, an INR on an anticoagulated patient that requires a medication adjustment, and a wound culture report. The list of examples is as long as the types of reports a physician receives in caring for patients.

None of the physicians who find themselves in situations in which a patient's diagnosis was missed or delayed because of a paperwork error ever intends for that oversight to occur, but physicians do fail to prevent the error from happening. These cases are not defensible because there is no plausible explanation that can be offered to a patient (or a jury) for how such a careless appearing error can occur.

These malpractice cases are among the easiest cases to prevent. A simple policy that no patient care information can be filed into the patient's medical record unless it is signed and dated by the physician can safeguard against such an occurrence in your practice. Recording the date of your review will provide a record of when the report was reviewed, which is sometimes important. Implement a rigid policy that every member of the staff must abide by. Periodically check to ensure that the policy is being followed by everyone in your practice. Have a specific method for training new or substitute staff on your policies. Keeping everyone in the practice informed of policies and procedures that impact patient care will provide a safety net that may help catch an error made by a well-intentioned employee who is not familiar with your office routines.

An added benefit of implementing a policy to document physician review of all incoming reports is that it will provide the physician with specific documentation of his or her review of the information. If a report includes abnormal results and follow-up is required, that information should also be documented. This can be done on the report itself or in the progress note.

---

A group practice includes four physicians who each have slightly different methods for handling the review of incoming reports. Three of the physicians require the staff to attach the report to the patient's chart. The fourth reviews the report and asks the staff to pull the patient's chart only if there is an abnormal finding that requires follow-up. Each physician has a medical assistant who is assigned to work primarily with him or her.

On a particular occasion, a medical assistant was working with the physician, who did not routinely receive charts when he reviewed reports. The medical assistant was covering for the physician's usual assistant who was out sick. The physician reviewed a mammogram report and wrote "let me see the chart" on the report. He then initialed and dated the report and placed it in his inbox for the medical assistant. He continued seeing patients for the remainder of the day. The medical assistant, who was accustomed to looking for the physician's signature as a signal that the report could be filed, saw the doctors' initials but did not read the instruction "let me see the chart" and filed the report in the chart. The patient did not return to the office for 12 months. At that time, the doctor reviewed the report. There was a 12-month delay in the diagnosis of this patient's breast cancer.

This case illustrates the need for standardization of policies and procedures in health care. Variance in administrative policies and procedures among individuals within a practice can breed confusion among staff and results in chaos. A practical barrier to standardization is that every practice is different. Variations in practices include the different needs of patients based on the size of the practice, specialty, the patient populations, and so forth. In spite of this, within a particular practice, standardization of policies and procedures is imperative. Whatever administrative systems you employ can be tweaked and tailored to your situation, but in order to be effective, risk management policies must be uniform and consistent throughout the practice.

# When It Comes to Test Results, Adopt a Policy That "No News Is No News"

A common but risky policy is to tell patients with pending test results that "no news is good news." This means that a patient would assume that if he or she does not hear from the physician that there is a problem with a test result that all is normal. This policy, which is designed to reduce "unnecessary" contacts with patients, undermines an important safeguard in closing the loop with a patient with outstanding test results.

The Agency for Healthcare Research and Quality has developed a Patient Fact Sheet: *20 Tips to Help Prevent Medical Errors.* One of its recommendations to patients is that, when it comes to test results, they should "not assume that no news is good news."[11] This recommendation provides a great opportunity to partner with patients. Decide how you wish to handle the communication of test results to patients, and then advise your patients what to expect. If it is burdensome to personally contact every patient who has a normal test result by phone, an alternative is to mail the patient a letter advising them that the results were normal. Documenting your contact with the patient (or keeping a copy of the letter, if one is sent) will also serve as a record of your contact with the patient. This documentation is especially critical if advice or alterations in the patient's treatment are given in response to the test results.

# Have a Procedure for Missed Appointments

A 40-year-old patient undergoes an elective arthroscopy in a freestanding surgery center. The patient is given an appointment for a postoperative visit in the orthopedist's office 14 days later. The patient misses that appointment.

There is no follow-up or any further contact from the patient. Eighteen months later, the orthopedist is sued by the patient's family. At that time, he learns that the patient suffered a pulmonary embolism and died 10 days post-op.

When the physician reviewed the patient's medical record after he was sued, he noticed that there was an entry in the record two weeks after the surgery that the patient "no showed" for the appointment. The surgeon was unaware of this event.

Missed appointments are events in a medical practice, and every practice should have a policy for managing them. The physician caring for the patient should be alerted that a patient has missed an appointment—the physician should not be expected to deduce that a patient on the appointment schedule did not appear for that appointment. In a busy practice, this could easily be overlooked. A member of the staff should be responsible for bringing this event to the physician's attention. An active evaluation of the patient's status should be made and a decision made about what type of follow-up will be initiated. For example, a patient who has missed the first postoperative visit should be contacted to determine why the appointment was missed. In most instances, the appointment probably requires rescheduling. (The patient would not have been asked to return unless there was a clinical indication to do so.) There may be situations in which the physician feels that it is not required that the patient be rescheduled, for example, a patient diagnosed with prostatitis who reports that he now feels well. The key here is that you will not know why the patient missed the appointment unless you have contact with him. An educated assessment of the situation is required to determine whether additional follow-up is warranted. In any event, the fact that the patient missed the appointment and follow-up actions taken by the practice should be documented.

# What Does It Mean When a Patient Misses an Appointment?

Sometimes a patient misses an appointment because he or she forgot about it. This occasionally happens with even the most compliant of patients. A way to decrease the number of missed appointments is to call patients a few days before the appointment to remind them of the appointment. Many practices that schedule appointments far in advance find that this is an effective way to reduce missed appointments and the resultant idle time they bring about.[12] In some situations, a missed appointment is a signal that you and the patient may not be in agreement with their diagnosis or that the patient is unable to follow the treatment plan.[13]

> Consider the obese patient with whom you discussed the importance of weight loss at the last visit, or a diabetic patient who you counseled on dietary issues and who does not wish to return because he or she knows that he or she has not followed your advice from the last visit. Alternatively, it may be a pediatric patient who you diagnosed with an ear infection who you recalled to ensure that the infection cleared. When the day for the follow-up visit arrives, if the child is doing better, a busy mother may think that the visit is unnecessary and decide to skip it.

Each missed appointment is an opportunity for the physician and patient to explore issues that are impacting on the patient's ability or willingness to carry out your recommendations. The patient's apparent rejection of your best medical advice may cause you to have some feelings of anger or hostility toward the patient. Although it may sometimes be the case that the patient is rejecting your advice, it may help to reframe the situation and think of the failure to follow your advice as an opportunity for education to correct misunderstandings. If you approach a missed appointment as an occasion to explore with the patient why he or she missed the appointment, you may learn some important information about the patient that may help you in caring for him or her.

Perhaps the patient did not fully appreciate the risk that he or she was assuming by not adequately controlling his or her blood sugar or taking his or her antihypertensive medication regularly. Maybe the parent did not fully understand why it is important to re-examine a child after an ear infection to be sure that it is resolved. There may also be issues in the patient's life that make it difficult for them to comply with your advice. For example, perhaps a patient with limited income is unable to afford the medications that you have prescribed for him or her.

Uncovering a previously unknown issue that blocks the patient's ability to comply with your advice may afford you an opportunity to modify the treatment plan to one that both you and the patient can live with. Although this may take extra time, if a discussion such as this can improve the patient's compliance overall, the patient's outcome will be better, and both you and the patient will be more satisfied with your relationship.[14,15]

You may occasionally encounter a patient who is simply noncompliant with your medical advice, and a missed appointment is a symptom of that noncompliance. It is easy to develop a negative attitude toward noncompliant patients—they often are frustrating to work with and drain your energy. This is not constructive for you or the patient. If, despite your best efforts, you and the patient cannot find a way to work together on common goals for their care, the best risk management strategy may be for you to have an honest conversation with the patient. During this conversation, you can explain that you do not feel that you and the patient are the best match and suggest that the patient find another physician who he or she might be more willing to work with. If this is the case, specific steps should be followed when discontinuing a physician–patient relationship. This procedure is beyond the scope of this chapter; however, your local medical society or professional liability insurer may have materials that outline the steps that should be taken when discontinuing a professional relationship with a patient.

# How Does a Patient Become Lost to Follow-Up?

Patients who become lost to follow-up usually leave the physician's office without making an appointment. Without a pending appointment, most practices cannot identify a patient who requires follow-up care. Risk management strategies for preventing patients from becoming lost to follow-up begin with ensuring that the patient has a clear understanding of when he or she is to return and the purpose of that follow-up visit. This information should be part of the plan recorded in the medical record. There should be an explicit system for this information to be relayed to the staff, who will sign the patient out at the conclusion of the visit.

In some situations, a patient may not require follow-up care (e.g., a patient who is seen for a routine physical with no outstanding problems or a surgical patient who is discharged after a successful procedure). There is very little to worry about in these types of situations. The understanding is that the patient will contact the doctor if he or she needs further care. In these instances, a helpful risk management strategy is to specifically note that advice in the record. It is then unambiguous that the patient will return prn.

On the other end of the spectrum is the patient who requires close monitoring and follow-up—a patient with a new diagnosis of hypertension who requires medication adjustments, a patient with a postoperative wound infection, a patient with pneumonia, or a patient with kidney disease who requires dialysis. These patients are usually fairly easy to keep track of because they make a follow-up appointment (which is scheduled in the near future) before they leave the physician's office. Because not all patients will make an appointment before leaving the office, a risk-reduction strategy to ensure that these patients are not lost to follow-up is to implement a system to identify and monitor patients who do not make an appointment before leaving the office. These patients should be monitored and, if necessary, contacted to schedule the follow-up appointment. The fact that the patient has an appointment allows the practice to keep track of him or her. The backstop to preventing these patients from becoming "lost to follow-up" is an effective system to follow up on missed appointments. These risk management systems work in concert and are only as effective as the weakest link in the system.

---

Consider a patient you are caring for who has a stable chronic condition (e.g., a hypertensive patient who has been stable, a diabetic who has been compliant with diet and medication recommendations, a stable glaucoma patient). Now think about patients in your practice who require monitoring but not active treatment (a patient with a breast pathology who is being monitored, a patient with a slightly elevated glucose, or an elevated PSA that you believe is from an infection).

---

These patients require follow-up care, but in an intermediate time interval. These patients are the mostly likely to be lost to follow-up because they frequently do not make an appointment before leaving the office.

A reliable system for preventing these patients from becoming lost to follow-up would be one that requires all patients to schedule the follow-up appointment before leaving the office; however, this has practical limitations. Not all patients are willing or able to schedule an appointment several months into the future before leaving the office. Also, unless the practice has a system to remind patients of these appointments, patients may miss the appointment because they forgot about it.

A more practical approach to improving compliance with recommendations for follow-up care may be to have a recall system for these patients.[16] For a recall system to be effective, the staff signing the patient out must know when the patient is due back and must enter the patient into the recall system. Usually, patients are sent a reminder notice four to six weeks before the scheduled follow-up interval and asked to schedule an appointment. Of course, these patients would have to be monitored, and if they do not respond to the recall notice, an assessment would need to be made about what additional follow-up is required. Recall systems are an effective risk management tool to keep track of patients who leave the office without an appointment. Documenting that the recall notice was sent will provide the practice with a record of their efforts to recall the patient at the appropriate interval.

# Implement a Patient Safety Program in Your Practice

Improving patient safety is an important focus in health care and will likely be a goal that we are perpetually working toward. The system you practice in is very complex, with an assortment of opportunities for error. One area where you can have a profound influence on improving patient safety is in your own office.

Improving patient safety should be a priority for your practice and must involve everyone in your practice. Ideally, the physician should be the champion for improving safety in his or her practice.[17] You set the tone in your office. The culture of your practice reflects your priorities and values. Make it a point to create a culture that emphasizes avoiding errors and rapidly catching and correcting errors when they cannot be avoided. Everyone in the practice must be part of this important effort. Patient safety and error reduction cannot be viewed as busywork; rather, it must be viewed as important work that impacts patient care. It is everyone's job. Bringing a passion for safety to your practice will serve to inspire your staff, who aim to please you and will follow your lead in making safety a priority. The most important thing that you can convey to your staff is that you care about your patients and want to do your best for them.

Developing a patient safety program in your practice begins with identifying an area in your practice or an aspect of your patient population that poses a risk for error.[17] Perhaps it is following up on patients referred for mammograms, patients who are being anticoagulated with a narrow margin between therapeutic levels and dangerous levels, or patients with pending biopsy reports. Perhaps it would begin with looking at various policies and procedures in your office. How do you track patients sent for outside testing or consultations? Does your system for missed appointments really accomplish what you intended it to? Do you have a recall system for patients who need ongoing care? A key facet of this evaluation is ensuring that your policies and procedures are achieving their intended goal. Step back and consider this: "What is the reason we are doing this?"

After you have identified an area that you are worried about, involve your office team in considering the various problems that could arise (e.g., the patient fails to go for the study, the report is lost, the results are received but not seen by the doctor, the patient is not notified of test results, etc.). Actively assess your existing polices and procedures to see whether these errors would be identified. What things can you do to improve your system? Constantly review, update, and modify systems. Over time, technology may change; as software improves, you may be able to streamline processes. Always strive for efficiency and perfection. The objective is to have carefully thought out systems that prevent and catch errors before they injure the patient.

Taking steps to prevent and catch errors to improve safety by enhancing patient care has the added benefit of preventing malpractice cases that result from these errors. This chapter has included examples of errors and oversights that resulted in injuries to patients made by excellent clinicians who lost sight of administrative details. Patients and juries will understand when a physician misses a subtle or complex diagnosis. They cannot easily forgive an administrative or paperwork error that causes an injury to a patient. Experience teaches us that the policies and procedures that prevent these errors and oversights do not come together without deliberate planning and thought. Because these procedures are not usually part of medical school education or residency training, they can easily be overlooked as a new physician enters practice and so many things require consideration. They can also be overlooked by a busy, experienced physician who delegates the management of the office to a staff member who is not aware of these risk management principles. The efficient and safe administration of a medical practice requires focused time and attention. A strategy to improve safety and prevent malpractice cases is to implement the risk management techniques outlined in this chapter in your practice.

*If you only learn methods, you will be tied to your methods, but if you learn principles, you can devise your own methods.*

# REFERENCES

1. Gandhi TK, Kachalia A, Thomas EJ, et al. Missed and delayed diagnoses in the ambulatory setting: a study of closed malpractice claims. *Ann Intern Med.* 2006;145(7):488–496.

2. Bates DW, Cullen DJ, Laird N, et al. Incidence of adverse drug events and potential adverse drug events: implications for prevention. *JAMA.* 1995;274:29–34.

3. Leape LL, Bates DW, Cullen DJ, et al. Systems analysis of adverse drug events. *JAMA.* 1995;274:35–43.

4. Kilo CM, Delio SA, Littell F. Office efficiency: managing a high volume practice. *Forum-Risk Manage Found Harvard Med Inst.* 2000;20(2):10–11.

5. Fraker TD, Marco AP. The practice setting: office, hospitals, and others. In: Nash DB, Skoufalos A, Hartman M, Horwitz H, eds. *Practicing Medicine in the 21st Century.* American College of Physician Executives. Tampa, FL; 2006:228.

6. New York State Education Department, Office of the Professions. Nursing. *Practice Alerts and Guidelines: Frequently Asked Practice Questions.* Available at: http://www.op.nysed.gov/nursepracticefaq.htm, accessed March 3, 2008.

7. Hickner JM, Fernald DH, Harris DM, et al. Communicating critical test results: issues and initiatives in the testing process in primary care physician offices. *Joint Commission J Qual Patient Safety.* 2005;31(2):81–89.

8. Poon EG, Gandhi TK, Sequist TD, et al. "I wish I had seen this test result earlier!": dissatisfaction with test result management systems in primary care. *Arch Intern Med.* 2004;164:2223–2228.

9. Boohaker EA, Ward RE, Uman JE, et al. Patient notification and follow-up of abnormal test results. *Arch Intern Med.* 1996;156:327–331.

10. Mold JW, Cacy DS, Dalbir DK. Management of laboratory test results in family practice. *J Fam Pract.* 2000;49:709–715.

11. Agency for Healthcare Research and Quality. *20 Tips to Help Prevent Medical Errors.* Agency for Healthcare Research and Quality; September 2000. AHRQ publication 00-P038[JBA1], Rockville, MD.

12. Hon KLE, Leung TF, Wong Y, Ma KC, Fok TF. Reasons for new referral non-attendance at a pediatric dermatology center: a telephone survey. *J Dermatol Treat.* 2005;16:113–116.

13. O'Connell D. The non-compliant patient and steps toward cooperation. *Forum-Risk Manage Found Harvard Med Inst.* 2000;20(2):18–19.

14. Stewart MA. Effective physician-patient communication and health outcomes: a review. *Can Med Assoc J.* 1995;152(9):1423–1433.

15. Piette JD, Heisler M, Wagner TH. Cost-related medication underuse: do patients with chronic illnesses tell their doctors? *Arch Intern Med.* 2004;164:1749–1755.

16. Rosser WW, McDowell I, Newell C. Use of reminders for preventive procedures in family medicine. *Can Med Assoc J.* 1991;145(7):807–814.

17. West DR, Westfall JM, Araya-Guerra R, et al. Using reported primary care errors to develop and implement patient safety interventions: a report from the ASIPS collaborative. *Adv Patient Safety.* 2005;3:105–119.

# Chapter 8

# The Challenge of the Patient in Transition

Marjorie O. Thomas

*. . . remember that there is always a patient and that you have not finished your work until you have taken care of the patient, not just the problem.*
Katharine Treadway, MD

A middle-aged male patient with a past medical history of asthma was treated by his primary care physician over many years. Over a weekend, he presented to a local emergency department with cold symptoms and increased coughing. He also reported difficulty breathing. A chest X-ray was performed. The radiology report recommended a CT to further evaluate a right upper-lobe finding.

The patient was discharged from the emergency department with a diagnosis of pneumonia and instructions to see his primary care physician in a few days. The patient saw his physician soon after discharge and advised him of his emergency department visit and pneumonia diagnosis. The physician never received a discharge summary and had no information concerning the CT recommendation.

About nine months later, the patient experienced a right-sided focal seizure. A CT of the brain led to the discovery of a metastatic lesion, and a primary right upper-lobe lesion was subsequently found.

Writing about medical errors, Drs. Robert Wachter and Kaveh Shojania assert, "You are far more likely to hear the reassuring words, 'Let me read your order back to you,' when you call your local Chinese take-out restaurant than we would be if we called a nurses' station of virtually any

U.S. hospital."[1] This is an uneasy truth given the relative risk of verifying a dinner order against verifying a medical order. Who would want to concede that the care and treatment of the infirm or the prevention of infirmity are too often left to chance? That, however, is precisely what happens when there is no plan or system to ensure that a handoff—the temporary or permanent transfer of the care of a patient—is handled correctly and completely. Maybe it will happen right this time, or maybe it won't. When it doesn't, the consequences can be dire.

Handoffs occur innumerable times each day in the care and treatment of patients. These transactions include hospital discharge and admission, a physician's transfer of his or her patient's care to another physician, the transfer of on-call responsibility within a practice or to physicians outside of the practice, an anesthesiologist's report to the nurse in the postanesthesia care unit, this nurse's handoff of the patient to an inpatient unit, a physician's transfer of a patient to a different hospital or a nursing home, and discharge of a patient to home health care or even back to the patient's or his or her family's care. The referral of a patient for consultation and the return of that patient to his or her physician as well as the reporting of critical laboratory and radiology results to the physician are also handoffs.[2] Where there is a lapse in these transitions, the patient's care may be adversely affected. In a recent publication of the World Health Organization, "hand-overs," as they are called in some countries, are characterized as "an international concern."[3]

At its core, the problem of handoffs is a problem of communication, mainly among the providers of care, but it often also involves communication with patients and their caregivers. In a report regarding these communication failures, Dr. Kathleen Sutcliffe et al. remind us that "clinical medicine . . . involves multiple handoffs with many places where critical information must be effectively communicated."[4] From their very important study of missed and delayed diagnoses arising from the ambulatory care setting, Dr. Tejal Gandhi et al. report that issues related to handoffs are a leading factor contributing to medical errors.[5]

In the care of the hospitalized patient, handoffs, or sign-outs as they are usually referred to in that setting, occur many times throughout the course of a day as a result of shift changes. These transfers of care are often marked by "communication failures," which "can lead to uncertainty in patient care decision making, potentially resulting in patient harm."[6] Dr. Alan Forster et al. help us understand the magnitude of the problem of handoffs in ambulatory care. They report that almost 20% of patients discharged from a hospitalization experienced an adverse event in the transition from hospital to home. Some of these problems were serious enough to cause permanent disabilities. A third of the adverse events were considered to be preventable, and for another third, their severity could have been ameliorated had they been addressed sooner.[7]

"Transitions in health care . . . are an inevitable by-product of technological and clinical progress" and they "are here to stay."[8]

If we can better understand the lapses that can potentially occur at these transitions and put into place measures to help prevent them, patients will receive safer and ultimately better care.

# Upon Admission

Dr. Cara Litvin helps us understand the frustration faced by the admitting physician who has a new patient before him or her and a dearth of information. She describes the admission of a young ventilator-dependent patient in a vegetative state to her New York City acute-care hospital, from a nursing home, for a newly diagnosed DVT. Her diligent search of the transfer documents is not rewarded with much useful information; however, she finds reference to a recent head CT. Her efforts to obtain a copy of the report of this study prove futile, and she must now subject the patient and the already overburdened healthcare system to another CT. Dr. Litvin's exasperation finds expression in these words:[9]

> These days, we can find the answer to almost any question immediately by doing a Google search, but unfathomably, it is still not possible for a physician in Manhattan to obtain a timely report of a study performed in another New York borough.

Another common problem with the patient who is being admitted to the hospital includes the transfer of information about the patient's medications. From a recent study, it was concluded that with more than half of older patients who are admitted and who are taking at least four medications, there are unintended medication discrepancies at the time of admission. Greater than a third of these errors had the potential to result in moderate or severe harm to the patients.[10] Concern about medication errors arising at transitions of care caused the Joint Commission on the Accreditation of Healthcare Organizations to issue an alert urging medication reconciliation at transitions of care.[11]

---

An 81-year-old petite female patient was admitted to a large community hospital where she underwent a laminectomy. Her very attentive primary care physician who had privileges at this hospital and who was well known there, prepared a dictated and transcribed summary of his patient's medical history and medications. This summary was placed in her chart at admission. The medications included 0.5 mg of Ativan for her Ménière's.

> In the preadmission process, the patient was asked by the hospital staff to list her medications. She included the Ativan, erroneously omitting the decimal point. The morning after surgery, her nurse in the postsurgical unit questioned the neurosurgeon's PA about the Ativan order, which was written as 5 mg. It seemed excessive to the nurse. The PA reduced the dose to 2 mg without reviewing the primary care physician's medication history or contacting him. Shortly after the 2 mg of Ativan were administered, the patient's family arrived on the unit. They found a dramatic change in their mother's sensorium. Difficult to arouse, she was somnolent. The medication error was subsequently identified.

In this case, the primary care physician did the responsible thing for his patient. The problem was that he was having a one-way conversation. He was speaking to the physicians, PAs, and nurses who would assume his patient's care, but they did not know he was speaking to them; therefore, they were not listening. It would appear that his preparation of a summary was not ordinary practice in this hospital, and thus, no one was aware of it, even though it was present in the patient's hospital chart. This one-sided delivery of information without the assurance that it has been received and therefore will be acted on is at the heart of the problems with handoffs in health care.

The issue of accurate patient information at admission has become of even greater concern with the burgeoning of one of medicine's newest specialists, the hospitalist. Physicians in this specialty are responsible for managing the care of hospitalized patients.[12] Usually, the patients are previously unknown to the hospitalist. Information from the patient's physician is essential in bringing this physician "up to speed." Certainly the hospitalist will obtain a history from the patient that will only be enhanced by the information that a physician familiar with the patient will be able to add.

Much has been written about the handoff of the hospitalist to the physician who will continue the patient's care after discharge. The literature that concerns information provided at admission, to the hospitalist, is far less robust; however, the potential for error where important information is not supplied to the hospitalist is just as significant. Therefore, the patient whose hospitalist has dependable information from the patient's physician is likely to receive better care during the hospitalization.

Sometimes a handoff at admission occurs at the request of the emergency physician or an admitting physician. With an unplanned admission where the patient's physician may not have had prior notice and may not have been able to provide information before admission, it is incumbent on the physicians who will care for the patient to contact his or her physician.

# At Discharge

A 50-year-old female patient with a significant medical history of hypertension and diabetes was admitted under the care of a hospitalist for congestive heart failure. Admission testing revealed anemia, and a lower GI bleed was discovered. A GI consult was requested. A colonoscopy was performed, and the patient was found to have three polyps. She was discharged home two days after admission.

The discharge summary was forwarded to the patient's primary care physician, however, it did not include any information concerning the pending pathology report, which was issued four days after the patient was discharged. She was seen in follow-up by her primary care physician on numerous occasions. She also had several visits to the hospital for unrelated complaints.

About 18 months after the colonoscopy, the patient presented to the emergency department of the same hospital with diarrhea and severe stomach pains and was admitted with a diagnosis of gastroenteritis. A few days later, she was diagnosed with metastatic colon cancer to the liver.

This case points to a number of concerns related to the handoff of the patient who is being discharged. The gastroenterologist received a pathology report with a diagnosis of polypoid adenocarcinoma. He assumed that the report would be placed in the hospital chart and that follow-up plans would be made between the hospitalist and the patient's primary care physician. The hospitalist prepared the obligatory discharge summary in which he made no mention of the pending pathology report.

The physicians who reviewed this case after the patient sued, raised concerns about her care over the 18 months between the admission at which the colonoscopy was performed and the later admission when the cancer was diagnosed. Although the discharge summary lacked specific information about the colonoscopy and the pending pathology report, it included that the patient had had a polypectomy and also that she required transfusions while she was hospitalized. Further consideration about these pieces of information may have led the primary care physician to discover the positive pathology from the colonoscopy.

This case reminds us of the critical importance of the delivery of information from the care of the hospitalized patient to the physician who is assuming the patient's care. Similar circumstances arise when a patient is hospitalized, for example, for a surgical procedure that will subsequently influence his or her medical care. The transfer of the care of the patient and the information crucial to that care must be seen as a collaborative process in which no one's job is complete until it is certain that the baton is truly passed from one hand to the other.

In their previously cited study, Dr. Forster and his colleagues reported that nearly 20% of patients experienced an adverse event in the transition from hospital to home.[7] Surprisingly, this was the case even though an electronic message, detailing medication changes, is sent from the hospital where the study was conducted to the primary physician at discharge. This study concludes that more specific information is necessary concerning what the physician who is assuming care is to do with regard to follow-up, when it is to be done, and any particular concerns about what he or she should watch for. These authors also make the very important recommendation of including the patient in this information loop. In the previously described case, the patient may have been able to point out to the primary care physician that the results of the colonoscopy were pending if she had been told at discharge that those results were not yet known.

The preparation of a discharge summary is not simply a ministerial function to be carried out by the discharging physician. Rather, it is a mode of communicating critical information between the physician who has been responsible for the patient's care and the physician who will be continuing that care. Changes in medication or other regimens have likely been made. Studies have been conducted. There are often more studies to be performed or further consultations to be requested. Any of these changes or plans requires that the receiving physician be provided with the details necessary for him or her to move forward with the care of the patient. The physician who is responsible for preparing a discharge summary must remember this. Although it is unclear how often this occurs, the American Academy of Family Physicians recommends that hospitalists dictate a discharge summary that is to be faxed to the family physician on the day of discharge.[13] This accelerated delivery would certainly be a boon to the care of the recently discharged patient.

Dr. Carlton Moore et al. in their report of a study concerning patients who are discharged with unresolved medical issues for which further workup is necessary, refer to the discharge summary as "usually . . . the common thread ensuring that patient care is appropriately transitioned" from the hospital to the outpatient setting. These researchers also found, not surprisingly, that where the recommended workup was documented in the discharge summary, it "increased the likelihood" that that workup would be completed; nevertheless, more than half of the discharge summaries did not include the recommended workup. This information was located elsewhere in the patients' hospital charts. Over a third of the recommended and documented workups were not carried out. These recommendations to which there was no response included CT scans where admission chest films showed pulmonary nodules and cases in which patients were admitted with chest pain, myocardial infarctions were ruled out, and the patients were to have stress tests. There would be unanimous agreement that the care of these patients was far from complete.[14]

It is not enough for a discharge summary to be dictated, transcribed, and faxed in a timely way to the primary care physician, as recommended by the American Academy of Family Physicians. If the discharged patient is to have a reasonable chance of receiving the recommended care, both the sender and receiver must take this document seriously. It must include the detailed information that the receiver needs to continue the care of the patient—the receiver must expect that it will and therefore read and respond to it as such. In one study, it was determined that patients were less likely to be readmitted if/when they are seen in follow up, the physician had already received the discharge summary.[15] As with any recommendation from a co-treating physician, the receiving physician may decide on a different course for good medical reason. To close the loop, however, such a decision requires comprehensive documentation in the patient's chart, including the physician's rationale for opting for a plan different from that proposed in the discharge summary.

Among the many consequences of incomplete transactions at handoff are delayed diagnoses, missed diagnoses, and injuries caused by medication errors. About half of patients for whom there was a workup error related to discontinuity from hospital to outpatient care required readmission.[16] These errors take a heavy toll on the health of patients as well as on the healthcare system. Many of them can be prevented if the primary care physician is provided with information that advises him or her specifically what is to be done, when it is to be done, and the dangers to watch for.[7]

We sometimes see cases in which the community physician, not having received a discharge summary for a patient being seen after hospitalization, will resort to taking the patient's word about his or her course in the hospital, including test results and follow-up recommendations. In most of those cases, the patient's report is favorable, including no need for additional studies or workup. That is the patient's interpretation of information received at discharge and, although he or she probably does not intend to deceive his or her physician, the information that he or she passes on may be far from accurate. Verification of clinical data reported by the patient is a must. It is the only way for the physician to be sure that he or she is acting in the best interest of the patient.

---

A middle-aged female patient, well known to her primary care physician, saw him in follow-up two days after a brief hospitalization. The patient had no written discharge information but reported to her physician that she had been admitted because of constipation and treated with an enema and that the constipation had not returned. She had been feeling fine since then.

The physician advised her to continue her medications, which included a diuretic and aspirin. Later that day, the patient fainted and was taken to the hospital, where she was found to have a massive gastrointestinal bleed. When her physician received the discharge summary from the earlier hospitalization, he noted that the patient had undergone a colonoscopy and that the discharge diagnosis was lower gastrointestinal bleed and diverticulosis.

---

It may appear ironic to suggest that it is also important to consider the patient and the family as participants in the patient's care and, therefore, that it is also necessary for there to be handoff to the patient at discharge. It is likely that he or she is leaving the hospital with a change in medication regimen or some other action he or she is to take before the first follow-up visit with the physician who is to continue his or her care. The patient needs information at discharge to do so. Drs. Eric Coleman and Robert Berenson assert that in many cases patients "do not understand essential steps in the management of their condition, and cannot contact appropriate healthcare practitioners for guidance."[17] Without adequate preparation for the management of what may be a new illness or, at a minimum, changes in their care, patients are discharged to be at least partially responsible for carrying out that care.[17] Although the patient should not be entrusted with the total responsibility of delivering the information necessary for continued care to the primary care physician, the patient should at least be given information concerning the recommended plan.[7]

This handoff information to the patient and family should be detailed and specific to the patient's treatment and condition at discharge. The general instructions usually provided to patients are likely inadequate for a patient whose condition requires specific follow-up care. Preferably, this information is provided in writing, not only to lessen the cognitive burden for a likely anxious patient, but also to provide a document to which they can refer.

An older cardiac patient, being discharged from a hospitalization, was advised about changes to his sizable medication regimen, including discontinuation of his "beta blocker." Not previously hearing that medication described in that manner, he arrived home with uncertainty about which medication he should stop taking.

Can we expect patients to carry out instructions or follow advice that is unclear and unspecific? Can we expect them to understand the technical terms and abbreviations commonly used in medicine? The patient or his or her family must be given clear instructions. They must understand what concerns to watch for and which ones indicate the need for contacting the physician or seeking emergency care. To help make sure that the patient is able to follow these instructions, he or she must be provided with the names and telephone numbers of the physicians or facilities he or she is to contact for clarification and questions in the event of an emergency and also for the recommended follow-up care.[18]

The patient's preparation for discharge must also take into account that patient's ability physically, and otherwise, to assume his or her care.[19]

In one case, an older, blind male patient was discharged with instructions and supplies for self-administration of Lovenox, as well as other medications. Both a pharmacist and a nurse counseled him at discharge. After several days at home, the patient called his doctor's office to say that although he had been discharged with several medications, including injections, he could not administer them because of his inability to read the instructions. Neither of the discharge instructors had recognized that the patient was blind.

Transitional deficiencies are experienced not only where patients are discharged to outpatient care but also in interinstitutional transfers. The same level of care must be exercised in these handoffs to prevent patients from suffering what are often devastating consequences.

A patient with a past medical history of atrial fibrillation was treated with Coumadin over many years. He was medically cleared for a total hip arthroplasty. His primary care physician wrote that postoperatively the patient was to be fully anticoagulated.

At the time of discharge from the hospital to a rehab facility, the patient's INR was subtherapeutic; however, the Coumadin dosage was not adjusted before discharge. While at the rehab facility, the patient suffered a stroke.

In this age of increasingly abbreviated hospital stays, it is not surprising that many patients are discharged with laboratory results pending. A test is performed because a physician considers it important to the care of the patient. Failure to respond to some test results may even have "catastrophic consequences"; nevertheless, the physician who is assuming the responsibility of that care may not have been informed that these results are to be expected.[20] "The baton of responsibility for patient care must be passed with confidence and certainty"[21]—confidence and certainty that the person to whom it is being passed has the information and ability to continue the patient's care.

# In Consultation

A 52-year-old male patient was seen by his primary care physician for an annual physical. The physician ordered tests, including a PSA. The report, which was received a few days later, showed an elevated PSA of 10. The physician referred the patient to a urologist; however, he did not provide the specialist with a copy of the laboratory report or a note with the reason for the consultation.

When the patient saw the urologist, he offered unrelated urological complaints for which the urologist treated him. The urologist prepared a report concerning his treatment of the patient and mailed it to a physician of the same last name as the referring physician; however, he was not the referring physician.

Approximately 14 months after the initial referral, the patient saw his endocrinologist, who drew a PSA that was also reported at approximately 10. The patient was again referred to the urologist, who diagnosed prostatic adenocarcinoma.

The practice of medicine requires the expertise of physicians of many specialties. For a patient to benefit from the knowledge and skills of these physicians, the patient will, even for brief periods of time, have portions of his or her care transferred from one physician to another. Without the bridge of communication, these specialists become "'silos' of care,"[22] isolated from crucial information and knowledge about the patient. The patient in this case was sent to the urologist without any of the necessary information. The urologist made no contact with the referring physician and accepted the patient's word about the reason for his referral.

Regardless of the brevity of the patient's time in the hands of a physician, if the physician's consultation is to be beneficial, necessary information must be transmitted to and received by the consulting physician. After the patient's return to the referring physician, the guidance of the consultant can only be considered and implemented if it is effectively communicated. "Multiple people caring for a given patient need a systematic process to facilitate communication and keep everyone in the same 'movie.'"[23] Unfortunately, the communication between providers often does not live up to these standards.

When the coordination and communication between the members of the team is not handled well, appearing almost seamless to the patient, it raises questions in the patient's mind about the competence of the team and the extent to which his or her care may be compromised by the poor communication. Irwin Press, in referring to those situations, speaks of the patient being "functionally dismembered, with the parts distributed to a variety of staff members." He adds that "this is unquestionably the most depersonalizing aspect of the entire clinical encounter" and is likely a factor that predisposes patients to file claims.[24]

Dr. Tejal Gandhi, in her evaluation of a case in which a patient's diagnosis of tuberculosis was delayed because of poor handoffs in which multiple providers were involved, says this:[25]

> The current test result tracking and follow-up systems in health
> care are inefficient and chaotic, with many opportunities for
> delays and losses to follow-up.

Continuing in her analysis of this patient whose diagnosis was substantially delayed in part because of poor communication and handoff, Dr. Gandhi points out that an abnormal CT result warranted a telephone call from the consulting physician (the radiologist) to the referring physician. Dr. Gandhi also points to the "diffused responsibility" where there are multiple physicians or other healthcare providers involved, which may lead to assumptions as to who will follow up on particular aspects of the patient's care. This concern serves to remind us that, arguably, the most important skill to ensure quality patient care, particularly where that care is being provided by multiple physicians, is effective communication. Many problems around handoffs arise from situations in which there is a lack of clarity.

A family physician referred his patient to an orthopedic surgeon for a left shoulder mass. The orthopedist's report to the referring physician included a plan for an MRI. The family physician was not sure whether the orthopedist expected that he (the family physician) would order the MRI or that the orthopedist would do so. The family physician did not contact the orthopedist to clarify this point.

When the patient returned to see the family physician a few months later, the mass was markedly increased in size. Workup was commenced, and the mass was found to be a high-grade malignancy.

Effective communication dictates that, when there is a lack of clarity, verification, not assumption, will help to ensure that the patient receives the proper care. To leave any important responsibility up in the air, assuming that someone else on the team will take care of it, is to take the chance that no one will take care of it. This problem manifests itself in cases in which there is a lack of follow-up, a lack of adjustment to a medication dose, or a change in a medication regimen. This lack of communication between physicians co-treating a patient often leaves the patient not knowing how to proceed or who will give directions about care.

Dr. Thomas Lee, writing about the paucity of information that often attends referrals and consultations, says that the "pressure for 'accountability' must be felt by both parties in the consultation relationship." He adds that patients are too often seen in consultation without the necessary information from prior evaluations.[26] One way of opening the lines of communication around referrals is—where a specific question is not clearly put to the consultant—for the consulting physician to be willing to ask the referring physician how he or she may be of help in the evaluation of the patient.[27] The issue of the ineffective transfer of information can be reduced to a very simple question. How can one be expected to carry out a responsibility without the information necessary to do so?

Inadequate clinical information negatively impacts the care of patients referred to physicians in any specialty. In some cases, even pathology examinations miss the diagnostic mark because of a lack of information about prior procedures and diagnoses. It is disheartening to learn that in some cases the consultant's reluctance to insist that the referring physician provide additional information may be because he or she does not want to offend the referring physician.[28]

# Finding a Better Way

There is much room for improvement in the way that handoffs occur in health care. This is, in part, reflected by its continued inclusion as a requirement in the National Patient Safety Goals. The requirement is to "implement a standardized approach to 'hand off' communications, including an opportunity to ask and respond to questions."[2] This "opportunity to ask and respond to questions" is key to improving communication at transitions of care, whether at a shift change, when a patient is being referred for consultation, or when a patient is being discharged from a hospitalization. The act of asking and responding to questions provides opportunities for clarification of information that is crucial to patient safety and improvement of the quality of care.

Drs. Wachter and Shojania rattle what may be an overconfidence in the promise of technological solutions to the problem of information transfer in healthcare. They remind us that although handoffs may benefit from computer communication, person-to-person communication will remain a necessity; therefore, those involved in the care of patients must find ways of improving in this area.[29] The healthcare industry is holding out much hope for the electronic medical record as a means of accessing information across the continuum of care, whether inpatient or outpatient. Although we must continue to work toward improving communication of medical information through these technological means, it is important to remember that individuals who make up the team and the team as a whole are central to the care of the patient.

No computer system, regardless of its sophistication, will replace the healthcare team and the information exchange that must occur between its members. "Even the fully wired hospital of the future will require thousands of oral handoffs each day."[29] These transfers of care will still take place between physician and physician, physician and nurse, physician and patient, and the myriad others who make up the healthcare team. Given that reality, everyone involved must work assiduously to improve personal communications, one discussion at a time and one handoff at a time.

In some institutions, staff has been instructed in the use of templates to aid in improving the verbal exchange of information, for example, where a nurse, resident, or other physician consults with a patient's attending physician by telephone. One such template is SBAR, an acronym to remind the user to describe the *s*ituation, provide *b*ackground information, and provide an *a*ssessment and a *r*ecommendation.[30] Formulations such as this one can be useful in helping the speaker organize his or her thoughts and the information that he or she is delivering.

Another example of a template used by the United States Forest Service in providing direction to fire fighters is described in the work of Dr. Sutcliffe et al. This five-part protocol recommends that the speaker offers the following information:

1. Here's what I think we face. (**SITUATION**)
2. Here's what I think we should do. (**TASK**)
3. Here's why. (**INTENT**)
4. Here's what we should keep our eye on. (**CONCERN**)
5. Now talk to me. Tell me if you don't understand, cannot do it, or see something I do not. (**CALIBRATE**)

To facilitate memorization, this template is referred to by the acronym STICC.[31] The specificity of the information required by STICC helps to ensure that critical information (such as what the person accepting care for the patient should be particularly concerned or vigilant about, recent changes in the patient's condition, anticipated changes, and the plan of care) is addressed.[32] Although these templates are mostly used in verbal communication, they may prove to be helpful in framing written communication between physicians, whether in a discharge summary or a report from a consulting physician.

Adding structure to sign-outs is another way of improving that aspect of the transferring of patient care.[33,34] The methodical delivery of this important clinical information that will permit the succeeding caregiver to know what occurred in the preceding period, what is anticipated, and what to watch for can only benefit the patient.

---

A 73-year-old patient with a history of hypertension, noninsulin-dependent diabetes, and chronic renal insufficiency was admitted for elective sigmoid resection and diverting colostomy. On the second postoperative day the patient was tachycardic, although she was receiving a low-dose beta blocker. That day she informed the nurse that she had developed left leg pain. Assuming that the pain was related to the epidural, which was placed preoperatively, the nurse called anesthesia, and they responded by decreasing the epidural rate. The surgical team was not called.

On the following day, the patient offered no complaints to the surgical team on morning rounds. Later that evening, the covering intern was called concerning the patient's left leg pain. No information about this intern's findings was relayed to the surgical team the following morning.

On postoperative day four, the patient complained to the nurse of mild chest discomfort. She was seen by the house staff within 20 minutes and by the attending physician several hours later. Her exam was unremarkable. A workup was initiated, but within an hour of the attending's visit, the patient's blood pressure fell; shortly thereafter, she had a pulseless electrical activity arrest and could not be resuscitated. A postmortem examination revealed pulmonary embolism.

---

Commenting on this case, Dr. Arpana Vidyarthi calls for the standardization of the sign-out process.[34] A standardized sign-out, including "structured written" information, could have changed the outcome in this patient's case.

A recitation of the information received in the exchange at handoffs, specifically at sign-outs, has also been found to improve communication. This is referred to as a read-back. The person who is receiving the information makes note of it and reads it back to the provider of the information as a way of confirming understanding.[3] This, like many of the techniques that improve communication, costs little, and its benefits are immeasurable, given that it has the potential to prevent injury and save lives. Read-back is the procedure often followed when a customer calls in a restaurant takeout order.

Improvements must also be made in the handoff that occurs when a patient is discharged from a hospital or from an emergency department visit. With over 35 million hospital admissions annually and 115 million emergency department visits,[35] there is much room for error and improvement. The content and timeliness of the discharge summary, so that it is available to the physician who will continue the patient's care, deserve attention. Dr. Sunil Kripalani et al. point out that the Joint Commission on the Accreditation of Healthcare Organizations requires that discharge summaries are completed within 30 days of discharge. These physicians raise the specter that this timeframe is too generous to help ensure patient safety, as most patients will be seen at a follow-up visit well before the discharge summary would be available. Drawing on some very early work, they propose that safety and efficiency would be improved by giving the discharged patient copies of the most pertinent data for delivery to the physician at the follow-up visit.[36] Certainly some patients will arrive at the visit having lost or forgotten these materials; however, this strategy, as an interim measure, is worth consideration.

To help improve handoffs to patients, whether from the emergency department, a hospitalization, or a patient returning home from an important visit with his physician, the previously described models may be useful. Consider STICC. All five points (a statement of the situation, what should be done, why it should be done, concerns about the patient's condition, and an assessment of understanding) are important to patient handoff. The fifth point, eliciting feedback from the patient, is invaluable in assessing the patient's understanding of the information with which he or she will return home.

Dr. Darrell Solet et al. evaluated the handoff process at the Indiana University School of Medicine and propose that educating senior medical students and residents in proper handoff methods may help to reduce errors. They conclude that "all physicians should be able to demonstrate minimal competency in communication in order to practice medicine in general and especially to perform handoffs."[37] Given the detriment poor communication poses to patient safety, this recommendation too merits serious consideration.

Hierarchical issues also have the potential to affect communication and, at handoff, between those who care for patients.[38] The teamwork training being undertaken by many healthcare organizations is one way to address this very significant barrier that impedes a junior person's ability or willingness to communicate information upward and affects a senior person's manner of communicating downward. Communication is central to the work of any team, and given that the quality of communication among team members is related to many factors concerning their work together, it is important that efforts are undertaken in health care to improve teamwork.[38] This area, which is beginning to receive well-deserved attention, holds much promise in helping to improve the coordination of patient care and transitions in the course of that care.

Good handoffs are not chance occurrences.[39] Handoff is a procedure that requires a plan and diligence. The time and space dedicated to handoffs should be protected from interruptions and shortcuts. Good handoffs permit the physician, nurse, or other healthcare provider who is transferring the care of the patient to go on to their rest or the care of other patients, knowing that they have carefully delivered the patient with the information that is necessary to continue his or her care. They have done what is necessary for that care to continue even in their absence. This safe delivery of the patient into the hands of the person who will continue their care is important even in the case of the retiring physician who must permanently hand off the care of his or her patients. One such physician wrote to his patient, "I will arrange personally for a new physician . . . to assume your care. . . . It has been a deep honor and privilege to serve as your physician." The ultimate handoff, well executed.

## REFERENCES

1. Wachter RM, Shojania KG. *Internal Bleeding: The Truth Behind America's Terrifying Epidemic of Medical Mistakes.* 1st ed. New York, NY: Rugged Land LLC; 2004: 177.
2. 2008 National Patient Safety Goals. Available at: http://www.jointcommission.org/PatientSafety/NationalPatientSafetyGoals/08_amb_npsgs.htm, accessed December 12, 2007.
3. World Health Organization. Patient safety solutions: communication during patient hand-overs. *World Health Organization: The Joint Commission.* 2007:1(solution 3).

4. Sutcliffe KM, Lewton E, Rosenthal MM. Communication failures: an insidious contributor to medical mishaps. *Acad Med.* 2004;79:187.
5. Gandhi TK, Kachalia A, Thomas EJ, et al. Missed and delayed diagnoses in the ambulatory setting: a study of closed malpractice claims. *Ann Intern Med.* 2006;145(7):488–496.
6. ECRI. Risk and quality management strategies 17: communication. *Health Risk Control.* 2006;(Suppl A):7.
7. Forster AJ, Murff HJ, Peterson JF. The incidence and severity of adverse events affecting patients after discharge from the hospital. *Ann Intern Med.* 2003;138:161–167.
8. Wachter RM, Shojania KG. *Internal Bleeding: The Truth Behind America's Terrifying Epidemic of Medical Mistakes.* 1st ed. New York, NY: Rugged Land LLC; 2004:167–168.
9. Litvin CB. In the dark: the case for electronic health records. *N Engl J Med.* 2007;356:2454.
10. Cornish PL, Knowles SR, Marchesano R, et al. Unintended medication discrepancies at the time of hospital admission. *Arch Intern Med.* 2005;165:424–429.
11. The Joint Commission. Sentinel event alert. *The Joint Commission.* 2006;issue 35.
12. Wachter RM, Goldman L. The emerging role of "hospitalists" in the American health care system. *N Engl J Med.* 1996;335:514–517.
13. American Academy of Family Physicians. Guidelines for interaction in "hospitalist" models—communication between the receiving inpatient care management physician and the referring primary care physician. Available at: http://www.aafp.org/online/en/home/policy/policies/h/hospitalists.html, accessed December 3, 2007.
14. Moore C, McGinn T, Halm E. Tying up loose ends: discharging patients with unresolved medical issues. *Arch Intern Med.* 2007;167:1305–1311.
15. Van Walraven C, Seth R, Austin PC, Laupacis A. Effect of discharge summary availability during post-discharge visits on hospital readmission. *J Gen Intern Med.* 2002;17:186–192.
16. Moore C, Wisnivesky J, Williams S, McGinn T. Medical errors related to discontinuity of care from an inpatient to an outpatient setting. *J Gen Intern Med.* 2003; 18:646–651.
17. Coleman EA, Berenson RA. Lost in transition: challenges and opportunities for improving the quality of transitional care. *Ann Intern Med.* 2004;140:533.
18. American Hospital Association. Office of General Counsel. *Discharging hospital patients; legal implications for institutional providers and health care professionals. Report of task force on legal issues in discharge planning.* Chicago, IL: American Hospital Association; 1987:61.
19. Agency fore Healthcare Research and Quality. Discharged blindly. Agency for Healthcare Research and Quality. Available at: http://www.webmm.ahrq.gov/case.aspx?caseID=111, accessed December 3, 2007.
20. Roy CL, Poon EG, Karson AS, et al. Patient safety concerns arising from test results that return after hospital discharge. *Ann Intern Med.* 2005;143:121–128.
21. Kripalani S, LeFevre F, Phillips CO, Williams MV, Basaviah P, Baker DW. Deficits in communication and information transfer between hospital-based and primary care physicians: implications for patient safety and continuity of care. *JAMA.* 2007;297(8):839.
22. Coleman EA, Berenson RA. Lost in transition: challenges and opportunities for improving the quality of transitional care. *Ann Intern Med.* 2004;140:533–536.

23. Groff H, Augello T. From theory to practice: an interview with Dr. Michael Leonard. *Forum-Risk Management Foundation of the Harvard Medical Institutions.* 2003;23(3):10.

24. Press I. The predisposition to file claims: the patient's perspective. *Law, Medicine & Health Care.* 1984(April):59.

25. Gandhi TK. Fumbled handoffs: one dropped ball after another. *Ann Intern Med.* 2005;142:355.

26. Lee TH. Consultation guidelines for primary care providers. *Forum-Risk Management Foundation of the Harvard Medical Institutions.* 2000;20(2):20.

27. Salerno SM, Hurst FP, Halvorson S, Mercado DL. Principles of effective consultation: an update for the 21st century consultant. *Arch Intern Med.* 2007;167: 271–275.

28. Sutcliffe KM, Lewton E, Rosenthal MM. Communication failures: an insidious contributor to medical mishaps. *Acad Med.* 2004;79:186–194.

29 Wachter RM, Shojania KG. *Internal Bleeding: The Truth Behind America's Terrifying Epidemic of Medical Mistakes.* 1st ed. New York, NY: Rugged Land LLC; 2004: 175–176.

30. SBAR—a communication technique for today's healthcare professionals. Available at: http://www.saferhealthcare.com/index.php?option=com_content&task=view&id=33, accessed December 13, 2007.

31. Sutcliffe KM, Lewton E, Rosenthal MM. Communication failures: an insidious contributor to medical mishaps. *Acad Med.* 2004;79:186–194.

32. Brigham Women's Hospital. Patient safety update: hand off policy enhances patient safety. *BWH Nurse.* Available at: http://www.brighamandwomens.org/publicaffairs/publications/DisplayNurse.aspx?articleid=775&issueDate=1/1/2007%2012: 00:00%20AM, accessed December 3, 2007.

33. Shojania KG, Fletcher KE, Saint S. Graduate medical education and patient safety: a busy—and occasionally hazardous—intersection. *Ann Intern Med.* 2006;145: 592–598.

34. Agency for Healthcare Research and Quality. *Fumbled handoff.* Available at: http://www.webmm.ahrq.gov/printview.aspx?caseID=55, accessed December 12, 2007.

35. American Hospital Association. Appendix 3–Supplementary Data Tables: Utilization and Volume. Available at: http://www.aha.org/aha/trendwatch/chartbook/07appendix3.pdf, accessed March 24, 2008.

36. Kripalani S, LeFevre F, Phillips CO, Williams MV, Basaviah P, Baker DW. Deficits in communication and information transfer between hospital-based and primary care physicians: implications for patient safety and continuity of care. *JAMA.* 2007;297(8):831–839.

37. Solet DJ, Norvell JM, Rutan GH, Frankel RM. Lost in translation: challenges and opportunities in physician-to-physician communication during patient handoffs. *Acad Med.* 2005;80:1095.

38. Helmreich RL. On error management: lessons from aviation. *BMJ.* 2000;320: 781–785.

39. Australian Medical Association Limited. Safe handover: safe patients. Guidance on clinical handover for clinicians and managers. Available at: http://www.ama.com.au/web.nsf/doc/WEEN-6XFDKN, accessed December 12, 2007.

# Chapter 9

# Don't Put Your Head in the Sand

Philip A. Robbins and Christine J. Quinn

*The important thing is not to stop questioning.*
Albert Einstein

A 17-year-old athlete underwent an ACL repair/reconstruction. On the second postoperative day, the patient's mother called the orthopedic surgeon because the patient's pain had increased. The orthopedist adjusted the pain medications over the phone. The next day (postoperative day three) the patient's mother called the orthopedist again and reported that the patient's foot was cold and bluish. The orthopedist advised the patient to come to his office for immediate evaluation. Upon examining the patient, the orthopedist noted swelling of the leg and sluggish capillary refill with normal pulses. He sent the patient to the emergency department for a duplex scan to rule out deep venous thrombosis (DVT). He also measured compartment pressures and ruled out compartment syndrome. Relieved, the orthopedist discharged the patient home.

The following evening the patient returned to the emergency department with increased swelling of the operative leg. The orthopedist measured compartment pressures again and found them to be elevated. Pulses were not present by Doppler. Thinking that the patient had a compartment syndrome, the orthopedist emergently took the patient to the operating room for a four-compartment fasciotomy. Postoperatively, pulses remained absent. A vascular consult was not obtained until the following day. At that time, an arteriogram was performed that revealed a false aneurysm in the popliteal artery. Several vascular procedures were performed, but ultimately, the patient required a below-the-knee amputation.

In reading about a 17-year-old athlete who ends up with an amputation after an ACL reconstruction because of a missed vascular injury, you may think that this surgeon must have had a fairly significant knowledge deficit. However, the surgeon caring for this patient was a well-trained orthopedic surgeon who had completed a fellowship in sports medicine. Although this was a rare complication, all orthopedic surgeons are trained to consider vascular injuries in the differential diagnosis of a postoperative complication, such as occurred here. You may have thought that this was a cavalier, arrogant surgeon who failed to make the correct diagnosis because he failed to respond to the patient's complaints; however, the surgeon caring for this patient was very conscientious. He was very responsive to the patient's complaints. His workup of this patient's complaints included an unscheduled evaluation of the patient, with measurement of compartment pressures in the emergency department on a holiday weekend.

Because this case had such a devastating outcome, it is a powerful teaching case that illustrates patterns that occur in many malpractice cases. Cases exist in which physicians have a gap in training or experience that leads them to make an error or miss a diagnosis. Some cases result from physicians taking on cases that are beyond the scope of their training and expertise, but in many more cases, the physicians involved in malpractice cases are well-trained, well-meaning, experienced, conscientious physicians who make cognitive errors that, in retrospect, seem unimaginable. Hindsight is 20/20.

If we characterize these errors as knowledge deficits, the way to prevent such problems from recurring would be to supplement the physician's training or to limit the physician's practice. Although these may be appropriate steps in some cases, in this case, neither of these would be an effective strategy. In all likelihood, the surgeon involved in this case will never have another outcome like this again. First, this is an extremely rare complication so that the odds of having two patients present like this is very low. Second, there is no doubt that this surgeon will always recall this case and would have a very low threshold for recognizing this situation if it were to arise again. The surgeon might even call for a vascular consultation when one is not necessary.

The main problems in this case include the orthopedist not considering other diagnoses and not asking for help when he did not understand what was happening with the patient. Essentially, the surgeon caring for the patient put his "head in the sand" and did not see the complication the patient developed until it was too late to salvage the patient's leg. If we want a better understanding of how mistakes are made by dedicated and skillful physicians, it may be instructive to look a little deeper and attempt to understand the cognitive errors made by the surgeon in the case. This chapter offers some insights that we hope will help you avoid similar catastrophes in your practice even if you do not perform surgery, as errors of a similar nature can occur in all specialties.

# Why Did This Physician Not Consider Other Diagnostic Options?

A brief review of heuristics may help guide our analysis. Shortcuts in reasoning are referred to as heuristics by cognitive psychologists. In his article *The Cognitive Psychology of Missed Diagnoses*, Dr. Redelmeier describes three shortcuts in reasoning that contribute to errors in diagnosis: the *availability heuristic*, the *anchoring heuristic*, and the *framing effect heuristic*.[1]

The availability heuristic implies that the physician chooses the obvious diagnosis rather than considering the less common diagnosis because the more obvious diagnosis comes to mind more easily (is more available).[1] During flu season, a pediatrician may be seeing many patients with body aches, headaches, and fever. The common diagnosis of flu may influence the pediatrician's thinking, causing him to overlook the less common diagnosis of meningitis.

---

In the case described, the orthopedist's familiarity with compartment syndrome and the rarity of a vascular injury occurring after an ACL reconstruction may have influenced his thinking. It was more likely that the patient had a compartment syndrome or a DVT than a vascular injury. As the case was analyzed, the surgeon admitted that he never even thought of a vascular injury as a possible cause of the patient's symptoms.

---

The *anchoring heuristic* is a shortcut that leads physicians to stay with the intended diagnosis after it is established. This may be because the physician has become invested in the initial diagnosis.[1] There have been many cases in which a surgeon continues to believe that a wound infection is superficial, despite growing evidence to the contrary.

---

In the case described, the orthopedist was thinking of compartment syndrome; when the compartment pressures were normal, he was reassured and sent the patient home. The surgeon was anchored to the compartment syndrome diagnosis, and when he ruled that out, he felt that the patient was fine and did not pursue other diagnoses, even though he had only ruled out a diagnosis he was anchored to and did not establish a diagnosis that explained the physical findings.

---

The third shortcut that is used in decision making in complex situations is known as the *framing effect heuristic*, in which people come to different decisions depending on how information is presented or framed.[1] For example, a patient presents to the emergency department with complaints of lower-back pain radiating to the lower extremities. The patient's bladder incontinence is not elicited by the emergency department physician and is not relayed to the ortho-pedist that is consulted over the phone. The orthopedist advises that the patient can be discharged and seen in his office the next day. If the information about bladder incontinence was conveyed to the orthopedic surgeon, he would have seen the patient immediately because of a possible cauda equina syndrome.

---

In the case described, the orthopedic surgeon caring for this patient did informally consult with a colleague in his practice about this patient; however, the colleague did not perform an independent evaluation of the patient. The informal consultation served as reassurance for the primary surgeon that his care was appropriate. This is not uncommon because the "consultant" is offering an opinion that is based solely on the information reported by the physician asking for the advice.

---

# What Can We Learn from This Case That Can Help Prevent Other Cases?

## Consider All Possible Differential Diagnoses

Early in our training we learn the process of differential diagnosis, which is the process of weighing the probability of one diagnosis versus the possibility of other diagnoses. In order to perform a differential diagnosis, there must be an availability of all possible diagnoses. In the case we described, one failure was the lack of availability of the diagnosis of a vascular injury to the orthopedic surgeon caring for the patient.

## Ask for Help If You Do Not Understand What Is Going on with a Patient

If you are not sure what is happening with a patient, consult with other physicians both within and outside of your own specialty. Do not be embarrassed to ask a colleague for help if you do not understand what is happening with the patient. These seem like obvious suggestions, yet in many cases they are not carried out. To explore why these simple risk-reduction strategies are sometimes hard to implement, let us review an aviation disaster from which we can learn some lessons.[2,3]

On March 27, 1977, a bomb exploded at the Canary Islands Los Palmas Airport. As a result of this event, many planes, including a KLM 747 and a Pan Am 747, were diverted to Tenerife's Los Rodeos Airport. After a long delay, the Los Palmas Airport was reopened, and both planes began preparing for take off. During this process, there was some confusion about the position of the planes on the runway, and whether or not they were cleared for take off. A junior officer of the KLM flight crew questioned the captain of the KLM flight about the position of the Pan Am 747 on the runway. The KLM captain, who was a very experienced pilot, dismissed the junior officer's concern and proceeded to take off. Shortly thereafter, the two 747s collided and exploded on the runway—583 lives were lost.

As you would imagine, this accident was thoroughly investigated, and several factors were identified as root causes of the accident. One of them included the dynamic between the captain and other members of the crew. The pilot of the KLM flight was one of the most senior pilots in the airline, and although the junior officer who questioned the pilot about the position of the other plane was also very highly trained and knowledgeable, the captain dismissed his concerns. As a result of this tragic accident, airline safety procedures were improved. There was an emphasis on training crews in communication techniques that prevent hierarchical barriers from blocking information flow.

## What Things May Influence a Physician's Willingness to Ask for Help?

The fields of aviation and medicine have many similar characteristics. Both require highly trained specialists to make crucial decisions in stressful time-pressured environments. Both professions also tend to have hierarchical chains of command that influence communication dynamics.

In the case of a complication/untoward event, the clinical decisions the physician makes may be influenced by hierarchical factors in relationships that impact on communication. "Communication is likely to be distorted or withheld in situations where there are hierarchical (e.g., power/status) differences between two communicators."[4] In the case of a resident, he or she may not speak up or offer an observation that would be helpful for the attending physician to be aware of, because he or she is concerned about how the attending physician may receive the information. Much like the captain of the KLM plane, a senior physician may ignore or reject information presented by a junior member of the team or "shoot the messenger" who bears bad news. This type of communication gap certainly hampers the flow of valuable information and can be the cause of errors in judgment.

There may also be situations in which a younger, less experienced surgeon may fear the embarrassment/humiliation of having a complication exposed to colleagues, peers, more senior physicians, and so forth, and may be unconsciously hoping that the worst-case scenario does not play out, resulting in a more conservative "watch and wait" approach in a patient for whom more aggressive intervention was clearly warranted.

---

In the case we described, the orthopedic surgeon was a member of a group that included several senior associates. This case occurred over a holiday week, and the senior partners were off for the holiday. One wonders if the orthopedic surgeon had had the opportunity to have a more senior partner examine the patient, might that more experienced physician have suggested a vascular consult early on? Of course, in order to prevent the framing effect heuristic, it would be important for the senior partner to actually examine the patient or at least ask questions beyond what the original surgeon was reporting.

---

At the other end of the spectrum, experienced physicians may be reluctant to ask younger physicians for help. They may be concerned that a junior associate or colleague may think less of them or that they have lost some of their acumen, are past their prime, and so forth, if they ask them for help. Medicine has been learning about this phenomenon from the aviation industry. Flight crews undergo a great deal of training to help flatten hierarchical influences that may make it difficult for senior pilots to ask for help from junior colleagues. In speaking about surgeons, Dr. William Berry noted, "We were trained to be soloists. We do not really like playing duets. In fact, we're more likely to see ourselves as the conductor with ultimate responsibility and complete authority."[5] This training may make it harder for an experienced surgeon to ask for help from a colleague. As the following case illustrates, experienced physicians may also be influenced by the fact that in many years of experience an unusual complication has never arisen (availability heuristic).

---

Consider the case of a 32-year-old patient who presented to the emergency department of a hospital with an elbow fracture. Both the attending orthopedist and the orthopedic resident saw the patient and noted that the patient's neurovascular status was intact. The patient was admitted, but because of scheduling issues, surgery was not planned until two days later.

On the night of admission, the patient was seen by the orthopedic resident for complaints of pain. The splint applied to the patient's arm was checked to ensure that there was no constriction. The patient's neurovascular status was again noted to be intact. During the night and throughout the next day, the patient required an unusually high amount of pain medication, including multiple doses of intravenous morphine. Because there was a low index of suspicion for a problem occurring, no one rounded on the patient until the evening, when it was noted by the attending orthopedist that the patient had limited mobility of the hand. A compartment syndrome was diagnosed, and an emergent fasciotomy was performed. Unfortunately, the patient developed muscle necrosis, which required multiple debridement surgeries. The patient lost significant function of the hand. This experienced orthopedist's judgment was influenced by the rarity of compartment syndrome after the particular type of elbow fracture the patient had sustained.

---

Other factors that might influence a physician's reluctance to ask for help include not wishing to burden a colleague with a complication. You may not wish to impose your complications on someone else. It may be difficult to ask for help, especially from someone in your own field. This can be embarrassing. You might also be trying to respect someone's time off on a weekend or a holiday.

Your ability and willingness to ask for help may also depend on where you are. Are you at a tertiary-care hospital or a small community hospital? Who is the expert in this situation? Is the needed expert someone at your hospital that you have easy access to, or will you need to transfer the patient to a tertiary center? In a small community hospital, there may be logistical barriers. For example, do you have a contact at the tertiary hospital who will accept the patient?

Your decision may also be influenced by who you would be asking for help. If this person is a known expert who everyone goes to when there is a problem, it may be the norm to ask this person for help, which may make it easier and more acceptable to ask for help. Alternatively, if the culture is to handle your own problems, this may be a barrier to asking a colleague for help. If you are thought of as the expert in your hospital, it may be harder for you to ask someone else for help.

Some situations may require a patient to be seen by a particular expert to address a complication. When laparoscopic cholecystectomies were new, a number of general surgeons had cases in which patients sustained common bile duct injuries during the procedure. Because these were complex repairs, it was often necessary to refer the patient to biliary surgeons who specialize in these repairs. There was a spate of claims where surgeons, without adequate training, attempted to repair these injuries that resulted in significant injuries to patients. Many of these cases subsequently resulted in malpractice cases.

Your willingness to ask for help may also depend on how requests for help are received. To illustrate this, it may be helpful to recall our experiences as residents. Perhaps you were responsible for a patient with a low urine output, or maybe you had a patient who you thought might need a blood transfusion. Recall how you may have been reluctant to call a chief resident to ask about that patient, if that resident had previously rebuffed or belittled you. Contrast that with your willingness to ask a question of an attending or chief resident who seemed to want to help you learn. A study by Sutcliffe and colleagues found that residents "were concerned about appearing incompetent in front of those with more power and they were hesitant to communicate information that was unfavorable or negative to themselves."[4] These same dynamics may carry over into private practice. If you have a comfortable relationship with a colleague, you may be more likely to discuss a difficult case with him or her and to ask for advice and counsel. If that person is difficult to approach, you may avoid or delay that conversation.

Sometimes you may be concerned that another physician with whom you consult or to whom you refer the patient may make you feel incompetent or indebted to him or her. You may also be concerned that this consultant may say something harmful to the patient about your care. This is a valid concern, especially in light of a study by Huycke and Huycke, which found 27% of callers to a malpractice law firm reported "an explicit recommendation by a healthcare provider to seek legal counsel."[6] Keep in mind, however, that if a patient is dissatisfied, he or she may seek out another opinion on his or her own. One way to mitigate against this is to handle the referral yourself. If you allow the patient to become dissatisfied and seek another opinion on his or her own, it is more likely that that person may criticize your care. If a patient is not doing well or if there is a complication, it may be prudent for you to refer the patient for another opinion yourself. This accomplishes a few things. First, it shows the patient that you are genuinely concerned about him or her and are doing your best to ensure that he or she gets the best possible care. Second, it may provide another perspective that may be helpful in your care of the patient. Finally, the second opinion may affirm that your treatment plan is correct, and this will serve to reassure both you and the patient.

Hierarchical and communication dynamics may unconsciously influence choices and decisions physicians make when caring for a patient with a complication. Of course, a professional must put these feelings aside and do what is necessary to care for the patient; being aware of these dynamics is a risk-reduction strategy in helping to avoid them.

## Deal with Complications Head On

Consider a patient who has undergone a total hip replacement. He returns to your office two-weeks postoperative with a wound that is draining but otherwise looks benign. The patient is on Lovenox for DVT prophylaxis, which can cause these wounds to drain for a longer period of time. This type of drainage is not unusual for a postoperative patient, and it is not unreasonable to have a low clinical index of suspicion for a wound infection in this circumstance.

What is in the back of the surgeon's mind when he sees this patient and he considers whether to culture the drainage? Is he weighing what he would do if he cultures the wound and the cultures come back positive with a possible containment? His concern is not wanting to take the patient back to the operating room to open the wound if it is not necessary.

Sometimes there may also be denial that delays the physician's recognition of a complication. Can the surgeon objectively consider the likelihood that he or she has made an error that is causing a patient a problem? We all know that we are not perfect and that every patient cannot have an optimal outcome, but on some level we do believe that our skill and experience bode well for our patients.

Intellectually, we may agree that 1% to 2% of patients who undergo a primary total hip replacement will have a postoperative infection,[7] but we may also believe that our complication rates are lower than average because of our skill and attention to detail. This may make it harder to recognize a problem when it develops. We may also be influenced by a sincere desire for our patients to do well. We do not wish for them to experience setbacks from complications that may require additional surgery or to subject them to additional pain or a prolonged recovery.

Consider a patient who had been noncompliant with your recommendations and now develops a complication. Perhaps it is a diabetic patient who has not followed your advice on diet or medications or a patient with chronic obstructive pulmonary disease (COPD) who continues to smoke or a surgical patient who has been weight bearing against your advice or a patient who got a cast or a wound wet.

If you suspect that a patient developed a complication because he or she was noncompliant with your recommendations, you may feel frustrated in caring for this patient. In some cases, you may even feel some anger toward the patient.

How do these feelings influence your interactions with the patient? Might you avoid them? Spend less time with them? Not listen as carefully to their complaints? Roter and Hall noted that "the frustration and the repetitiveness associated with treating patients with chronic conditions may reduce physicians' liking for them."[8] Their studies also showed that physicians curtailed social conversations with sicker patients, which was predictive of lower satisfaction.[8] Interestingly, Dr. Hall and her colleagues also found that sicker patients liked their doctors less.[8,9] This decreased satisfaction on both sides of the physician–patient relationship may increase the likelihood that the patient may sue the physician caring for them in the face of an unexpected or disappointing outcome.

## It Is Important to Realistically Guide Patient Expectations

Consider a patient who is coming to you for a total knee replacement. He has a friend who you successfully operated on last year and who had an excellent result. This patient is very active and anticipates returning to playing tennis in six months as his friend did. What if the patient does not have the same result as his friend? What if the knee is stiff after the surgery and requires additional physical therapy? What happens if the knee develops an infection and requires additional surgery? Is the patient prepared for this potential adverse outcome?

Sometimes you may encounter a patient who is asking for a procedure because a friend had it or he or she read about it on the Internet. He or she may come to you with some misinformation or an inflated optimism of what a particular procedure can do for them. If his or her clinical situation is different or more complex than the friend he or she is comparing himself or herself to and the outcome he or she is hoping for might not be realistic, it is important to ensure that he or she understands why his or her situation is different. Additionally, the patient may have a complication that can result in an adverse outcome with patient disappointment.

When a patient experiences a complication, a physician may worry that the patient may sue him; however, when we consider the number of complications that occur, we know that very few patients who suffer a complication sue their doctor. Many variables factor into a patient's decision to sue the physician who cared for him or her. There are also many variables that influence whether a case has merit from a medical perspective. Often, a key issue in a malpractice case is determining whether the outcome the patient has experienced is the result of an acceptable complication or is the result of an error in their care. Sometimes this is very hard to determine. For this reason, prevention of a malpractice case really begins at the start of your relationship with the patient. Be sure that the patient has a realistic understanding of his or her illness and the options available for treatment. If willing to undergo surgery, he or she should have a realistic expectation of what the surgery can accomplish, what the most frequently encountered complications are, and what the recovery period will be like. Documentation of this discussion is an important part of this consultation with the patient and a critical risk management strategy. If there is ever a question about the content of this discussion, your contemporaneous documentation of this discussion will be invaluable.

---

Consider the overweight patient who presents for liposuction and shows the plastic surgeon a picture of a shapely model in a small bikini, or the young man with a bump on his nose who feels that rhinoplasty will improve his social life.

---

These are examples of patients who may have unrealistic expectations. Each patient must be evaluated on the basis of his or her goals for the planned procedure. If these goals are not in concert with the physician's anticipated outcome, proceeding will invariably yield an unhappy patient. If the patient is disappointed by his or her outcome, he or she may become angry. Patients who are angry might express this anger by suing their physician. This is particularly true where a complication occurs or the risk-reward relationship is not favorable.

---

For example, a patient with intermittent back pain controlled with nonsteroidal anti-inflammatory medication might be a poor choice for spine surgery; a patient who suffers a complication from a simple scar revision will be particularly disgruntled if there is an unfavorable result.

---

Often, lawsuits are a result of unrealistic expectations. These are examples of situations that should alert us to at least think twice before taking on certain patients. There is nothing wrong with telling patients that you do not think that you can help them or that you feel that a procedure is not indicated. This risk management strategy may even prevent a lawsuit.

# How Can You Mitigate the Risk of a Malpractice Lawsuit If a Patient Has a Complication?

## Breaking Bad News to a Patient Who Has Had a Complication

---

Consider the case of a very active 55-year-old athletic female who undergoes a right total knee replacement. At two-weeks postop, she returns to your office with a draining wound that is obviously infected. You must tell this patient that she will need to be readmitted to the hospital immediately for a surgical procedure to irrigate and debride the wound and that she will require 6 weeks of intravenous antibiotic therapy. You must also inform her that if the infection does not clear there is a possibility that the knee prosthesis may have to be removed.

---

### *Communication with the Patient and the Family Is Essential*

Breaking bad news to a patient is never a pleasant job. Physicians who take care of cancer patients face this experience on a regular basis. Dr. Vandekieft comments, "Physicians also have their own issues about breaking bad news. It is an unpleasant task. Physicians do not wish to take hope away from the patient. They may be fearful of the patient's or family's reaction to the news, or uncertain how to deal with an intense emotional response."[10] He continues:

Historically, the emphasis on the biomedical model in medical training places more value on technical proficiency than on communication skills. Therefore, physicians may feel unprepared for the intensity of breaking bad news, or they may unjustifiably feel that they have failed the patient. The cumulative effect of these factors is physician uncertainty and discomfort, and a resultant tendency to disengage from situations in which they are called on to break bad news.

To understand better why patients sue their doctors, Dr. Beckman and his colleagues looked at depositions from plaintiffs (patients who sued their doctors). They found that "the most common relationship complaint arising from the depositions was the feeling of being deserted and feeling alone. Most often, plaintiffs described the experience of trying unsuccessfully to contact the practitioner. Attempts involved answering services, nurses on inpatient units, unkept promises to return to the bedside, or return calls."[11]

---

In the infection case we described, it is obvious that the surgeon seeing the patient would break the news to the patient as part of the visit; however, many clinical situations are not as straightforward. Sometimes there may be a temptation to allow a surrogate to break bad news to the patient, especially if you are not in the hospital when the problem is discovered.

---

Wherever possible, you should be the one breaking the news to the patient. If you delegate this discussion to someone else, the patient may feel abandoned. "The physician's *presence* may be the assurance that the patient needs."[12]

This is a crucial conversation, and you should have it with the patient as soon as reasonably possible. If you delay this conversation, you risk having others answering the patient's questions in your absence. Patients who are confused or worried about their condition will ask almost anyone they encounter about their condition/situation. This may be detrimental because these other caregivers may not have all of the information you have about the situation and may give the patient inaccurate or even erroneous information. After the patient has developed a viewpoint, it may be harder for you to correct his or her understanding of the situation. If you do not handle this conversation skillfully, the patient may even perceive you as defensive and may begin to wonder whether you are withholding information from them. This may put you and the patient on a path that is difficult to recover from.

It is also important to understand that the patient may not be able to process all of the information that you are sharing at once. This difficult conversation may actually be a series of conversations in which it is necessary for you to repeat explanations to the patient over time. It may be painful and frustrating for you to have to repeat this information, but it is best if you can address the patient's concerns personally and help him or her build on the understanding of the situation with each conversation. The information that you share with the patient must be consistent. Your goal in these situations is to prevent misunderstandings. If a patient perceives that you withheld information from him or her, he or she likely will feel angry toward you. If you learn additional information over time, you should explain to the patient why and how the additional information became available.

---

In the infection case described previously, it would be helpful to explain to the patient when the culture reports are expected back and at what intervals you will be able to make clinical determinations concerning the treatment of the infection. This will help provide the patient with some guideposts in her treatment and help pave the way for sharing progress reports on the status of the infection.

---

You should also recognize that the patient may want his or her family or other significant people to be involved in his or her care, and with the patient's permission, you should communicate with that person(s) as often as needed. "Having another person present provides the patient with a sense of support and a belief that he or she does not have to deal with the crisis alone."[13] Keep in mind that families play a significant role in a patient's decision to sue their doctor; thus, alienating or antagonizing a family member may actually increase the risk of a lawsuit. If you find that there are several family members involved and that information is not being shared so that you are providing the same information over and over again to different people, it is reasonable to ask the patient to appoint one or two family members as spokespersons who will relay information to other family members.

## Avoid the Perception of Abandonment

Keeping in mind that the concept of abandonment is really about the patient's perception of being abandoned by his or her doctor in a time of need, another risk management strategy that is sometimes overlooked is keeping patients informed of your own schedule. Dr. Beckman's study also reported that patients negatively perceive "the loss of contact with the 'expert hired to perform a procedure or surgery' who is replaced on follow-up visits by a junior member of the team, typically a resident."[11]

In the inpatient setting, it is particularly important to prepare patients for changes in coverage. If you plan to be away for the weekend or for vacation, a conference, and so forth, it is prudent to let patients know about this in advance so that they are not surprised by your absence. Giving them information about how you will provide the covering doctor with information about their situation will reassure patients and decrease their anxiety about the transition. If it is reasonable, you may also wish to tell the patient that the covering doctor can reach you while you are away, if necessary. Some physicians have found it helpful to provide patients with a direct number where they can be reached over a weekend or holiday if there is a problem. These physicians have reported that very few patients actually call them, and the goodwill generated by providing a patient with this type of access is incalculable. Alternatively, you may wish to call the patient who you are concerned about to check with them over a weekend or a holiday. Imagine the reaction of a patient (and their loved ones) to receiving this type of personal care and concern from their physician.

In the outpatient setting, you must keep your office staff and partners informed about a patient who has had a complication. For example, your staff should know that if that particular patient calls for an appointment or with a question, he or she should be given reasonable priority. You would not want all of the work you did to repair a fragile relationship with a patient to be undermined by a mishandled call back or billing issue, due to a communication failure between you and your office team. It may seem burdensome and time consuming to attend to these small details, but the time it takes to address them up front pales in comparison to the time it would take to defend a malpractice action. Although all of your patients should be treated with courtesy and respect, patients who have had a complication or an unexpected outcome require and should receive special attention from both you and your staff.

## Dealing with Angry and Difficult Patients and Families

---

Imagine that you are seeing the patient who had the infected knee replacement in your office two weeks after the hospitalization to treat the infection. To your surprise, the patient is very angry and expresses that she is very discouraged because she expected that by now she would be able to travel. At this visit, the patient is accompanied by a family member who you have not met previously and who wants to know how much longer it will be before the patient will be "back to normal."

---

When a patient has a complication or an unexpected outcome, he or she may become angry at you. Sometimes this anger is not expressed immediately, which means that it may catch you by surprise at a follow-up visit. The opportunity to be aware of this anger and to understand better its source is another reason that it is important to continue to ensure that you are the person seeing a patient who has had a less than ideal outcome. The patient may have feelings of loss, as a result of their less than optimal outcome, which are expressed as anger. There may be a natural temptation to avoid this unpleasantness by passing this patient on to a subordinate or an assistant. This is especially easy to justify when you are busy and you fear that the patient will take up more time than you allotted for the visit. Try to resist this temptation. The paradox is that the more you wish you could avoid the patient the more important it is for you to see him or her. "Helping the patients work through their reactions will not only allow them to feel supported and establish a positive tone for the remainder of the treatment."[13]

Although you may feel that you have done all that you can for the patient and said everything that you can say to explain what happened, keep in mind that patients may not process all of the information you offer them in one encounter and may require repeated explanations of how their injury occurred. "According to what is known about anxiety and information processing, anxiety is likely to interfere with patients' ability to obtain the very information they seek from physicians."[14] Taking the time to listen to the patient's concerns and fears may resolve some of the anger or at least help the patient recognize that his or her anger should not be directed at you. If the patient feels your compassion and understands that you are doing all you can for him or her, the anger may be blunted. You may be concerned that this type of discussion will take a significant amount of time; however, according to Fogarty et al.: "The physician's expression of enhanced compassion took approximately 40 seconds."[14] Imagine that spending an additional 40 seconds with a patient could possibly make the difference in the patient's decision to sue you after a complication.

In order to be sure that you are available to spend the required amount of time with a patient who has suffered a complication, you should keep your staff informed of patients who may require extra time and attention from both you and them. Your staff members can support you in implementing this risk management strategy if they are aware of the patient who has suffered a complication and if they are sensitive to this patient's needs. For example, try to schedule the patient at a time when you are able to spend the requisite time with him or her to answer questions and address concerns. It may also be helpful if you invite the patient to have a family member or significant other participate in the discussions. It can be very beneficial to have a second person hear what you are telling the patient—that person may also serve as a support to the patient who is anxious. Because many patients say they sue to get information,[15] you do not want the patient to sense that you are withholding information from them; thus, do your best to answer all of the patient's questions honestly.

You may find yourself in a situation in which the patient's prognosis is grim, and grief over the loss is very appropriate. Dr. Quill and his colleagues have suggested that "joining with the patient and family in the expression of a wish that their circumstances were different"[16] may be helpful. They suggest that this type of statement may also be useful in many scenarios in which bad news is delivered to a patient. They specifically suggest that in situations in which the patient has experienced a complication, the physician "should emphasize a willingness to work together and to do one's best"[16] to help the patient move forward.

Having had the opportunity to review many malpractice cases has provided us with an opportunity to gain some insight into how malpractice cases evolve when patients have unexpected results or complications. Our work with physicians involved in malpractice cases has been instructive. We believe that physicians who apply risk management principles in handling situations in which patients have unexpected outcomes can often prevent malpractice cases.

If your patient's course is not unfolding as expected, you can decrease the risk of a malpractice suit by not becoming complacent. Be on your toes at all times. Be aware of cognitive errors; look for alternative diagnoses if all of the facts do not fit the clinical presentation. Ask for help, and get other opinions when the situation is unusual or complex. Be mindful of how your ego can influence your decisions. Try to be cognizant of situations in which your ego may be hampering your judgment. Try not to put your "head in the sand" when things are not going as planned. Your goal is to recognize complications as they are unfolding so that you can react and mitigate the injury to the patient.

Because it is not possible to entirely prevent complications from occurring with each of our patients, it is also critical to employ and work toward mastering strategies that will assist you in dealing effectively with patients who experience unexpected and disappointing results.

Keep in mind that not all patients who experience complications with adverse outcomes sue their physicians. Nurture your relationships with all of your patients. Also, pay special attention to your relationship with a patient who has had a disappointing outcome. Spend extra time answering his or her questions. Ensure that all members of your team are aware of and are sensitive to that patient's needs. Maintaining a strong relationship with the patient's family will be helpful in the long run.

We hope we have offered you some guidance to help you avoid the pitfalls we described in this chapter. Remaining vigilant in our efforts to recognize and treat complications promptly is good for our patients and provides us with an added dividend of preventing malpractice lawsuits against us.

*The important thing is not to stop questioning.*

# REFERENCES

1. Redelmeier DA. The cognitive psychology of missed diagnoses. *Ann Intern Med.* 2005;142:115–120.
2. Worst air disaster of all time. Aviation Sri Lanka. Available at: http://atcsl.tripod.com/world_aircrashes.htm, accessed September 7, 2007.
3. Pizzi L, Goldfarb NI, Nash DB. Crew resource management and its application in medicine. In: *Making Health Care Safer: A Critical Analysis of Patient Safety Practices.* Agency for Healthcare Research and Quality. AHRQ 01-E058. Available at: http://www.ahrq.gov/clinic/ptsafety/chap44.htm, accessed September 7, 2007.
4. Sutcliffe KM, Lewton E, Rosenthal MM. Communication failures: an insidious contributor to medical mishaps. *Acad Med.* 2004;79:186–194.
5. Berry W. I'm a surgeon, not a teammate. *Forum-Risk Manage Found Harvard Med Inst.* 2003;23(3):16–18.
6. Huycke LI, Huycke MM. Characteristics of potential plaintiffs in malpractice litigation. *Ann Intern Med.* 1994;120:792–798.
7. Vaccaro AR. *Orthopaedic Knowledge Update 8.* Rosemont, IL: American Academy of Orthopaedic Surgeons; 2005:418.
8. Roter DL, Hall JA. *Doctors Talking with Patients/Patients Talking with Doctors: Improving Communication in Medical Visits.* 2nd ed. Westport, CT: Praeger Publishers; 2006.
9. Hall JA, Horgan TG, Stein TS, Roter DL. Liking in the physician-patient relationship. *Patient Educ Couns.* 2002;48:69–77.
10. Vanderkieft GK. Breaking bad news. *Am Fam Physician.* 2001;64:1975–1978.
11. Beckman HB, Markakis KM, Suchman AL, Frankel RM. The doctor-patient relationship and malpractice. *Arch Intern Med.* 1994;154:1365–1370.
12. Broyard A. *Intoxicated by My Illness, and Other Writings on Life and Death.* New York, NY: Clarkson N. Potter, Inc; 1992. Quoted by: Adson MA. An endangered ethic—the capacity for caring. *Mayo Clin Proc.* 1995;70:495–500.
13. Ptacek JT, Eberhardt TL. Breaking bad news: a review of the literature. *JAMA.* 1996;276:496–502.
14. Fogarty LA, Curbow BA, Wingard JR, McDonnell K, Somerfield MR. Can 40 seconds of compassion reduce patient anxiety? *J Clin Oncol.* 1999;17:371–379.
15. Vincent C, Young M, Phillips A. Why do people sue doctors? A study of patients and relatives taking legal action. *Lancet.* 1994;343:1609–1613.
16. Quill TE, Arnold RM, Platt F. "I wish things were different": expressing wishes in response to loss, futility, and unrealistic hopes. *Ann Intern Med.* 2001;135:551–555.

# Chapter 10

# Disclosure

James W. Tuffin and Geraldine M. Donohue

*For nothing is hidden that will not be disclosed, nor is anything secret that will not become known and come to light.*
Luke 8:17 (NRSV)

A surgeon called his malpractice insurer seeking guidance. He related that he performed a cholecystectomy on a middle-aged female patient. She was discharged and thought to be without complication. She then made some complaints to her primary care physician that prompted an order for an X-ray. The radiologist called the surgeon to alert him that a clip appeared to be out of place on the X-ray. The radiologist and primary care physician deferred to the surgeon for further communication with the patient. The surgeon told the patient that he needed to operate again because of a "complication." An open Roux-en-Y procedure was needed to repair the bile duct. The patient was told that the surgery for the complication was "successful." She seemed grateful and satisfied with the information that she received. She was doing well on a postoperative visit to the surgeon's office. The surgeon has now received a letter from the patient's attorney, with her signed authorization for the release of all records. He is wondering whether he should call the patient to explain what happened.

D octors are courageous. They are able to hold another person's living heart, treat frightening infections, and be present at the beginning and end of life. They had the courage to put their education and training ahead of the pleasures enjoyed by those who pursue less demanding occupations without guarantee of material reward. They must also have the courage to confront and tell the truth, even when it does not seem to be in their interest to do so.

In the 19th century, a physician faced "no tribunal other than his own conscience to adjudge penalties for carelessness or neglect."[1] The second half of the 20th century saw an explosion of tort litigation, state-imposed professional discipline structures, modern hospital credentialing procedures, HMO reviews, higher education of the patient population, and the patients' rights movement. Physicians are now scrutinized as never before.

Disclosure of medical errors is a practical, if unpleasant, reality. Whether the physicians involved are helped or hurt by the disclosure is not relevant to the disclosure decision. Ethical considerations, patients' needs, legal requirements, and prevention of future errors all take precedence over any adverse consequences for physicians involved in the error.

Disclosure requirements challenge basic instincts. Anyone who owns a television and views law or detective programs hears the constant warning that "anything you say can and will be used against you in a court of law." Hardwired with this common wisdom and able to cite numerous anecdotes of bizarre judicial rulings in apparently frivolous lawsuits, many health professionals are understandably skeptical if told that they may benefit from the voluntary disclosure of a medical error. They understandably ask why they should disclose.

Thinking about disclosing medical errors asks the deepest questions about the physician–patient relationship. The accepted mores of the market place, *caveat emptor*, clearly do not work in this context. Once the economic and legal curtains are pulled back, the patient is most often naked and defenseless before the physician. The patient lacks the training and skills necessary to help himself or herself; he or she must rely on the expertise and professionalism of the doctor. Thus, many courts describe the relationship as a fiduciary one, or one of high confidence and trust. If we look at the situation as only a contract, the physician's promise to exercise reasonable professional care and diligence also fails to satisfy. Whatever one thinks of the legal remedies available to an aggrieved patient or family, money—even too much money—cannot erase pain, eliminate a disability, or bring back the dead. The ideal is a relationship of supreme trust and confidence. Like all ideals, it is never demonstrated perfectly.

Stated broadly, there are two reasons for disclosing medical errors: (1) to fulfill the rights and meet the needs of the patient involved in the error and (2) to meet the needs of society—and the healing professions—to avoid future errors.

Laws and regulations requiring disclosure are most often focused on events that occur in hospitals or other state-licensed facilities. Private physician offices may not be regulated with the same level of specificity.

# A Changing Culture

Leaders of the patient safety movement, such as Leape, Berwick, and Marx, have been instrumental in influencing the changing culture of error disclosure in medical practice today.[2-4] The staggeringly high statistics of morbidity and mortality caused by medical error from the Institute of Medicine report has only served to strengthen their missions. Physicians and all members of the healthcare team need to be able to discuss openly medical mistakes in the clinical environment without fear of punishment. This changing culture is the critical path to bringing the discussion of the error to the bedside.

The following case illustrates an open environment for the disclosure of errors within the healthcare team:

> A pediatrician calls her malpractice insurer seeking guidance. A nurse administered an initial dose of a vaccine from a prepackaged syringe that was intended for the second dose. The error was immediately recognized. Because the second dose is half of the initial dose, a second injection was used to complete the initial dose. With the patient still in the office, the pediatrician wants to review what she will say as she lets the mother know that an error necessitated the second injection.

This practice instilled an open environment for the disclosure and discussion of medical errors. A professional member of the pediatrician's team made a mistake and immediately alerted the physician to the error. The pediatrician was unsure of how to proceed with disclosure of the event to the infant's mother and contacted her insurer for assistance.

In this case, the doctor saw her insurer as a resource; the call was not made to comply with contract requirements. Specific discussion of insurance issues comes later. Depending on the nature of the circumstances and the timing of the adverse event, the doctor may be more comfortable and confident to seek guidance before proceeding with disclosing the error to the patient.

In *Forgive and Remember: Managing Medial Failure*, Charles Bosk writes of an attending surgeon's reflections of the importance of disclosure, particularly within the healthcare team:[5]

> Now in this business it takes a lot of self confidence, a lot of maturity, to admit errors. But that's not the issue. No mistakes are minor. All have a mortality and a morbidity. Say I have a patient who comes back from the operating room and he doesn't urinate. And say my intern doesn't notice or he decides it is nothing serious and he

doesn't catherize the guy and he doesn't tell me. Well, this guy's bladder fills up. There's a foreign body and foreign bodies can cause infections; infection can become sepsis; sepsis can cause death. So the intern's mistake here can cause this guy hundreds of dollars in extra hospitalization and it could cost him his life. All mistakes have costs attached to them. Now a certain amount is inevitable. But it is the obligation of everyone involved in patient care to minimize mistakes. The way to do that is by full and total disclosure.

# Ethical Reasons for Disclosure

The relationship of a patient to a physician is one of high trust and confidence. The patient relies on the physician's knowledge, skill, and judgment and depends on the physician for information. Nevertheless, the adult patient retains the ultimate right of decision. Modern laws concerning "informed consent" acknowledge patient autonomy and require the physician to educate the patient to facilitate decision making.[6]

The American Medical Association codified a physicians' ethical obligation to disclose the relevant facts when errors result in harm:[7]

> It is a fundamental ethical requirement that a physician should at all times deal honestly and openly with patients. Patients have a right to know their past and present medical status and to be free of any mistaken beliefs concerning their conditions. Situations occasionally occur in which a patient suffers significant medical complications that may have resulted from the physician's mistake or judgment. In these situations, the physician is ethically required to inform the patient of all the facts necessary to ensure understanding of what has occurred. Only through full disclosure is a patient able to make informed decisions regarding future medical care. Ethical responsibility includes informing patients of changes in their diagnoses resulting from retrospective review of test results or any other information. This obligation holds even though the patient's medical treatment or therapeutic options may not be altered by the new information. Concern regarding legal liability which might result following truthful disclosure should not affect the physician's honesty with a patient. (I, II, III, IV) Issued March 1981; Updated June 1994.

This policy goes beyond providing the patient with information to facilitate informed decision making; disclosure may be required "even though the patient's medical treatment or therapeutic options may not be altered." It acknowledges that the relationship between the patient and the physician is a relationship of trust that must be based on truth.

# Legal Reasons for Disclosure

One of the most disheartening situations the physician can face is making an error, apologetically disclosing it to the patient, in a timely manner, only to have a lawsuit be initiated. The physician can do everything possible medically, ethically, and legally for the patient, oftentimes while observing no lasting injury and yet find no escape from litigation. Such was the situation in the following case:

> While the patient was still in the recovery area, the orthopedic surgeon realized that arthroscopy was performed on the wrong knee. The surgeon called his malpractice insurer for advice and immediately informed the patient of the error. The surgeon apologized, and the patient was eventually put in touch with the insurer to discuss compensation. The patient flatly rejected offers of what the surgeon and insurer thought was a reasonable compensation. It did not appear that the patient sustained any permanent disability or significant injury.

The patient sued. Investigators videotaped the patient engaging in activities clearly inconsistent with the patient's subjective claims of pain and disability. Nevertheless, the surgeon was subjected to a humiliating trial, and the court permitted the plaintiff to submit a claim for punitive damages. Such circumstances, however, occur infrequently.

Laws or regulations may require disclosure of an error to the patient. These rules do not necessarily have disclosure of medical errors as their specific purpose. For example, New York hospital regulations provide that the patient has the right to do the following:[7]

> Obtain from the responsible medical staff member complete current information concerning his/her diagnosis, treatment and prognosis in terms the patient can be reasonably expected to understand. The patient shall be advised of any change in health status, including harm or injury, the cause for the change and the recommended course of treatment. The information shall be made available to an appropriate person on the patient's behalf

and documented in the patient's medical record, if the patient is not competent to receive such information.

This obviously requires disclosure of an error that results in harm or injury. California's law requiring reporting of adverse events to the state requires that the "facility shall inform the patient or the party responsible for the patient of the adverse event by the time the report is made."[8]

When weighing disclosure, the easiest rule to apply is most often the Golden Rule. If one can expect the patient to feel upset or betrayed when the facts come to light at a later date, the error should be forthrightly discussed at the earliest appropriate time. A physician who is brought to court will find very little sympathy if it is shown that pertinent information was withheld from the patient.

Withholding information about an error may impact the physician's psychological functioning. If a physician was to conceal an error, there are some states that have a "discovery rule" statute of limitations, where the patient's time to bring legal action is extended until the patient learns of the injury. In other states, the statute of limitations may be extended if the physician fraudulently conceals information from the patient.[9] Physicians who have readily disclosed mistakes to their patients have reported a great sense of unburdening and relief that comes from the honest and forthright discussion.

The instinct for self-preservation and its corollary, fear, will sometimes lead a physician to resort to deception. Every malpractice attorney has war stories about altered records. All will agree that this is one of the most self-destructive things that a physician can do.

---

A patient coded and expired in the hospital. The family claimed that the doctors, including the pulmonary consultant, failed to recognize and deal with the patient's acidosis. The partner of the pulmonary consultant was not involved in the hospital care or the lawsuit but was called for a deposition to read office notes. The records showed typical medical visits, with interval histories, blood pressures, the patient's weight, and other pertinent data. The examiner then asked the doctor whether copies of the record were sent out before the lawsuit. The answer was ultimately yes. The lawyer confronted the doctor with a copy of the records, which lacked the recorded blood pressures and other routine information. The lawyer asked the doctor when the additional information was added to the chart. The doctor said something about not recalling, and the doctor's lawyer called for an adjournment. The partner decided that the prudent thing was to settle the lawsuit.

---

In one situation, a physician had been found to embellish a consultation report to suggest ruling out mesenteric ischemia after an autopsy showed a necrotic bowel. In another instance, a physician was found to have added false information to the medical record showing that the patient was given advice to repeat an X-ray. In one rather extreme case, a doctor rewrote an entire chart on forms that did not exist at the time of the treatment. Because these activities are antithetical to the ideal of trust and confidence, they are invariably fatal to any legal defense.

A most troublesome situation that happens far too often is the truthful addition to the medical record when the physician is faced with a letter from an attorney requesting a medical record or when faced with a Summons & Complaint. In reviewing the documentation in the patient's medical record, the physician may feel justified to "make the record fit the actual care delivered." There is no justification; this is alteration of a legal document. What can the physician do to try to defend his or her position? The physician should contact his or her malpractice insurer or, in the situation of a lawsuit, his or her defense attorney and work that additional information into the case.

# Will Disclosing an Error Affect My Malpractice Insurance?

Some physicians mistakenly cite concerns about malpractice insurance as a reason not to disclose the facts surrounding an error. They cite policy provisions that exist in some polices to the effect that "the insured shall not concede liability or agree to pay damages." These clauses generally prevent the insured from formally binding the insurer to a court judgment or claim settlement without the insurer's consent. They do not invalidate insurance coverage when the insured fulfills professional, legal, or ethical obligations to provide accurate information to the patient. The physician should also be aware of any requirements in his or her particular insurance policy regarding the reporting of incidents or potential claims. It may be in his or her interest to report an error to the insurer even if it is uncertain that the patient will actually make a claim.

# What About HIPAA?

The HIPAA privacy rule is no impediment to the disclosure of medical errors. The privacy rule encourages disclosure to the patient. HIPAA specifically permits the use and disclosure of protected health information as required by state regulations and to carry out a facility's quality-improvement and error-prevention programs. The privacy rule also permits physicians to share information with liability insurers.

# Managing Disclosure

Earlier in the chapter, a pediatrician was faced with disclosing to a mother of an infant that the vaccination, intended to be handled with one injection, required two injections. The child received the correct vaccination and the correct dose and route; however, two half-dose injections, the equivalent of one dose, were administered in error.

When the injury or "damage" to the patient is minimal, the disclosure tends to become a less fiery issue for most physicians; however, in the case of this pediatrician, she became concerned as to how to proceed and what words to use to the infant's mother. Providing information about how the nurse made the error, explaining that there was little consequence to the infant with the exception of an additional "stick," and putting forth a sincere apology are crucial.

Parents do not want to hear that even the most minor of errors happened to their children. After an error has occurred, the parents will need to re-establish faith and trust in the pediatrician and staff. The honesty demonstrated in the disclosure conversation can work to mend what has the potential of being a tattered relationship if the parent discovers that the vaccination required only one injection. Then trust will be bruised, possibly beyond repair.

In our work with thousands of physicians who were in attendance at workshops on disclosure of adverse outcomes, there was the rare dispute that disclosure of an error was not indicated. Opinions were strongly expressed that the patient must be told about the adverse event; however, when asked to role play how to have the disclosure conversation with patients, the physicians fell silent. Physicians recognized that it was difficult to break the news of a medical error to a hypothetical patient in a "safe" classroom setting and acknowledged the profound strain on them to have this conversation in reality.

According to Upadhyay and associates,[10] 90% of physician participants indicated that they always or frequently disclosed information to their patients after an adverse medical event. When an adverse event happens, it is regrettable for both patient and physician. The patient will be filled with myriad powerful emotions, and the physician will be overwhelmed with distress, disbelief, and guilt. The conversation that will follow is of vital importance and must be handled with skill.

# The Impact of the Event

When a medical error or adverse situation has occurred, the physician will feel devastated. He or she will be flooded with concerns about his or her competence as a physician. Fears of the ramifications of the mishap or error will begin to overwhelm the physician. Can I regain my patient's trust? Will my patient forgive me? Can I forgive myself? Will I be able to continue to practice? What if my colleagues learn of this? Will my reputation be ruined? Will I be sued?

Such fears must not deter the physician from disclosing the event to the patient; however, the physician needs to manage these emotions before meeting with his or her patient/family to discuss the situation. This is an arduous but necessary chore so the physician can feel in control when with his or her patient. The patient will be frightened and needs to see that the physician is confident, displaying that a human error happened but showing that his or her competence remains intact. Also, the patient should not be further burdened by his or her physician's emotional state.

In *The Lost Art of Healing*, world-renowned cardiologist Bernard Lown discusses disclosure:[11]

> When I am proved wrong, as happens, alas, far too frequently, I parade it, announce it to colleagues, especially to my young students. I take heart the words of the poet Yevtushenko:
>
> > And all mistakes, sins that have been secreted
> > Pound themselves like epileptics,
> > Saying: 'That which is not expressed will be forgotten,
> > And what is forgotten will happen again.'
>
> Acknowledged mistakes provide potent learning experiences. Admitting them helps ensure that they will not be repeated. The humbling avowal of error prevents doctors from confusing their mission with a divine one. We possess no omniscient powers, only intuition, experience, and a patina of knowledge. These are most effective when one is constantly probing to advance the interest of an ailing human being.

# What Do Patients Want to Know?

Learning of a medical error from the patient's perspective creates a multitude of emotions, including sadness, anxiety, depression, frustration, and anger. Research has shown that the way the disclosure of the error is handled can either help or hinder the patient's response to the injury.[12] Patients reported that a physician's disclosure of the error and an honest and compassionate apology would leave them less distressed.[12]

The foundation of the physician–patient relationship is based on trust, faith, and honesty. Concealment of an error leads to anger, rage, and often malpractice litigation. Patients want physicians to be open about the error and to offer as much information as possible rather than to be placed in the position of asking multiple questions.[12] Patients want reassurance that they will not be held financially responsible for the error. A consistent finding in the research of Gallagher and associates was that patients want to know that learning has occurred from the error and that there are plans for preventing such errors in the future.

## The Significance of Timing and Setting

The physician should consider that if he or she does not talk to the patient about the error, it is quite likely that someone else—nurse, resident, hospital administrator, or even the patient in the next bed—will. By taking early ownership of the situation, the physician can ensure that the information is presented accurately and in a noninflammatory way.

A prolonged hesitation to discuss the situation may be viewed by the patient as an attempt to conceal the details of his or her clinical course. At the same time, often prompted by guilt feelings, the physician can move too rapidly to a conversation of disclosure of events only to later learn that he or she was not entirely or at all responsible for their occurrence. The conversation should not take place until the physician is clear and definite about the details of the case.

Medical environments are less than ideal for having delicate conversations. In the case of disclosure of a medical error, it is incumbent on the physician to locate an available office or other space that will provide privacy and comfort. This may even require asking for additional resources to ensure the proper setting such as moving a bedridden patient to a private visiting area or room for the discussion.

## Who Should Be Included?

When considering who should be included in this difficult and delicate conversation, remember that the powerful bond between the physician and his or her patient should not be diluted. Alone or with others, the physician must be the individual who speaks directly to the patient/family to disclose the details of the adverse event. Depending on the severity of the event, the physician may wish to invite members from the administration of the hospital.

Most hospitals today have a system in place and a team available for such incidents. The team is made of many disciplines and serves multiple purposes to help the physician with this essential conversation. Administrators of the hospital are often present to unburden the patient of financial responsibility for the mishap as well as to lend support to the physician. In some circumstances, there is concern that anger will erupt from patients or families, and the physician should not be alone in such an event. As the chapter proceeds, "who will be included" will become more meaningful as it relates to a specific clinical case.

## The Disclosure Conversation

No physician wants to face a patient's family to report a catastrophic outcome, but the situation is particularly grueling when it occurs as a result of a preventable error. Consider the following case and the conversation that followed with the family.

## A Case of Wrongful Death

A 61-year-old female with a history of hypertension and on a diuretic and calcium channel blocker was scheduled for a screening colonoscopy at her local hospital. Accompanied by her husband, the patient arrived at 8 a.m. for preprocedure blood work with a colonoscopy scheduled for 12 p.m. The physician, behind in his schedule, began the procedure at 1:30 p.m.

Conscious sedation protocol was initiated; the rhythm strip initially appeared normal, with a heart rate of 65 and blood pressure of 100/70. Shortly into the procedure, the monitor suddenly went off, and the patient was in ventricular fibrillation with no detectable blood pressure. The patient became pulseless, and resuscitative measures were immediately attempted; however, the patient was unable to be revived.

It was then discovered that the patient's blood work was abnormal. The patient was hypokalemic. The physician failed to check the findings before proceeding with the procedure. If the blood work had been reviewed before the procedure, the procedure would have been postponed until the patient's potassium returned to the normal range.

The physician quickly recognized that because of the patient's diuretic along with the colonoscopy prep, blood work prior to the procedure was of particular significance, as she was at risk for an electrolyte imbalance. His demanding schedule, in combination with not wanting to keep his patient—already prepped and NPO—waiting any longer, side tracked him. He was filled with remorse for his error and was also terrified. The patient's husband remained in the waiting area, and the physician had to go speak with him.

The husband looked concerned as the physician solemnly approached him in the waiting room. The physician took the husband to a small, unoccupied office for privacy. The following words were offered:

> I know you have been waiting for a long time. The procedure was long and more difficult than we expected. Your wife began to experience cardiac symptoms that were immediately picked up by the cardiac monitor and the colonoscopy quickly became secondary; we turned our focus to your wife's heart. I am deeply sorry to tell you that your wife experienced the most serious cardiac arrhythmia, called ventricular fibrillation, causing her heart to stop. We did everything we possibly could but we could not revive her. I am so very sorry.

The husband began to weep and asked to see his wife.

This is not a conversation of disclosure. This is a conversation of breaking bad news. After some time had passed, the patient's husband tried to contact the physician. The husband was perplexed as to how he could walk into a hospital with his wife at his side and walk out alone, forever. He wanted to speak with the doctor and learn more about what happened. The physician never returned the husband's calls. This made the husband skeptical. He began to wonder whether he was informed about all of the facts.

Without answers and angered by the absence of a call back from his late wife's physician, he sought the counsel of an attorney. The medical record told the story that his wife's death was not only likely quite preventable but that the physician omitted relevant details of the case to the husband in order to perhaps conceal an error. Learning of this, the husband felt betrayed and enraged, and a lawsuit eventuated.

Contrast this conversation with a *disclosure* discussion using the same clinical scenario:

> I know you have been waiting for a long time. The procedure was long and more difficult than we expected. Your wife began to experience cardiac symptoms that were immediately picked up by the cardiac monitor and the colonoscopy quickly became secondary; we turned our focus to your wife's heart. I am deeply sorry to tell you that your wife experienced the most serious cardiac

arrhythmia, called ventricular fibrillation, causing her heart to stop. We did everything we possibly could but we could not revive her. I am so very sorry.

I have something particularly painful to tell you. You must know the details of what occurred. The blood work your wife had drawn this morning was never checked prior to the procedure. The blood work had one important abnormal finding that I believe could have contributed to your wife's heart problem. I would not have gone forward with the colonoscopy today if I had seen the blood work. I can't begin to tell you how very sorry I am.

Tearfully, the husband asked if he could see his wife.

This is a conversation of full disclosure of a medical error. The physician knew he would have postponed the procedure if he had reviewed the blood work and had seen the potassium level. How would this change the events going forward? The physician would have taken the ethically correct action. The physician has to learn to live with this mistake the remainder of his life. The patient's family may or may not be sympathetic to him. There may be recognition that doctors' human frailties can result in catastrophic results. Regardless of the response and subsequent outcome from the family, the physician was obligated to disclose the clinical facts and did so.

If the patient's family decided to bring a lawsuit against the physician, settlement would be an easier course. The plaintiff's attorney would not have such leverage as in a case of concealment of a medical mistake. There would be an absence of betrayal. Perhaps, most important of all, the physician would have his self-respect. Although the early disclosure will not prevent a malpractice claim or disciplinary action against the physician, it will remove a highly inflammatory element from the situation.

## Failure to Diagnose an Epidural Lesion

A 23-year-old female arrives in the emergency department complaining of cardiac distress and with a rapid heart rate. The patient's heart rate had gone as high as 140, and although panic attack was suspected, the patient was admitted to a telemetry unit to rule out arrhythmia.

The patient's cardiac symptoms spontaneously resolved; however, she began to complain of intense neck pain. By the following morning, she described the neck pain as "agonizing." Her physician sent her for an MRI of the neck, which was read as normal. The physician discharged the patient with a plan that a family member would take her home after 5 p.m. Later that afternoon, a nurse enters the room as the patient is complaining of difficulty breathing and suddenly goes into respiratory arrest. The patient was successfully intubated and brought to ICU. The patient awakened, was cognitively intact but with an inability to move any extremity and could not be weaned from the ventilator.

A repeat MRI of the neck revealed an epidural lesion. In comparison to the original films, the abscess was present but not appreciated.

---

The patient was informed by the ICU attending physician and the radiologist that a medical error occurred. The attending physician in the ICU had established a good relationship with the patient and as a result wanted to be the one to inform her of the error. Before she could learn it from any other source, he wanted to be sure that she heard the devastating news from a trusted person. The radiologist agreed, because it was his error, to be present for the disclosure as well.

When two doctors meet with a patient, it must be agreed on which person will take the lead in the conversation. Because the ICU physician had far more experience than the radiologist in such distressing and delicate matters, they agreed that he would be the one to inform the patient. The radiologist offered a sincere apology. He also explained that he believed he read her MRI thoroughly and made a mistake for which he had no explanation.

A hospital administrator, a social worker, and a risk manager joined in the meeting but were not initially present. This was intentional, as the ICU physician felt that too many people, particularly a sea of unfamiliar faces, would only serve to frighten the patient. At the same time, real answers would be required to questions surrounding continued care and billing.

According to ethicist John Banja, "In instances where the hospital comes forward and admits blame—especially where the harmed party might not have even known error occurred—the harmed party is much less likely to go to court and ask for the sun, moon and stars in damages. Indeed, out-of-court settlements, whose damage awards are more amicably and reasonably reached, are the norm. On the other hand, in instances where harm causing error was intentionally concealed from the harmed party but who found out anyway, he or she will very likely request punitive damages in addition to the usual request for compensation for pain and suffering."[13]

Later, in the course of the patient's care, she wanted to make sure this mistake would not occur to another patient. This is a common phenomenon among those involved in medical errors. The injured person wants to have a role in protecting future patients from falling victim to the same error.

The decision of who should be present at a meeting is made by the team. The patient and family, as members of the healthcare team, should have a voice in who they would like at the meeting. Sometimes members representing a religious affiliation may be requested. Learning of a medical error that has significantly altered the life of a person or loved one can produce powerful emotions, including anger, rage, and explosiveness.

Social workers may be helpful to the patient and family to manage and work through their emotions. Depending on the nature of certain circumstances, family members may give out signals that controlling their anger may be particularly difficult with the potential for harm to come to members of the healthcare team. Security should be on notice and available if needed.

# A Case of a Lap Burn

A woman was scheduled for an elective diagnostic laparoscopy for dysfunctional uterine bleeding. After accessing the abdomen with the trocar without complication, the surgeon inserted the laparoscope but found that she needed to reposition the trocar. She removed the laparoscope and placed it on the tray in front of her. After adjusting the trocar, she picked up the laparoscope and noticed that the drapes were melted where the distal tip of the scope had been placed. The drapes had been covering the patient, and on examination revealed a second-degree burn of the thigh. The burn healed without any scarring.[14]

This case was submitted anonymously to the Agency for Healthcare Research and Quality[14] for commentary on reduction of fires and burns in the surgical setting. There is no information provided about the physician's disclosure conversation with the patient.

The disclosure ought to be self-evident in this case, as the patient will find a burn on her lower extremity; however, explanations have been used to avoid responsibility for the injury. For example, words have been used such as "in order to manage your procedure safely it became unavoidable" or "patients at times have incurred a slight burn from the instrumentation" or "we will watch that burn but know that it will heal rapidly, nothing to be concerned about," which serves to evade responsibility for the error and implies that the injury was expected. The patient is entitled to a forthright explanation of the facts surrounding the error.

# In Closing

All errors, minor and major, are serious to the patient. All errors require genuinely apologetic explanations and information about plans that are underway to protect future patients from having to endure the same mistakes. The practice of medicine is an art and a science. It is a profession comprised of the brightest, best trained, and educated individuals; however, in the end, at best, physicians are still only human. Errors will happen and must be discussed within the profession and with the patient. Physicians devote their lives to helping countless patients whose illnesses they successfully treat and whose lives they save. The occurrence of errors is but a miniscule part of what occurs in their work.

Hergott addresses the difficulties physicians experience with having an adverse outcome over the course of a medical career:[15]

> We remember forever the suture that tore through, the obstetric delivery that went bad, or advancing the angiographic catheter 1 millimeter too far. But we quickly forget the decision to order a lung scan that clarifies the diagnosis and saves a life in a subtle case of pulmonary embolism. Or proceeding with a biopsy on a doubtful skin lesion that turns out to be melanoma. Or the decision most often successfully made, not to test at all but to depend on our clinical assessment, itself based on expertise we also take for granted but which is in fact the product of intensive, prolonged, and ongoing study and practice. Perhaps it is because we expect to succeed almost every time that we barely notice when we do. It is the preponderance of our successes over any failures, after all, that allows us to continue in the difficult life of medical practice.

## REFERENCES

1. *Medical Ethics and Etiquette*. The Code of Ethics adopted by the American Medical Association, with commentaries by Flint A. New York, NY: Appelton & Co; 1893: Ch. I, Art. I, § 1, D. Available at: http://books.google.com/books?id=mvyGtbrwpZoC&printsec=frontcover&dq=Medical+Ethics+and+Etiquette#PPP7,M1, accessed December 12, 2007.
2. Leape LL. Error in medicine. *JAMA*. 1994;272(23):1851–1857.
3. Marx D. *Patient Safety and the "Just Culture": A Primer for Health Care Executives*. New York, NY: Trustees of Columbia University, 2001. Available at: http://www.mers-tm.net/support/marx_primer.pdf, accessed December 12, 2007.
4. Berwick DM. Institute for healthcare improvement: people. Available at: http://ihi.org/ihi/aboutus/people.aspx, accessed December 12, 2007.

5. Bosk CL. *Forgive and Remember: Managing Medical Failure.* 2nd ed. Chicago, IL: University of Chicago Press; 2003:60–61.
6. Eg, New York Public Health Law § 2805-d.
7. New York Code of Rules and Regulations §405.7(b)(8). American Medical Association, Code of Ethics, E-8.12. Available at: http://www.ama-assn.org, accessed September 4, 2007.
8. Cal. Health and Safety Code § 1279.1(c).
9. *Simcuski v. Saeli,* 44 N.Y.2d 442, 377 N.E.2d 713, 406 N.Y.S.2d 259 (N.Y. May 04, 1978).
10. Upadhyay A, York S, Macaulay W, McGrory B, Robbennolt J, Bal BS. Medical malpractice in hip and knee arthroplasty. *J Arthroplasty.* 2007;22(6):2–7.
11. Lown B. *The Lost Art of Healing.* Boston, MA: Houghton Mifflin; 1996:108.
12. Gallagher TH, Waterman AD, Ebers AG, Fraser VJ, Levinson W. Patients' and physicians' attitudes regarding the disclosure of medical errors. *JAMA.* 2003;289(8): 1001–1007.
13. Banja J. Moral courage in medicine-disclosing medical error. Center for Ethics, Emory University. 2000–2001. Posted by John Banja Feb 1, 2001. Available at: http://www.ethics.emory.edu/content/view/205/98/, accessed December 12, 2007.
14. Agency for Health Care Research and Quality. Available at: http: www.webmm. ahrq.gov/, accessed April 18, 2008.
15. Hergott LJ. Playing the moonlight sonata from memory: celebrating the wonders of our difficult life. *JAMA.* 2002;288(20):2516.

# Chapter 11

# Apology and Forgiveness

Geraldine M. Donohue

*One of the most profound human interactions is the offering and accepting of apologies.*

Aaron Lazare, MD

She was an extremely fit, slender, 24-year-old female who presented with classic symptoms of appendicitis: pain in the lower right abdomen, nausea, fever, and an elevated white blood count. After obtaining informed consent, I took her to the OR to do an exploratory laparoscopy, expecting it to result in a laparoscopic appendectomy. Because I was operating in a teaching hospital, I allowed a third-year surgical resident to make the umbilical incision—not an unusual degree of responsibility for his position. His technique was not perfect, and after inserting the laparoscope, what we saw would make the heart of any surgeon skip a beat: an abdomen filling with blood from an injured artery.[1]

The surgeon masterfully converted to an open procedure and with the rapid arrival of a vascular surgeon the bleeding was quickly stopped and the appendix ultimately removed. Shortly thereafter, a candid conversation ensued between the surgeon and the patient's family in which the surgeon fully disclosed the unanticipated events that transpired during the surgery.[2]

The patient's course was longer and more complicated than expected, and discharge from the hospital came nine days later. The patient recovered well, although in a follow-up visit with the surgeon, she had some minor concern as to the healing of the scar. He was pleased with the healing; however, he offered the patient a referral to a plastic surgeon if she so desired.[2] In the surgeon's words, he described what followed:

> The next time I heard from her, it was in the form of a malpractice suit. I was incredulous! How could she do this when I saved her life? After much discussion with my attorney and malpractice insurer, we decided to fight the case. I was delighted that we were going to "defend and deny" this claim. If I'd had any idea what was to come, I would not have been so gleeful.[3]

The trial began before an audience of the surgeon's most supportive people in his life: parents, siblings, a few close friends, and his partner. Opening arguments were described as a source of humiliation with commentary from the plaintiff's attorney as to his incompetence as a physician and his breech of duty to his patient, of which the surgeon said left his head "reeling."[4] The comment that struck most deeply, however, came directly from his patient:

> I sued because he acted like what had happened to me was no big deal. One time when I saw him in the office after this happened, he actually put his feet up on the desk while we talked. He just didn't care.[4]

The surgeon wrote this:

> That comment hit me like the heat from a blast furnace. It wasn't the injury and outcome that had led to that miserable day in court—it was her perception that I didn't care. My actions had communicated apathy, and that was what landed me in court, not the medical complication.[4]

In his groundbreaking book, *Healing Words: The Power of Apology in Medicine*, Dr. Michael Woods writes poignantly that as his attorneys were congratulating each other after two weeks of legal debate that resulted in a victory, he felt the battle had been won but that he had lost the war.[2] According to Woods:

> I think the entire experience made me begin to ponder exactly how and when the entire medical profession had lost a very basic form of human kindness: the ability to offer a heartfelt, authentic *I'm sorry*.[5]

# The Arc of Apology and Forgiveness

When things do not go as planned, communicating caring, understanding, and apologizing can dramatically affect the physician–patient relationship. In his momentous book *On Apology*, Dr. Aaron Lazare states, "Apologies have the power to heal humiliations and grudges, remove the desire for vengeance, and generate forgiveness on the part of the offended parties."[6] In the doctor–patient relationship, apology takes on even greater importance and complexity.

"Apologies have a potential for healing that is matched only by the difficulty most people have in offering them."[7] Physicians may not apologize easily. Feelings of embarrassment, guilt, and grief that surface when a patient has been harmed, even when fault is not clear, can become a barrier for doctors and prevent effective communication after a medical error.[8] Physicians have often been warned that apologizing is an admission of legal liability, "At the time when such communications might be most valued by a patient."[7]

Recent trends in encouraging apology may imply that apology can preclude the need for a patient or family to seek legal counsel. It is too early to make such assurances; however, early studies have proved promising. For example, the University of Michigan Health System, the Veterans Affairs Medical Center, and COPIC have all had great success in decreasing lawsuits, attributed to the institution of policies and/or programs based on disclosure of errors.[2] Woods takes such encouraging results further as he writes, "The primary focus of these programs is risk management, not apology for apology's sake. I believe that spontaneous, authentic apology, offered as a genuine attempt to heal the physician–patient relationship, accompanied by disclosure, would be even more effective."[9]

Woods quotes Richard Boothman, JD, known for the design and implementation of successful disclosure programs:

> My own approach evolved after watching those reactions [of patients who have been dealt with fairly and respectfully, and with open communication], and I became bolder in reassuring our staff that if they would only concentrate on better patient communication and safer patient care, the claims would take care of themselves.[10]

The following case illustrates how a family responded when there was an absence of apology from a physician with whom they had a long-standing relationship:

---

A 22-year-old graduate student, still under the care of his pediatrician, was repeatedly seen for persistent complaints of headache, fatigue, and nausea. The physician would reassure him that he was fine and experiencing the "signs of stress that come with the pressures of being a student." At their last visit together, he made a recommendation for the patient to see a therapist. The patient did not believe he required psychotherapy; however, he complied with his doctor's recommendation. The patient was unable to connect the headaches to stress or anxiety. Ultimately, the patient's parents took him to a neurologist where on MRI a pituitary tumor was discovered.

The patient received a copy of a letter the neurologist sent to his pediatrician informing him of the presence of the tumor, the patient's increasing symptoms, including visual disturbance, and indicating that neurosurgery would be likely.

The patient underwent surgical removal of the tumor with a good recovery. The family never again heard from the pediatrician; the patient's mother decided to call him. The physician said, "Stress is what I see most commonly with complaints that your son had. If I had to work up every complaint of a headache or stomachache like it was stemming from a catastrophic illness, we would have a lot of unneeded testing and worry." The mother found this an unacceptable response when her son had endured unrelenting pain and underwent unnecessary psychotherapy treatment. A lawsuit eventuated.

---

One can envision two silhouettes, patient and physician, back to back. The doctor, upon receipt of the report, had a painful discovery that a young man he had treated for years had a pituitary tumor. For the moment, it takes his breath away. He questions everything he could remember about the office visits, the young patient's symptoms, how he listened to him and tried to provide reassurance, or how he had perhaps failed to listen and now began to question his own competency. He wants to reach out to them. He instinctively picks up the phone to call, only to put the receiver back on the hook, suddenly feeling like his hands are tied. What would he say? Are they angry with him? He read and re-read his patient's medical record to the point that he could recite his writings. Did the symptoms he was given warrant the suspicion of a tumor? What has the neurologist said to the family? Has he already been implicated in missing the diagnosis? How can he face his patient now? Shame, embarrassment, fear of liability, and denial are only a few of the powerful elements that prevented that call from going through.

What is happening with the patient and the family? They are given unsettling news. It was not stress and anxiety. The patient requires surgery for a tumor. Things move rapidly: new physicians to meet, a hospitalization, an operation, worry and fear, and then all is all right; however, they keep returning to the absence of a dedicated and trusted figure, so much a part of their lives for so many years. Why didn't he call after learning of the tumor? Didn't he care? Didn't he want to be of any help? Didn't he want to say that maybe he could have done more testing before sending a patient for therapy? He saw us through so many rough illnesses in the past. We had such gratitude for him. Didn't he know we loved him? Didn't he think we would forgive him?

Denial can be at play for both physician and patient. The pediatrician may be hoping, rightly or wrongly, that another pediatrician in his shoes would not have entertained a diagnosis of a pituitary tumor. Therefore, he has nothing to apologize for. The family is in denial too. How could the doctor that has always been there for them leave them now? They are yearning for acknowledgment, for respect, and for an apology. They even consider that maybe the doctor never got the letter from the neurologist and does not know the events that have transpired. Then they find the physician is defensive and unapologetic.

Their hopes that he just did not know what happened are shattered. The patient and family are now angry. Whether the pediatrician is responsible for the error ultimately or not, the age-old idiom "adding insult to injury" is fitting. The parents entrusted their son to his care and now believe, mistakenly, that he didn't care after all. The legal system is introduced into the doctor's world. A lawsuit is one of the most disturbing, gut-wrenching, agonizing events that a physician may face. What if only the pediatrician had placed that call?

# Rooted in Rearing and Culture

The 1970 best-selling novel and motion picture introduced a phrase that dashed across America: "Love means never having to say you're sorry." In spite of the hype that followed, discussions ensued as to what the phrase, written by Erich Segal, really meant. It could imply that within the safe and trusted bond of unconditional love, some things can be overlooked. Mistakes can happen within the confines of loving relationships, and in the absence of apologies, relationships continue to survive. Individuals could have behaved better than they did; nevertheless, there is no demand for apologies. Although children are customarily raised to say "I'm sorry" for hurtful behaviors, what is witnessed within the home environment influences the ability to be apologetic as an adult. In some families, apologies need not be said in words but can be displayed through other means of communication, for example, through the use of humor.

For physicians who were raised with such family dynamics, the already difficult task of apologizing becomes compounded. The bond between the physician and patient is professional, not personal, and one in which, if an error occurs, an apology is required. The following illustrates a physician who was unable to say that he was sorry:

---

A female patient had gynecological surgery, and a metal clip was mistakenly retained. Discovered on X-ray, the patient had to undergo an additional procedure for removal of the foreign object. In the physician's office, during a follow-up visit, the doctor gave the patient one of his business cards. On the back of the card he added the words "also specializes in metal clips." The patient saw no humor in this gesture.

---

The physician likely did not know how to express his sorrow for putting his patient through anxiety, worry, and the risks associated with an additional procedure. When he recognized his mistake, he did not know how to discuss this in a meaningful, serious, and contrite manner with his patient. His attempt at humor offended his patient, and a lawsuit was soon initiated.

The influence of cultural conditioning helps to explain why some people are less able to apologize than others:

> We are discouraged from taking responsibility for our actions and apologizing for our wrongdoing because we have been raised in a culture that causes us to fear making mistakes. Those who make mistakes are seen as losers, and because of the highly competitive nature of our culture, achieving and winning are valued far more than courtesy, kindness, and a concern for the consequences of our actions. Some people even believe that apologizing is a sign of weakness, and not apologizing is a recommended strategy for staying in control.[11]

Particular characteristics have been attributed to those who have trouble apologizing. These traits include the following: being raised to not show any signs of weakness, perfectionism, the need to be right, having a tendency to judge others, and difficulty with empathy.[12] As a physician, Woods comments that this list "aligns with mine."[13] He writes, "No wonder the simple words 'I'm sorry' are among the hardest for doctors to say."[13]

> An ordinary apology of the sort delivered routinely in the course of daily life can trip up the most skilled surgeon. It can confound medical practitioners who possess some of society's most brilliant minds. In their role as healers, doctors should be master empathizers.[13]

For some physicians, apologizing comes more easily. An orthopedic surgeon gave the following account of what his life was like as a youngster and what led to his passion for medicine:[14]

> I've always wanted to be a doctor . . . since I was 8 years old. My uncle was a physician . . . an old time physician. . . . he had an

office downstairs in his house. His caring for his patients had a great influence upon me at that early age. When I was 14 or 15 I started volunteering at the hospital . . . I hung around the emergency room and got to meet the orthopedist in the emergency room. Back in the 60s there wasn't the strictness in place as there certainly is now and I benefited from it. As a volunteer, I ended up helping out in the operating room when they needed an extra pair of hands and ended up holding a lot of legs for the orthopedists . . . I just always wanted to be a doctor . . .

As a physician, he apologizes freely, "Regardless of the cause or fault of the suffering of the patient because I am sorry. . . I'm very sorry and feel for my patients when they run into unexpected complications or are unhappy with a result. . . . you have to put yourself in your patient's shoes or the shoes of their loved ones . . . try to feel what they must be going through. . . you have to in order to be a good doctor."[14]

The orthopedic surgeon poignantly described the events of an unexpected outcome with a teenage boy, over 25 years ago, as if the situation had just occurred today:[14]

---

He was 16, and he came into the emergency room from a moped accident. He was a passenger on a moped, put his foot down, and broke his femur while the moped was moving. He came into the emergency room, and I put him into skeletal traction, which was what was done back in the late 70s. So I put him into traction, and the next morning I came in to see him and he was complaining of a little shortness of breath and had signs of respiratory distress.

I asked for a chest X-ray and the medical and pediatric consults. In the course of getting the testing done, he went into acute respiratory distress and was transferred to the critical care unit. He had what we suspected . . . a fat embolus. He was put on Heparin, and unfortunately, he just didn't respond. He didn't respond to anything. I would see him in the morning and talk to the family and then in the afternoon, after I finished my rounds and surgery, I would go back to hospital and spend time sitting with the family in the waiting room or at the bedside, talking to them quietly. We were all hoping that he would get better, but his course continued to deteriorate and nothing really prevented or improved his condition; tragically, he succumbed to death a month later. We did everything that could possibly be done at that time.

For 30 days I spent a good portion of each day with the family at my patient's bedside . . . listening, answering their questions, trying

> to coordinate with the other doctors so they knew what was going on and . . . saying I was sorry. I couldn't prevent a fat embolism, but I could apologize for it happening . . . so I did, all of the time . . . because I was sorry . . . sorry for his suffering . . . sorry for the unforeseen complication . . . sorry for his family's anguish . . . and sorry a youngster died too young. I could cry now just thinking about him.

Sarah Lawrence-Lightfoot, author and educator, identified *attention* as one of six dimensions of respect. When patients are not responding to medical treatment, physicians can often be uncertain about what to do. Feeling helpless, doctors need to battle the temptation to retreat, and they need to come forward with respectful care. As this young patient's condition was deteriorating and hope was diminishing, the orthopedist offered to the patient and family his *attention*. He attended to their needs by his presence and availability. His actions illustrate the meaning of the *attending* physician.[15]

The physician's colleagues believed that in the litigious environment of the late 70s a lawsuit would ultimately be instituted against him because a 16 year old boy died in the hospital, after weeks of suffering. The orthopedist was never sued. He believes that physicians cannot properly deliver care to their patients if they are constantly worried about being sued. He stated:[14]

> If you do surgery and the outcome isn't as expected and complications happen . . . you truly feel sorry . . . whether it was in or out of your control. You are always still sorry it happened. You did your best, and unfortunately, the result wasn't what you expected and you have to admit it. If you did something wrong you absolutely need to fess up to it and say you're sorry. You can never just dismiss it as these things happen. Getting sued is a fact of life if you practice medicine in the US. It cannot and must not affect how you practice. You have to have empathy . . . and when you say you're sorry, it has to be heartfelt . . . It is healing for your patient and really for you too.

# When Things Go Wrong

Patient safety champion, Dr. Lucien Leape, spearheaded a project in 2005 that opened discussion with physicians, risk managers, hospital administrators, attorneys, and soon patients and families as well to examine the need to dissolve the resistances to apologizing when errors occur. This led to the creation of the consensus statement *When Things Go Wrong: Responding to*

*Adverse Events.*[16] Divided into three sections—(1) the patient and family experience, (2) the caregiver experience, and (3) management of the event—this document is a guide for the physician when adverse outcomes occur.

Navigating through uncharted waters, Leape had little idea as to what to expect as invitations went out for the first meeting on the discussion of the power of apology.[17] The response was overwhelming, and a second meeting was required on the same day. The meetings took place at Harvard, and excerpts from the discussions include the following.

From Leape:[17]

> We're really delighted to see so many people here. It really makes us feel this is an idea whose time has come. Long overdue we would say, but at least we're here.
>
> We coined the term "second victim." The patient who is injured is the first victim. The caregiver who causes the injury is the second victim because if the injury is serious, the feelings of shame and guilt can be quite profound. But I would say there's a third victim and that's the relationship. Because an injury is a threat to trust, and trust is the cornerstone of the physician–patient relationship. Without trust there is no relationship. That trust, I believe is a sacred trust. It's what makes medicine different from every profession. It's what makes medicine a calling, and not a career.
>
> The patient wants to know what happened, they want to hear the doctor say "I'm sorry"; and they want the doctor to tell them what's going to be done to make sure the same thing doesn't happen to anyone else.

Doctors have been cautioned in the past from admitting liability to patients in case a lawsuit was filed and those words would be used against them.[17]

A physician in the audience raised a question:

> This presentation is a real relief to me, because it feels to me that that's my natural tendency. Even though the shame and guilt is overwhelming at times, it helps me to apologize. I don't mean to sound skeptical, but can I just confirm—if you do apologize, I believe that you would reduce the number of lawsuits against you—but if a family does choose to go ahead and file a lawsuit, will your admission that you made a mistake, can that still be used against you in court?

Leape shared with the audience a conversation a plaintiff's attorney had with him in which he learned of two key elements about apology from a legal perspective. The first was that two thirds of the plaintiff attorneys' clients would go away if doctors and hospitals told them what happened and apologized.[17] Leape continued[17]:

> The second thing he said is, when you're in a malpractice trial, when you get toward the last day, it's usually pretty obvious how it's going to turn out. So—this is the trial lawyer—you get the doctor up on the stand for one last time, and you say, "Now, Dr. Smith, when this happened did you tell the patient you were sorry?" And he says, "Well, no I didn't."

As one can imagine, the physician loses sympathy in the eyes of the jury as they listen to the absence of an expression of contrition to the patient. Currently, approximately 30 states have enacted evidentiary rules that make expressions of sympathy after an accident or error inadmissible in civil court to prove liability.[18] "This body of legislation, referred to as 'I'm sorry' laws, encourages full disclosure of mistakes or errors in judgment by eliminating physicians' and hospitals' fear that their admissions will be used against them in a court of law."[18]

## The Healing Power of Apologies

In personal relationships, when one individual injures another, the question of intent comes into play. Lazare speaks of questions that are raised such as "was the action intentional" or "was the action a means of getting revenge."[19] An effective apology can heal even in severely frayed personal relationships in which matters of selfishness and malice existed.[19]

In contrast, in the professional relationship, between physician and patient, the element of intent is removed. Injuries to patients are accidental. When medical errors happen, it is widely believed that they are the result of a multitude of complex reasons. When analyzed, in the end, it may often be distilled down to "to err is human." Although unintentional, the patient and/or family have been victim to suffering and an apology must follow. The properly delivered apology can restore self-respect and dignity and return a feeling of safety and trust to the relationship.[19] What follows in the next section are elements that the physician may find helpful when faced with the need to apologize to his or her patient.

## Essential Elements of an Effective Apology

Lazare delineates four necessary components to an effective apology.[19] Within the physician–patient relationship, apologizing must be delivered properly and with sincerity in order for it to be meaningful and healing.

## Acknowledging the Offense

Physicians need to be forthright when disclosing a medical error and not minimize or dilute their involvement in the event. Lazare believes that acknowledging one's responsibility is the most essential component in the apology process.[19]

Apologizing can fail if the physician falls into such linguistic traps as saying "I'm sorry for what happened yesterday" or "I'm sorry for anything I did" or just a vague and general "I'm sorry."[19] On the surface, the physician may believe that the apology was put forward. The patient is left feeling an inadequacy in the apology without having been provided with the details surrounding the need for the apology.[19]

## Remorse

The patient must feel that the physician is remorseful about the error. Lazare writes of the importance of remorse; he defines it as, "I mean the deep, painful regret that is part of the guilt people experience when they have done something wrong. To feel remorse for an action is to accept responsibility for the harm caused by it."[20] Remorse is tied to one's conscience with a chastising that occurs that one will never repeat such a mistake.[19]

Authenticity is central to the expression of remorse. If the same error is repeated and an apology again follows, it will leave the patient questioning whether the initial apology was ever sincere.[19]

Humility is a central element in the apology process, as defined by Lazare[21]:

> Apologizing is an act of humility since it is an acknowledgment of making a mistake and expressing remorse. Such humility contributes to restoring the dignity of the offended party. Apologizing without humility, and even worse, by expressing arrogance or hubris, transforms the intended apology into an insult.

## Explanations

An explanation of what occurred is an essential part of the apology process.[19] Lazare believes that the explanation must satisfactorily address the sincerity of the apology and not evade further responsibility for the mistake. He includes a list of expressions to avoid that would only serve to dilute the delivery of an effective apology such as, "I was not myself" or "I was overtired" or "I was preoccupied" or "I was under stress."[22]

When a patient or family receives the needed information for what transpired, they can stop wondering about what happened and can begin to grieve the loss endured.[19]

## Reparations

"For some apologies, reparations can be the dominant feature of the apology, because they completely restore the loss."[23] This is perhaps one of the more challenging difficulties a physician can face if the nature of the loss cannot be repaired or restored. If there is available reparation that is not offered, then the apology has failed.[19]

In the absence of fully recovering the loss, the physician should offer every means available to lessen the extent of the injury and reduce the likelihood of further complications. This often means consulting with other physicians, perhaps from other specialties.

The patient who has incurred a medical error needs comfort, support, and questions answered. The patient should not be allowed to experience a further loss of trust in the sacred physician–patient relationship. The physician's presence should be strongly felt by the patient as he or she shoulders the burden of the injury together.

# The Shared Experience

Patients, like most people, can be forgiving if they have experienced an error. In the absence of an apology, patients will have difficulty with forgiveness. Why is the apology so important to the patient's forgiveness? Lazare writes this[24]:

> The fundamental reason for this demand is that apology meets the psychological needs of the offended party. It restores the damage that was done. It heals a wound that will not heal spontaneously.

Lazare notes that the literature is far vaster on forgiveness than on apology.[19] He suggests that people find the forgiveness process easier than the apology process.[19] "Although the analysis of any given apology involves many variables, the act of apologizing is often a simple task, an intuitive and spontaneous act which is usually gratifying to both parties."[25]

> An effective apology is one of the most profound healing processes between individuals, groups, or nations. It may restore damaged relationships or even strengthen previously unsatisfactory relationships. For the offender, offering an apology may diminish guilt, shame, and the fear of retaliation. For the offended party, receiving an apology may remove a grudge with its corrosive anger, thereby facilitating forgiveness and reconciliation. With such healing qualities, apologies should be considered among the most profound behaviors of humankind.[26]

# REFERENCES

1. Woods MS. *Healing words. The power of apology in medicine.* 2nd ed. Oakbrook Terrace, Ill: Joint Commission Resources; 2007:13.
2. Woods MS. *Healing words. The power of apology in medicine.* 2nd ed. Oakbrook Terrace, Ill: Joint Commission Resources; 2007.
3. Woods MS. *Healing words. The power of apology in medicine.* 2nd ed. Oakbrook Terrace, Ill: Joint Commission Resources; 2007:14.
4. Woods MS. *Healing words. The power of apology in medicine.* 2nd ed. Oakbrook Terrace, Ill: Joint Commission Resources; 2007:15.
5. Woods MS. *Healing words. The power of apology in medicine.* 2nd ed. Oakbrook Terrace, Ill: Joint Commission Resources; 2007:16.
6. Lazare A. *On Apology.* New York, NY: Oxford University Press; 2004:1.
7. Frenkel DN, Liebman CB. Words that heal [editorial]. *Ann of Intern Med.* 2004;140:482.
8. Frenkel DN, Liebman CB. Words that heal [editorial]. *Ann of Intern Med.* 2004;140:482–483.
9. Woods MS. *Healing words. The power of apology in medicine.* 2nd ed. Oakbrook Terrace, Ill: Joint Commission Resources; 2007:86.
10. Woods MS. *Healing words. The power of apology in medicine.* 2nd ed. Oakbrook Terrace, Ill: Joint Commission Resources; 2007:84.
11. Engel B. *The Power of Apology: Healing Steps to Transform All Your Relationships.* New York, NY: John Wiley & Sons, Inc.; 2001:39.
12. Engel B. *The Power of Apology: Healing Steps to Transform All Your Relationships.* New York, NY: John Wiley & Sons, Inc.; 2001:47.
13. Woods MS. *Healing words. The power of apology in medicine.* 2nd ed. Oakbrook Terrace, Ill: Joint Commission Resources; 2007:41.
14. Anonymous. Interview with the author (GMD). September 26, 2007.
15. Lawrence-Lightfoot S. *Respect: An Exploration.* Cambridge, MA: Perseus Books; 2000.
16. Massachusetts Coalition for the Prevention of Medical Errors. *When Things Go Wrong Responding to Adverse Events: A Consensus Statement of the Harvard Hospitals.* Burlington, MA: Massachusetts Coalition for the Prevention of Medical Errors; 2006.
17. The power of apology. June 2005. Available at: http://www.rmf.harvard.edu/patientsafety/resource/archive/0506/feature1.asp, accessed February 4, 2006.
18. Bender FF. "I'm sorry" laws and medical liability. *Virtual Mentor.* 2007;9(4):300–304. Available at: http://virtualmentor.ama-assn.org/2007/04/hlaw1-0704.html, accessed December 12, 2007.
19. Lazare A. *On Apology.* New York, NY: Oxford University Press; 2004.
20. Lazare A. *On Apology.* New York, NY: Oxford University Press; 2004:107–108.
21. Lazare A. *On Apology.* New York, NY: Oxford University Press; 2004:116.
22. Lazare A. *On Apology.* New York, NY: Oxford University Press; 2004:125.
23. Lazare A. *On Apology.* New York, NY: Oxford University Press; 2004:127.
24. Lazare A. *On Apology.* New York, NY: Oxford University Press; 2004:242.
25. Lazare A. *On Apology.* New York, NY: Oxford University Press; 2004:248.
26. Lazare A. Apology in medical practice: an emerging clinical skill. *JAMA.* 2006; 296(11):1401.

# Chapter 12

# Lessons Learned:
# A Physician's Perspective

Seth Goldberg and Christine J. Quinn

*We are what we repeatedly do. Excellence then is not an act but a habit.*

Aristotle

---

A 52-year-old chronically obese, hypertensive, hypercholesterolemic patient was treated by his primary care physician (PCP) for eight years with moderate results. During the first two years of his care with the primary care physician, he was sent for cardiology referrals because of an abnormal EKG (R/O old myocardial infarction [MI]). Two thallium stress tests were normal, and cardiology declined to follow the patient. The patient had routine annual EKGs over the next four years, which showed no change.

Two years after his last EKG, the patient was seen in the primary care doctor's office for complaints of "chest congestion, cough, sore throat, discomfort in chest and elevated temperature." The lungs were clear to auscultation. The patient was diagnosed with bronchitis. The next day the patient died at home. An autopsy was performed that reported a large, acute MI 24 to 72 hours old.

---

Many factors can influence the decision whether a medical malpractice case should be defended or settled. A key factor in this decision is an assessment of whether the standard of care was met. To make this determination, a retrospective expert review of the case is required. Usually, the expert who reviews the case is a board-certified physician who practices in the same specialty as the physician who has been sued. Published guidelines and standards of care promulgated by specialty societies and governmental agencies are relied on. In addition, the usual custom and practice in a community are considered. There are times when judgment issues are gray and different physicians could approach a clinical situation in different ways that would still be defensible.

If we are able to analyze and dissect the causes of malpractice cases and publicize them to the community of practitioners, then these cases can provide major corrective signals for physicians in their practices. In this chapter we hope to share, through illustrative examples, some lessons that we have learned in reviewing thousands of malpractice cases. Our goal is to provide insights that may help to prevent such occurrences in your own practice.

# Adequate Documentation Is Part of the Standard of Care

The failure to diagnose a MI case that opened this chapter concerns a patient with multiple cardiac risk factors who appeared at his PCP's office for an intercurrent visit with symptoms suggestive of bronchitis. Although the physician's note was very brief, the elevated temperature, chest congestion, cough, and sore throat appear, even in retrospect, to be very suggestive of bronchitis. The patient apparently also was suffering from an acute MI at this time. Looking back, the physician stated that, despite the chest complaints, no EKG was performed at the last visit because the acute symptoms were so suggestive of bronchitis.

The history of the present illness documented for this visit was, as might be expected, extremely brief. The physician only reiterated the chief complaint, which included the phrase "chest discomfort," as initially recorded by his staff. In particular, there was no discussion or amplification of the phrase "chest discomfort" documented by the physician.

A basic standard of care that is often overlooked in a busy clinical practice is the documentation of a proper history. Abbreviating the entire history into a few words and combining it with a presumptive diagnosis under the heading "impression" does not meet this standard. Neither does omitting answers to the few most relevant questions relating to the chief complaint to support the eventual diagnosis. For example, consider questions such as these: Was the sputum mucopurulent? What sort of chest "discomfort" was the patient experiencing? In retrospect, one might wonder whether the answers the patient provided were consistent with the diagnosis of bronchitis. These questions are easy to ask and document; however, in this case, omission of the patient's responses became painful and expensive for both the patient and the physician.

Because the patient had not had a routine physical in the two years preceding this visit, the most recent EKG was two years old. During an intercurrent sick visit for bronchitis, it is not necessarily a deviation from community standards to defer an EKG until the next annual physical, even if an EKG is overdue; however, the failure to investigate and document the history of "chest discomfort" in the history of the present illness, coupled with the failure to perform an EKG in the face of a potentially serious complaint, made a damaging case against this physician. The failure to investigate these complaints in a patient with multiple cardiac risk factors also contributed to an impression that this physician in a busy practice was willing to waive basic standards of obtaining and documenting a history to save time.

A frequently overlooked benefit of writing a proper note is that the physician is forced to reflect and focus on the patient's complaints and history of the present illness. Especially in a hectic clinical environment, taking a few moments to write a clear note can provide an opportunity to clarify the physician's thinking, protecting both the patient and the physician.

# You Are Responsible for Care Provided Under Your Supervision

A 54-year-old woman slipped on the ice and sustained a Colles fracture of the right wrist. She was splinted in the emergency department and referred to an orthopedist's office. Two days later she was seen by a physician assistant (PA) when the supervising orthopedist was in the operating room. The patient had an X-ray and was casted. The films were only seen by the PA, who felt that the position of the fracture was adequate and did not require reduction. The patient returned to the orthopedist's office two weeks later and was again seen only by the PA, who again failed to recognize the poor position of the fracture on the X-ray. The patient was seen by the supervising orthopedist six weeks after the injury. At that time, he recognized that the fracture was malpositioned, which then required open reduction and internal fixation.

The use of allied health professionals in the delivery of health care is expanding and with good reason. They are highly skilled professionals; however, allied health professionals do not have the same training and experience as physicians. In this case, the physician assistant made an error and deviated from accepted standards of orthopedic care by misinterpreting this patient's injury as a minimally displaced Colles fracture. The PA did not recognize that this fracture was malpositioned and warranted corrective intervention.

Beginning with Dr. Lucian Leape's 1994 article, errors in medicine have been comprehensively discussed and categorized.[1] We can use this classification of the types of errors that occur in medicine to help guide our analysis of this case. The first error was made by the PA in this case and is an example of what Dr. Leape described as a knowledge-based error.[1] The PA likely had a knowledge or experience gap that resulted in his not recognizing that the fracture was poorly positioned. Dr. Leape noted that these errors are seldom recognized by the professional involved.[1]

Malpractice cases involving allied health professionals and physicians often concern a failure of the allied health professional to recognize that a situation requires consultation with their supervising or collaborating physician. It can, of course, be very dangerous for the patient and the physician, who is ultimately responsible for the patient's care when a nurse practitioner, physician assistant, or nurse is not aware that he or she is in a situation that exceeds his or her knowledge or skill.

In discussing human errors, Dr. James Reason makes a very strong case that the longstanding "person approach," which focuses on blaming individuals for errors (although emotionally satisfying) does not acknowledge that the same set of circumstances can repeatedly cause similar errors, regardless of the people involved.[2] This case illustrates that point. The supervising orthopedist contributed to the error that injured this patient by not having instituted a system to promptly review the X-rays in all fracture cases treated by the PA. This is what Dr. Leape called a latent error, that is, the absence of a system designed to identify and correct immediate errors (also called active errors) before catastrophic consequences occur.[1] It was the coincidence of these two types of errors that caused injury to the patient.

In this case, a plaintiff's attorney will ask about the systems that the supervising orthopedist had put into place to ensure that patients seen in his practice received quality care and to reduce the risk of errors that cause injuries to patients. From a risk-reduction standpoint, physicians and practices that employ physician assistants and nurse practitioners must develop formal protocols and practices of supervision and consultation that minimize risk to the patient.

This highlights an inflammatory element of this case. The patient was referred by the emergency department to an orthopedist and came to the orthopedist's office for evaluation as instructed. The patient was seen by the physician assistant employed by the orthopedic surgeon. The patient had a right to expect that the care she received would meet the standard of care that an orthopedist would provide. The orthopedist had an obligation to ensure the timely review of the care provided by the physician assistant. This case also brings up the notion that the practice of medicine, like so many human endeavors, is often redundantly constructed so that a single error is often recoverable. This has been called a "Swiss cheese" model by Dr. James Reason because coincidence or alignment of multiple deviations (holes) must occur for truly catastrophic results to evolve.[2] A consequence of this model is that although cutting a single corner or a single minor error does not usually lead to disaster, unfortunately, over a period of time, a pattern of practice can develop in which one shortcut is layered on top of another until the entire structure becomes an accident waiting to happen. In the vast majority of paid malpractice claims that we have seen, we can identify multiple components that chronically increased the risk of error. A major advantage of stressing failures of the system rather than focusing on blaming individuals for errors is that natural corrective strategies come to mind. This approach identifies the problematic patterns and risky practices that should be looked for and against which systems of management and supervision of staff need to be devised. Adopting the philosophy of professionals in the field of error prevention also means choosing the view that error-reduction systems are never complete and can always benefit from reassessment.

# Even Considered Departures from Standards of Care Are Difficult to Defend

An older ophthalmologist in limited practice saw a 45-year-old bilateral glaucoma patient for several years. He had been treating him with conservative medical and laser treatment with mixed results. When first seen, the patient already had almost complete loss of visual field in one eye, with an essentially normal visual field in the other eye. During this treatment period, the physician felt that referral to a glaucoma subspecialist was not indicated because of the low probability of success of surgery and the possibility of loss of vision in the remaining good eye. He felt that most subspecialists might overindicate the patient for surgery. The experts who reviewed the case for the defense opined that the surgical therapy (trabeculectomy) was in fact indicated and had been the standard of care for most or all of the time of the treatment.

This case would be very difficult or impossible to defend according to several ophthalmologists who retrospectively reviewed it for the defense because the ophthalmologist caring for this patient held medical opinions that were obsolete. These reviewing ophthalmologists strongly disagreed with the treating doctor's opinion that surgical intervention was too risky for this patient. In attempting to defend this case, an obvious weakness was that the patient, now plaintiff, could, without much difficulty, obtain several supporting opinions from qualified experts to testify that the ophthalmologist had not met the standard of care for this patient.

Even at the time, the ophthalmologist was aware that his treatment was likely controversial; however, his perspective was that he was acting in the patient's best interest by sparing him from hearing about alternative but risky surgical options. In modern medicine, there are often circumstances in which a variety of treatment options are available to treat a condition. For example, the treatment of prostate or breast cancer can include a number of choices that include various options and combinations of surgery, radiation, and chemotherapy. Other situations include the type of stents chosen for cardiac procedures, the question of surgical indications in many subspecialties, and the off-label use of medications. Unless there is a clear deviation, such as occurred in this case, these types of situations rarely lead to malpractice suits. The question these situations raise is how much is the physician obligated to disclose to the patient regarding alternative therapies?

The basic principle of disclosure is that the patient deserves a fair chance to hear and understand both sides of the issue. In this case, the physician would have to disclose to the patient that he is offering a controversial and nonstandard treatment option by not referring the patient to a glaucoma specialist. An effective risk-reduction strategy in a circumstance such as this would be to send the patient for a second opinion. This would give the patient the opportunity to hear about other available options from the providers of these therapies.

In this case, the patient might have been so fearful of having surgery that he may have even declined the second opinion. As long as it is an informed decision, a patient has a right to choose or refuse treatment. Whenever a patient declines a second opinion or refuses treatment, it is a golden opportunity for patient education. Often patients refuse treatment because of a flawed understanding of the value and the risks of the recommended treatment.

When a patient declines or is hesitant about agreeing to a treatment, the physician has an opportunity to reassess the patient's understanding of his or her illness and treatment options. This type of dialogue can be an opportunity for the physician to build on the patient's knowledge of his or her illness and correct any misunderstandings that the patient may have about his or her condition and the options available to treat it. The end result of this process may still be that the patient refuses your advice; however, at least you can be comfortable that the refusal is based on adequate knowledge. From a risk management point of view, contemporaneous, comprehensive documentation of this important discussion is imperative. The note summarizing this discussion with the patient should include a summary of your recommendation and the reason why the patient declined your advice. In this case, these standards were not followed, and despite the best of motives, the patient was injured, and the doctor was unable to defend the case.

# Ensure That Your Fail-Safe Systems Work

A 52-year-old woman with a history of fibrocystic disease and multiple bilateral cysts appeared at a radiologist's office as scheduled for a follow-up mammogram. The patient had a sister with breast cancer. The radiologist's intake form included a notation, apparently made by a member of the staff, that the patient had apparently discovered "a palpable lump" between the time that the mammogram was scheduled and the patient's appointment.

The radiologist was apparently not aware of this new information despite the fact that it was recorded on the intake form. The mammogram report lists the indication as "screening" and does not mention the lump or the patient's history. Therefore, when the mammogram showed no apparent mass or evidence of malignancy, the patient was merely advised to return for follow-up studies in one year. At that time, the patient was diagnosed with microinvasive carcinoma.

In this case, a change occurred in the patient's status between the time when she scheduled the screening mammography and the time she appeared for the study. Although the radiologist's intake form included a note in what appeared to be the staff's handwriting of "palpable lump," it is possible that the practice's computer records documenting the indication/type of mammography were not then updated to reflect this new information.

The American College of Radiology standard for a patient who has a palpable lump is that the patient should have a *diagnostic* mammogram (which is different from the *screening* mammogram that this patient had). In contrast to a screening mammogram, a diagnostic mammogram requires that the study "is performed under the direct supervision" of a physician, and that additional views and a possible physical exam to establish the location of the purported lesion be performed.[3,4] This standard was not met in this case.

Another weakness in this case was that multiple questions of the radiology intake form were left blank. This highlights a common problem that arises when a practice adopts a form to document information. Forms can be very useful risk management tools if they are used correctly. Well-designed forms can be an efficient way to facilitate and standardize the collection and documentation of important information that is necessary for the care of the patient; however, as with any tool, if forms are not used properly, problems can result. Two of the most common pitfalls of using forms to collect information are not completing the form, and failing to review the information recorded on the form. Unfortunately, both of these pitfalls were encountered in this case, and they contributed to errors in this case.

A preprinted form gives the impression that the information requested on the form is important to the patient's evaluation and care. The conclusion most reviewers (and jurors) will draw is that if the form asks for information it must be significant. Jury members may view it as negligence if the information requested on the form is not obtained. They will also likely consider it an error if the information provided is not reviewed and considered in the patient's care. The first risk-reduction point, therefore, is that forms should be completed in their entirety. Information that is not applicable or negative should be noted on the form. Every blank space should be completed. The second point is that information provided on the form should be reviewed by the clinician. This review must be documented. Many clinicians accomplish this by initialing or signing and dating the form as they review it. Alternatively, a specific comment about the information can be included in the report of the study or the note of the encounter.

In this case, there was also a communication failure within the team providing this patient's care. Important clinical information (the fact that the patient had a palpable lump) was known to certain members of the team, but this information was not effectively transmitted to the physician reading the study.

The healthcare industry is learning about improving safety from other high-risk industries, such as aviation. In reviewing some of the root causes of airline disasters, investigators learned that critical information was often not being shared with senior members of the crew because of hierarchical communication barriers. For example, junior members of the crew were afraid to speak to a senior member of the crew because no clear lines of communication were set up to facilitate this type of communication. In fact, unsolicited communication with the captain was often discouraged.[5]

To reduce this source of error, the aviation industry has placed a great deal of emphasis on facilitating communication of information between team members. Aviation crews are now required to undergo very rigorous training called Crew Resource Management (CRM) to enhance and strengthen communication skills among team members. All members of airline crews are trained to recognize that members of the crew often have critical information that the captain should be aware of. Surgical teams and emergency department teams in several hospitals have adopted these models with success.[6–8]

In this case, it appears that there were several team members (the receptionist, nurse, and technician) who did not review the intake form with the patient, did not appreciate the significance of the new complaint of a palpable lump, or were inhibited from communicating this finding effectively to the radiologist. Identification and correction of this apparent oversight by any member of the staff might have led them to alert the physician to this change in the patient's status and may have modified the physician's approach to reading this study.

This failure appears to have been compounded when the technician and the radiologist each failed to review the handwritten intake form when performing the studies and reading the films. A good fail-safe measure would have been for this form to be attached routinely and prominently to the reading jacket or folder and initialed by each professional after their reviews. This could serve as documentation of the physician's review of the information provided by the patient on a form to confirm that the physician has indeed reviewed the information on the form.

Practical experience in medicine teaches us that a few percent of any given method of defense against error will fail. Real safety, therefore, requires multiple independent, fail-safe mechanisms.

# There Is No Substitute for a Complete History

## Search Further if an Unexpected Pattern Occurs

A pediatrician was seeing an infant since birth for routine well-child check-ups. When the infant was six months old, in an apparently unrelated matter, the pediatrician was notified by the Department of Health that three of his patients, who, unknown to him at the time turned out to live in the same household as the infant, had recent positive conversion of tuberculin skin tests (TST). Although the pediatrician prophylactically treated the affected family members with INH, he failed to inquire about other members of their household, which included the infant.

Over the next eight months, the infant was seen by the same pediatrician and was diagnosed on several visits with recurrent bronchitis, cough, and colds, culminating in visits to the local hospital emergency department three times over a two-week period for vomiting and fever. After the infant suffered seizures, a CT showed a high-density area in the right parietal lobe. A pediatric neurologist noted that the child was delayed in milestones, that the CSF was abnormal, and that there was TB in the family. The child is currently profoundly retarded, requires a gastric feeding tube, and lives in a long-term care facility.

---

In this case of failure to diagnose TB meningitis, there were two distinct errors involving two groups of patients. The experts who reviewed the case for the defense felt that the pediatrician caring for this infant had at least two opportunities to take a proper history, which could have prevented the injury. The first opportunity was to take a more detailed history from the parent/guardian of three other members of the household who were being treated prophylactically for TB with INH. The second opportunity was to obtain a more complete family and social history of the infant, either initially or when he became recurrently ill.

According to the pediatricians who retrospectively reviewed this case, the standard of care requires that additions to the family and social history should be obtained for patients who recently converted their TST status. This would include asking who the other members of the patient's household are. Asking this simple question could have prevented this tragedy. In this case, the pediatrician may have assumed that the local Department of Health had done contact tracing and tuberculin skin testing of all household contacts; however, the availability of contact tracing depends on the geographic location of the patients. It would have behooved the pediatrician to inquire whether the adult contagious member of the household had been identified and treated. Furthermore, this discussion should have been documented in the chart.

It is unclear why the pediatrician failed to ask the appropriate questions. Perhaps the pediatrician was unaware of this standard of care. Many physician errors arise in situations in which the physician is in an unfamiliar territory; a way to avoid these types of errors is to consult with a colleague or a reference, in this case the American Academy of Pediatrics Red Book, an infectious disease colleague, or the Department of Health for information about case tracing.

The second aspect of this case is the evaluation of an infant who is becoming chronically ill over a period of months with what may be an infectious disease. Even if the connection to the other family members who had been exposed to TB had not been made previously, one would have anticipated that the pediatrician caring for the patient would have asked the mother questions about the health of other members of the household and documented her responses. If, as part of a comprehensive review and reexamination of a "failing to improve" patient he had asked the infant's mother about the family and social history and in particular, questions in the review of systems relating to TB exposure, this diagnosis may have been made much earlier; then the injury to the infant would have been avoided.

Frequently, malpractice cases occur after a patient deteriorated secondary to a serious undiagnosed cause that was unrecognized by the treating physician. Very often these patients repeatedly returned to the office or, as in this case, to both the primary provider's office and the emergency department with a variety of progressively serious complaints. Usually, the most likely initial diagnosis is that of a benign, self-limited disease; however, with persistent failure to improve, the probability of other initially less likely but more serious diagnoses increases. The difficult question then arises. When are indications present for a comprehensive review and reassessment or referral of the patient? Often, these cases become situations of missing the forest for the trees, and identifying these patients is difficult.

In this case, the primary physician focused exclusively on the presenting complaint at each visit in the series without looking at the bigger picture of the patient's overall deteriorating status and history. This type of situation can also occur when multiple providers, here the local hospital emergency department physicians, are also evaluating the patient at episodic visits. Because medical records are generally not easily available to multiple providers in different institutions who are caring for a patient, the physician must compensate by either prolonging his or her history, or assigning staff to obtain the records from other providers.

It is important to keep in mind that juries evaluating a malpractice case will wonder: *what simple and inexpensive actions, requiring only a modest amount of additional effort, could have been taken that would have prevented the injury that caused the lawsuit.* In a case like this, the jury may have a hard time understanding how a patient who is being seen regularly for care and who was not improving does not warrant a comprehensive evaluation or referral. This can be an inflammatory aspect of a case if the jury comes to believe that the physician could have taken the time to comprehensively review the situation, which would have made the diagnosis apparent.

This is not "defensive medicine," as the term is frequently used in a pejorative sense (i.e., it is not related to marginally relevant tests). Rather, it focuses on highly relevant questions of an expanded history. A carefully documented review would go a long way to establish that the physician is trying his or her best to provide good care to the patient, who in retrospect is becoming seriously ill. An excellent alternative risk-reduction strategy would be to refer the patient to a consultant who can take a fresh look at the patient if he or she is not improving.

# If You Provide Specialty Care, You Are Held to the Standard of the Specialist

A healthy 42-year-old male EMT was followed by his internist for many years. At one intercurrent visit for a viral syndrome, the patient also complained of anxiety, feelings of panic, and marital stress. The internist started the patient on an antidepressant and recommended psychotherapy with a psychologist. The patient began the medication and started to see the psychologist within the month.

For the next three years, the internist managed the medication, and the patient continued to see the psychologist, repeatedly speaking of increasing depression, panic, poor sleep, night terrors, difficulty going to work, and discord with his wife. The internist responded to these symptoms by changing the patient's medication. The internist and the psychologist never spoke directly; however, the psychologist indirectly communicated his recommendations for medication changes to the internist via the patient.

Ultimately, the patient exhausted trials on SSRIs, and atypical antidepressants were then begun. Benzodiazepines had been added to the regimen, as was medication for insomnia, with little relief. The internist was unaware that the patient had expressed strong suicidal ideation, albeit in the absence of thoughts about plans, to the psychologist. Both were also unaware that the patient had a large gun collection at home.

The patient could no longer continue working and was preparing to separate from his wife. The internist and the psychologist never communicated directly about the deteriorating status of this patient. At home, one evening, the patient committed suicide by gunshot to the head.

This case revolves around the failure of the primary care physician to refer the patient to a psychiatrist in the face of worsening psychiatric symptoms despite maximal therapy after multiple changes in medication. Although simple depression is commonly treated by primary care physicians, the question in this case is this: When does a patient pass the threshold for referral to a psychiatrist? The primary care physician's initial plan to begin treatment with antidepressants and to refer the patient for psychotherapy was reasonable, even retrospectively; however, as time went on, the patient's deteriorating clinical course and family and work stressors argue for the need to refer the patient to a psychiatrist.

In general, one can reasonably expect in cases in which patients are not responding to current therapy that the physician would at some point perform a global review of the patient's status. It is in the best interest of both the patient and the physician that the case be evaluated and managed in the light of possible adverse outcomes. If this had been done, referral to a specialist, in this case a psychiatrist, seems likely.

The psychiatric experts who retrospectively reviewed the case for the defense felt that the medications prescribed for this patient by the internist were actually inappropriate and even contraindicated. They also noted that the prescribing physician did not document his own assessment of suicide ideation/intent/plans in any of his notes.

This case illustrates an important risk management point: If you provide care to a patient that a specialist usually provides, you are held to the standard of the specialist. In this case, the internist assumed the role of a psychiatrist when he continued to prescribe numerous psychotropic medications for a patient whose status was deteriorating while relying too heavily on the psychotherapist for guidance about the medications. Because the psychotherapist is not licensed to prescribe medications, the internist's reliance on his advice for these medications placed the patient and both of the practitioners at risk. This is related to the other troubling aspect of this case, namely that the prescribing physician and the psychotherapist did not communicate directly with each other about this patient who was not improving and in fact was deteriorating. This brings out the gap between the care actually provided and the standard of care a psychiatrist would have provided to a similar patient, which would have included a more focused history, different medications, and, at a late stage, evaluation for possible admission.

# Record Alteration Changes the Focus of the Case

A 31-year-old previously healthy male was admitted to an emergency department for right lower abdominal pain and appendiceal symptoms. The patient underwent an open appendectomy.

The postoperative diagnosis was acute perforated appendicitis with peritoneal abscess. Pathological final diagnosis was mucinous cystadenoma (mucocele of the appendix with acute inflammation and perforation). Routine outpatient surgical follow-up was unremarkable.

Two years later, after a motor vehicle accident, the patient had a CT of the abdomen, which showed ascites. Shortly thereafter, the patient was seen for the first time by an internist. A repeat CT scan also showed ascites, etiology unknown. The internist promptly referred the patient to gastroenterology and surgery for evaluation. Both specialists saw the patient once and felt that no further follow-up was necessary.

The patient returned to the primary care physician's office 15 months later. At that time, he had a weight loss of 30 pounds and increasing abdominal distention for six months. The patient was diagnosed with late-stage pseudomyxoma peritonei, and he died at the age of 37 years.

---

Because the internist referred the patient at the initial visit to specialists for evaluation of persistent ascites, the bulk of the liability for the delay, if any, in diagnosing this patient's pseudomyxoma peritonei, would have normally been with the specialists. This patient had a very unusual disease, and the general rule is that a primary physician is able to rely on the specialists with whom he or she consults for advice; however, the defense of this case took an unexpected adverse turn.

As part of sending the patient to the gastroenterologist, the internist ordered a carcinoembryonic antigen (CEA) test. It was returned with a value of 15 (normal for nonsmoker is less than 2.5). The patient had stopped smoking five years earlier. When the case proceeded to depositions, a copy of the gastroenterologist's records was produced. At that time, it was noted that a copy of the laboratory report was contained in the gastroenterologist's records (it had been sent to the gastroenterologist by the internist when he referred the patient for the GI evaluation). This report was different from records provided by the internist to both the plaintiff and the defense attorneys.

When copies of the internist's medical records were reviewed by the experts for the defense, apparently the lower half of a page of the laboratory report, which contained the critical CEA findings, had been obscured; therefore, the existence of the CEA marker results was not known to the expert reviewers or the internist's defense attorneys.

This discrepancy in the records changed the focus of the case. The internist now had to explain how this discrepancy occurred. His explanation was that a member of his staff had made a copying error and that the CEA result was inadvertently obscured when the laboratory report was copied. It appeared to the plaintiff, and even to the other co-defendant physicians, that this laboratory report had been deliberately altered. This called the professionalism, honesty, and credibility of the internist into question. The internist now had to address this issue, and the focus of the case was no longer about the appropriate care he provided to the patient, but now centered on the details of his practice's procedures for copying records.

The possibility that the records had been altered also introduced the threat of additional legal consequences (beyond a payment in the malpractice claim) for the internist. If it is proven that the internist, or someone under his control, "deleted" or "removed" a true entry in the record, he or she can be charged with the crime of falsifying a business record. In New York state, Penal Law Section 175.005 provides for a penalty of up to a year in jail. Additionally, a conviction would lead to disciplinary review by the state licensure board, with penalties ranging from censure to license revocation.

As to consequences in a civil trial, many courts are striking the answer of a defendant who destroys evidence or manipulates it in such a fashion as to alter the truth as to what occurred. When an answer is stricken, the jury is told that the issue of liability has been decided in favor of the patient and that the only issue before them is to calculate the amount of damages to be awarded. More importantly, if an answer is stricken for fraudulent conduct, there may be severe insurance implications, such as the triggering of exclusion for fraud, thereby vitiating malpractice coverage for the physician.

# Ineffective Communication Between Physicians Can Result in Injuries to Patients

A 70-year-old man presented to an otolaryngologist with a friable granulomatous nasal mass. Biopsy diagnosis was fragments of complex papilloma with moderate to severe cytological atypia/high-grade dysplasia. No evidence of invasive tumor was seen.

Three months later, the patient was seen by another otolaryngologist (at a different institution), whose initial impression was R/O carcinoma. A CT scan showed a large polyp involving the left lower anterior nasal turbinate. Neither the report nor the slides from the original procedure were obtained.

Five months after the initial biopsy, the patient underwent definitive excision by the second otolaryngologist. The form submitted to pathology with this specimen noted this: "Deviated nasal septum. Sinusitis. R/O inverting papilloma." During this time, the pathology department was short staffed. Although the specimen was submitted entirely, as a result of the benign-appearing history given to the pathologist, only a single level was obtained for histology. Final pathological diagnosis was squamous papilloma with moderate dysplasia. Although the pathology department also had a policy that cancer cases were automatically reviewed by a second pathologist, no such review occurred in this case because only moderate dysplasia was noted.

Six months later, the patient had a recurrence. At that time, the otolaryngologist requested a review of the slides from the definitive surgery. As a result of this request, deeper recuts were made. After examining these recut slides, the pathologist issued an amended report stating that the deeper sections revealed foci of papillary carcinoma rather than the previously reported squamous papilloma with dysplasia. The patient subsequently underwent three surgeries and radiation therapy. He has been free of recurrence, but because of his physical appearance, he lives the life of a hermit.

---

As you might imagine, many pathology and radiology malpractice cases focus on the interpretation of the specimen or study. These cases are often difficult to defend because they typically concern a diagnostic conclusion that was later found to be incorrect. Many of these errors, which are indisputable in retrospect, are a consequence of fatigue and overwork. In this case, the pathology department was understaffed. The pressure of having to read additional studies to compensate for the shortage of staff probably contributed to the diagnostic error made in this case.

In today's environment, there are many reasons why physicians work under conditions that are suboptimal for patient safety. These practice patterns are typically difficult for an individual practitioner to modify. Nevertheless, it is important to acknowledge that the volume of specimens or films a physician interprets, and the policies and procedures under which they work, may be major risk factors for an error and subsequently a malpractice case. The higher the volume, the greater the likelihood of making a cognitive error due to distraction, fatigue, and so forth. Even more dangerous is weakening of a safety procedure to accommodate the higher work flow.

In addition to volume, there are also other practice patterns that may contribute to diagnostic errors. These are usually more within the direct control of the physicians involved in the patient's care. For example, in many cases, communication between physicians caring for a patient has been allowed to degrade over time from the ideal to become incomplete or ineffective or non-existent. In this case, the pathologist would have been much better prepared to read the slides and alerted to order deeper sections had he known that this was a recurrent lesion with a previous diagnosis of squamous papilloma with severe dysplasia. If the surgeon had provided this information to the pathologist, this error and subsequent injury to the patient would likely have been avoided.

The second otolaryngologist did not obtain the previous reports or slides before the definitive surgery. Obtaining this information often requires diligence and effort. In order to prevent cases such as this, many institutions have policies that require the review of previous pathology reports or slides when dealing with a neoplastic lesion. If this was done in this case, it would likely have prevented the misdiagnosis that injured this patient. Alternatively, a pathology intake form, which asked whether previous surgeries had been performed, might have provided useful information for the pathologist reading these slides.

This case serves as a good illustration of the difference between the gold standard of care that we all strive to provide to our patients, and the less than optimal care that patients sometimes receive. A benchmark for the gold standard is the type of care that we would want a member of our family to receive if he or she were the patient.

If this patient was a member of our family when he was seen at the second institution, we would want the care to include a review of the initial pathology report and an independent review of the slides. We would want there to be a personal discussion between the surgeon and the pathologist about the patient, his diagnosis, and the plan of care. We might even feel that a second biopsy and/or presentation at a tumor conference were indicated, as is done at many tertiary care centers.

Instead, in this malpractice case, the jury would be told about a cumulative series of shortcuts taken by the second surgeon and the pathologist, which likely led to an avoidable catastrophic injury for this patient. For example, suppose the plaintiff's attorney could establish that the pathology form was actually filled out by the circulating nurse on the basis of the preoperative operating room schedule. The plaintiff's attorney would also tell the jury that this case was representative of a pattern and practice by these physicians of failing to adhere fully to widely accepted standards that were known by both specialists and that were recognizable and correctable long before the events that led to this case unfolded. Finally, the jury would be encouraged to believe that awarding a very large amount of money would send a signal to the physicians involved, and the medical community at large, that these sorts of money-saving departures from best practices were unacceptable.

In conclusion, standards originally taught to us in medical school and residency training become the basis for community practice standards, which are then legally recognized in malpractice cases. In many instances, these high standards come under pressure immediately on graduation. It requires commitment and deliberate planning by the individual practitioner to maintain these standards in their daily clinical practice.

In this chapter, we have described cases that illustrate the dangers that arise from actions that can be interpreted as deviations from and the neglecting of generally accepted standards of care. For example, a standard homily taught in medical school is that 80% of diagnosis is related to obtaining and documenting a proper history. In some of the cases we described here, one risk-reduction strategy to avoid the unintended deviation from standards of care would have been for the physician to commit to an internal requirement and plan to *always* obtain and document a proper history of the present illness. Without this commitment, there is a risk that time pressures could influence the physician's ability to take a proper history, to document that history in the chart, and to review and reflect on that history. This erosion of standards would eventually lead to an increased systemic risk of not making a proper diagnosis.

These few cases indicate some of what can be learned by carefully considering and analyzing errors made by real physicians in actual clinical practice. These physicians are intelligent and work hard; nonetheless, these same types of errors occur repeatedly.

We believe that if physicians, including those in training, have an opportunity to review a large quantity of errors like these analyzed in a similar way, they could learn from these very painful experiences of others and practice better and safer medicine in the future.

*Excellence is an art won by training and habituation.*
*We do not act rightly because we have virtue or excellence,*
*but rather we have those because we have acted rightly.*
*We are what we repeatedly do. Excellence, then, is not an act but a habit.*
Aristotle

# REFERENCES

1. Leape LL. Error in medicine. *JAMA*. 1994;272(23):1851–1857.
2. Reason J. Human error: models and management. *BMJ*. 2000;320:768–770.
3. The American College of Radiology. *ACR Practice Guideline for the Performance of Screening Mammography*. Available at: http://www.acr.org/SecondaryMainMenu Categories/quality_safety/guidelines/breast/screening_mammography.aspx, accessed March 13, 2008.
4. The American College of Radiology. *ACR Practice Guideline for the Performance of Diagnostic Mammography*. Available at: http://www.acr.org/SecondaryMainMenu Categories/quality_safety/guidelines/breast/diagnostic_mammography.aspx, accessed March 13, 2008.
5 Powell SM, Haskins RN, Sanders W. Improving patient safety and quality of care using aviation CRM. *Patient Safety & Quality Healthcare*. July/August 2005. Available at: http://www.psqh.com/julaug05/delivering.html, accessed October 22, 2007.
6. Rivers RM, Swain D, Nixon WR. Using aviation safety measures to enhance patient outcomes. *AORN Journal*. 2003;77(1):158–162.
7. Garza M. Can aviation safety methods cut obstetric errors? *OB-GYN Malpractice Prev*. 2004;11(8):57–64.
8. Morey JC, Simon R, Jay GD, et al. Error reduction and performance improvement in the emergency department through formal teamwork training: evaluation results of the MedTeams project. *Health Serv Res*. 2002:37(6):1553–1581.

# Chapter 13

# Lessons Learned Defending Physicians: The Attorney's Perspective

## Roy F. Kaufman and Marjorie O. Thomas

*Clients don't care how much you know until they know how much you care.*

Author Unknown

A cardiologist was on trial for failing to diagnose heart disease in a 52-year-old mother of two teenage children. The patient, who experienced chest pain, had been discharged from the emergency room after an unremarkable EKG and negative enzyme studies. The cardiologist saw the patient in his office and recommended that the patient undergo a Thallium stress test on a nonemergent basis. Approximately 1 week later, before the patient had the recommended test, she was found dead in her bed by her 14-year-old daughter. The autopsy revealed an acute coronary dissection, a rare and usually untreatable condition.

While conferencing the case, I discussed with both my client and the expert the best way to illustrate the mechanism of a coronary artery dissection. During the trial, we all agreed that the jury did not seem to be grasping either the severity of the condition or its rapid onset. Together, we devised a model using Velcro to show the lumen of an artery wall, and during the trial, the expert used this model in front of the jury to show how this condition causes a sudden and catastrophic event. The sound of the Velcro separating not only got the jury's attention—it focused them onto the demonstrative evidence. In a case in which the plaintiff's attorneys sought a multimillion dollar recovery for their client's estate, the jury, focusing on the simple demonstrative evidence, returned a verdict in favor of the cardiologist.

---

D efending physicians, for over a quarter century, has taught us invaluable lessons about how juries react, witnesses perform, and evidence is viewed. In this chapter, we hope to share those stories and the lessons we have learned.

## Juries Are Audiences

To paraphrase an old children's book, all you really need to know about trials can be learned from sitting on a jury. A number of years ago, after I was admitted to practice and had already tried numerous cases, I was summoned for jury duty. In our jurisdiction, attorneys (and healthcare professionals) had previously been exempt from jury service. I spent the entire time of my jury service looking, listening, and observing the inner workings of a system, which few attorneys (up to that time) had had a chance to experience. The best analogy would be a surgeon being brought into a trauma center as a patient without ever letting on that he or she was a physician.

For the past 10 years, during every jury selection, I recount my own jury duty experience. It provides an immediate bond with the jurors, letting them know that I was one of them and that I am aware of what is discussed after the jury room door is closed. Most of those discussions center on how the witness came across, whether he or she was straight with the jury or was trying to con them into believing that something that they knew from common sense could not be correct. Some conversations are petty, commenting on the dress of the parties or the jewelry worn. I heard one juror comment that the physician wore such an expensive watch that he could easily afford whatever the plaintiff was seeking. The lesson here is that despite the court's admonition to the contrary, cases are decided on more than just the evidence, and those participating in the process need to be aware that this is what they face.

Most importantly, the jurors discuss whether the witness is the kind of physician that they would seek for care and almost always evaluate the case as if they were the ones receiving the care. This may not be the appropriate standard, but it helps one to understand better the thinking of the people in the jury box.

Since my own jury experience, I have spent countless hours advising clients how to communicate with a jury, but also giving them some insight into how the message is received. Juries are, in the end, an audience. They look and listen and, most of all, respond to what is happening before them.

Physicians appearing before a jury have the unique and disquieting experience of having their actions judged, usually for the first time, by someone other than a peer. Knowing who your audience is can help to avoid potentially embarrassing and costly mistakes.

# You're Not "Preaching to the Choir"

Two surgeons were sued for failing to timely operate on a 63-year-old husband and father of three adult children. The patient had undergone a difficult endoscopic retrograde cholangiographic procedure, at which time a very small retroperitoneal perforation occurred; it was quickly and properly diagnosed. The surgeons were called in by the gastroenterologist, and a decision was made to defer the risky and difficult repair while they monitored the patient's clinical course. Over the next 72 hours, the patient was closely monitored, and the hospital notes clearly documented the patient's waxing and waning symptoms. Surgery was performed on the third day after the perforation; however, the patient eventually succumbed to sepsis.

The issue at trial was whether the surgeons acted appropriately in deciding to treat the patient with conservative management of the small perforation in the hope that there would be spontaneous closure. Plaintiff's counsel, as he is entitled to do, called one of the surgeons as his first witness and proceeded to cross-examine him on the notes in the hospital chart, which recorded the monitoring of the patient's progress during the critical hours after the perforation. The most compelling notes were written by the nursing staff who monitored the patient's vital signs, complaints, and symptoms.

In response to a question highlighting a particularly damaging nurse's entry about the deterioration of the patient's clinical course, the surgeon told the jury, in a condescending tone, that he doesn't read nurses' notes, that they are not helpful to a physician, and clearly implied that they are useless. The widow, a registered nurse now working in special education, was not the only one offended by these comments.

After a seven-figure verdict in favor of the plaintiff, the jury told me how callous and insensitive this well-credentialed and experienced physician came across. Although none of the jurors were nurses, many of them had dear friends and relatives who were. They felt that the surgeon did not appreciate and understand the nurse's role in the healthcare continuum. More importantly, the nurse's observation provided yet another perspective as to the patient's condition, something critically important in deciding whether surgical intervention was necessary. As Dr. Linda Aiken and her colleagues put it, "Registered nurses constitute an around-the-clock surveillance system in hospitals for early detection and prompt intervention when patients' conditions deteriorate."[1]

The lesson here is that the message must be one that can be appreciated, understood, and respected by the audience. If the audience (in this instance, the jury) loses respect for the person delivering it, the message will never be accepted. In this instance, the jury is likely to be able to appreciate and understand the key and crucial role of nurses on the healthcare team and is also likely to lose respect for the defendant physician who minimizes, no less denigrates, that role.

It is not uncommon to have a defendant physician called by the plaintiff's counsel as the first witness during a trial. Because the plaintiff then has the opportunity to cross-examine the witness before his or her attorney can rehabilitate him or her, the plaintiff's attorney's goal is to have the jury's first impression of the witness be a negative one. In this case, the mission was accomplished.

## Juries Watch Everything

Many years ago, I was trying a case in a venue in which most of the selected jurors came from economically disadvantaged neighborhoods. During the trial, the judge instructed the jury that the case must be decided on the facts, what occurs on the witness stand, and that the jury was not to be swayed by any other factor—a common instruction to the jury.

The case involved a young woman who was alleging that the defendant orthodontist was negligent in not referring her for routine dental care during the four years that she was wearing braces. The child, an adult at the time of trial, sustained severe areas of decalcification of the enamel, resulting in a disfiguring smile requiring costly cosmetic veneers. The orthodontist documented in the records consistently that the child was missing office visits and showed evidence of poor oral hygiene, however there was no mention of referrals to a general dentist in the notes.

The orthodontist was a most pleasant gentleman in his mid to late 60s; he was adamant about defending the case. As a result, the case proceeded to trial. The venue was about 50 miles from his residence, in the county where his practice was maintained.

Despite my constant requests, the defendant showed up on only 1 day of the trial—the day he was asked to testify. His wife, nearly half his age and bedecked with a trove of jewels and fur, accompanied him to court. Although the orthodontist was an effective witness, the jury, four of whom were women, spent most of the time staring, with some disdain, at the visitor in the back of the courtroom.

I learned a valuable lesson that day, one that I share with clients to this day. Jurors notice everything that occurs in a courtroom. They look at who is there, who is not, and despite the court's instructions to the contrary, these observations have an impact on their decision making.

When physician clients ask about our chance of success at trial, I now routinely ask them in response, "How often are you going to attend the trial?" "How committed are you to assisting in your defense?" The success of the case is usually a function of those two factors.

Most trial attorneys do not wish to have their clients sit beside them at the attorney's table. Some trial attorneys consider the presence of their client at the attorney's table as a distraction to hearing the testimony and viewing the evidence. My own opinion is that the client sitting at the defense table makes them the center of attention; their every movement and reaction viewed by the jury.

When you, the physician-defendant sits in the back of the courtroom, the jury knows you are there; they know that you are interested and that you can, during the breaks in testimony, consult with the attorney as needed. Family members should provide emotional support . . . at home. At trial, they prove to be a distraction and, in some cases, can actually hinder the defense. For example, in a wrongful death action, when the plaintiff's surviving spouse sits alone in the back of the courtroom grieving over the loss of their loved one, the sight of a devoted couple sitting together serves only to reinforce the plaintiff's loss.

# Juries Love Visual Evidence

Years ago, in the days of smoke-filled courtrooms, a trial attorney's biggest obstacle was how to get the jury's attention. It was not uncommon to find at least one or two jurors and, possibly the judge, dozing off in the middle of the afternoon during a witness's reading of a record or description of a complex medical issue. Multimedia technology has changed the way evidence is presented and allows for these presentations to be engaging. Voluminous medical records are displayed using computers and shown to the jury with both highlighting and magnification. Radiological films and photographic enlargements of pathology specimens, portrayed with the use of computer technology, can bring clarity to even the most complex issues. Depositions can and are routinely videotaped, preserving the testimony of those who may not be available at the time of trial. These videotapes bring life where it has been lost and illustrate the most vulnerable aspect of witnesses' testimony; their body language.

As demonstrated in the "Velcro case" with which this chapter opens, evidence does not always have to be fancy or expensive; the most effective evidence is the kind that grabs the jury's attention and reinforces the principles that they are meant to demonstrate. Juries now expect and demand an opportunity to see material that relates to the testimony they will have heard before they go into the jury deliberation room. The images of the medical records and X-rays, projected onto screens large enough for the jury to view this evidence as it is being discussed, rather than the words, become the focus of the jury's attention, making the integrity of the record of paramount importance. Such a picture, literal and figurative, will remain with the jurors as they deliberate.

---

We often refer to a case in which the physician, after being sued, rewrote his records for the sake of greater clarity. As it turned out, the new notes were written on forms marketed by a company that was able to corroborate the plaintiff's attorney's suspicions regarding the authenticity of the records. The forms were not yet in circulation at the time of the visits in question.

---

Enlarged copies of these notes with the publication date and the dates of treatment highlighted would certainly stand out in the minds of any jury hearing this case.

## Honesty Counts

What happens in the rare occasion when there is no medical record, not because it was lost but because it never existed?

---

A psychiatrist was on trial for the death of a 58-year-old husband and father of four minor children, based on a claim that he failed to diagnose depression, which resulted in suicide.

The patient saw the psychiatrist for approximately two years, during which time he prescribed controlled substances for the patient's depression, anxiety, and sleep problems; however, at the patient's request (because of the sensitive issues discussed), no notes were made during the visits and no medical record was maintained. The only record of the visits was the carbon copies of the prescriptions for the controlled substances and the appointment diaries showing when appointments were made or canceled.

At trial, the psychiatrist testified that the patient had no previous history of suicide attempts, continuously denied suicidal ideation, and posed no suicidal threat. Because there were no records to support this testimony, the psychiatrist relied on his independent recollection. Fortunately, for this physician's defense, the family members all testified that there were no signs of an impending suicide.

When asked why he did not maintain a medical record (as required under the law[2]), the psychiatrist honestly told the jury that he respected the patient's wish for privacy, and although it would not have changed his treatment, he now realized that he was wrong in failing to maintain a record. Although the physician still faced charges by the state licensing board for failing to maintain a record, his honest and sincere testimony about why he did what he did resulted in the jury exonerating him of any negligence in this multimillion dollar case.

The importance of a complete medical record cannot be overemphasized. It is not only required by almost every jurisdiction as a matter of law, but it provides the practitioner with the ability to refresh his or her recollection based upon its contents. We sometimes encounter cases in which physicians explain that they did not follow their usual course (e.g., keep a medical record, document a particularly sensitive piece of information in the patient's history, or insist that a patient be seen before issuing a prescription based on the patient's complaint) to please an importunate patient. The patient's best interest is not served if the physician acquiesces to the patient's wishes to do that which is illegal or against the established standard of care.

Although records of visits are routinely maintained, many physicians are still reticent to document phone calls with patients and with other physicians concerning their shared patient. These conversations and the documentation concerning them form the basis of many claims and defenses. Whether they are recorded in separate logs or eventually noted in the patient's chart, the effort to create a record of these telephone contacts has proven their worth in cases in which the care of the patient and the defense of the case turned on that one note about that one conversation.

# Cases Don't Always Settle

One of the common misconceptions is that when a case involves a clear departure from accepted practice the case will always settle. Oftentimes, such cases do not settle either before trial or at trial because the plaintiff's counsel, feeling emboldened, demands a sum of money that is disproportionate to the claimed injury. In those instances, the case must proceed to trial and not merely for the purpose of reducing the plaintiff's demand. Sometimes the trial is the only way to resolve the matter.

---

An obstetrician was sued for failing to diagnose conjoined twins. The relevant issue involved the interpretation of a sonogram, which was performed in the obstetrician's office at 19 weeks. The patient had an additional sonogram performed at 26 weeks by another obstetrician, at which time the anomalies were diagnosed. The patient, presented with her options, chose to travel to a Midwestern clinic where a third-trimester termination was legally performed.

When the plaintiff's counsel demanded a seven-figure settlement for the physical and emotional damages sustained by his client, the case proceeded to trial. At trial, the obstetrician, a warm and caring physician with many years of experience, testified that he had no excuse for failing to diagnose this condition. Rather, he offered an explanation, which he told the jury did not excuse the misdiagnosis. Because he used an older machine for his ultrasound examination, he told the jury that if the heads, arms, and legs are aligned in a parallel manner, the image can appear as one fetus. Because the twins shared multiple internal organs, they could not be separated and most likely, given the time that this case occurred, would not have survived childbirth.

---

After considering all of the evidence and the plaintiff's demand, the jury returned a verdict in favor of the plaintiff for $800, the cost the plaintiff incurred for traveling expenses to undergo the pregnancy termination. The jury discounted the plaintiff's emotional injuries, finding that she would have experienced similar feelings even if she chose a termination during the second trimester.

Although almost every case presents obstacles, the lesson is that all cases need to be vigorously prepared for trial. Complete, thorough medical records and a genuinely warm and caring physician who is involved in the process and prepared for trial are invaluable assets.

# Expert Testimony Is Not Always Needed

Under our system, issues of law, such as what will be allowed to be admitted as evidence, are determined by the court or judge presiding over the case; however, issues of fact, that is, where the parties disagree as to what actually occurred, are determined by the jury—unless the parties agree to waive a jury.

---

A 35-year-old male presented to an orthopedic surgeon for an arthroscopy for a torn medial meniscus. The operation was uneventful, and on the first postoperative visit, the patient and his wife, a registered nurse, were seen in the physician's office. At that time, the patient, who did not have a fever, had fluid aspirated from his knee. The orthopedist considered the aspirate unremarkable and did not send it for culture. The patient went on to develop a septic knee and had multiple surgeries, culminating in a total knee replacement.

The patient and his wife claimed that the aspiration performed in the office was done under unsterile conditions and that the orthopedic surgeon did not wear gloves, did not adequately prepare the skin with antiseptic, and used a multiuse vial of an anesthetic to inject the joint.

During depositions, the plaintiff and his wife gave conflicting testimony as to what occurred in the physician's office. They gave different accounts about where everyone was standing, what everyone wore, and which side of the examining table the physician was standing on. More importantly, as to the size and color of the multiuse vial, different descriptions were given.

Because our expert would have testified that if unsterile technique was used, that was a departure from accepted medical practice, and that the introduction of an organism into the joint could account for the plaintiff's injuries, the only real question for the jury was whether the events occurred as the plaintiffs claimed.

---

On summation, I asked the jury this: "If the plaintiff has the burden of proving how the aspiration and injection occurred, how can they have met that burden when they cannot agree amongst themselves as to what occurred?" The jury returned a verdict in favor of the physician.

Although routine matters such as wearing gloves and creating a sterile field are not customarily documented, the lesson here is that by conforming to a routine custom and practice, the physician can rely on his or her usual practice when testifying as to what occurred. The strength of that testimony depends on the witness's (the physician's) ability to communicate with the jury.

Although it is unusual to find a situation where the plaintiffs disagree among themselves, it is not unusual to have such disagreements when multiple physicians are sued. Different versions of the same facts by individuals involved in the same care and treatment almost always result in unsuccessful outcomes for the defense.

# Kiss Your Defense Goodbye

There is nothing more frustrating to a defense attorney than having to settle a medically defensible case because the medical record has been altered. Plaintiffs' attorneys usually work under the premise that all medical records are altered. They will, therefore, go to great expense to hire forensic document analysts to prove that different inks were used in a single entry or that paper was not available on the date the entry was written, all in the hope that if an alteration is proven the defense will be discredited.[3] Sometimes, however, the records alone are all that is needed because alterations to the medical record are often apparent when looked at in the context of the total record.

For a trial attorney representing the physician, the altered record presents obstacles on many levels—from potential criminal liability for falsifying a business record to insurance issues, which may mean that the physician is denied coverage in a case in which he or she has altered records, to the personal exposure likely when a punitive verdict exceeds available insurance coverage. Also, courts take a very dim view of physicians whose records are found to be altered. In one such case, the opinion handed down by an appeals court included this stark conclusion:[5]

> We hold, therefore, that a deliberate falsification by a physician of his patient's medical record . . . must be regarded as gross malpractice endangering the health or life of his patient.

Experience tells us that most physicians are concerned that a jury will not believe them if the record does not accurately record all that transpired as to visits, conversations, recommendations, and treatment. The truth is that the record can never memorialize *all* that occurred and that, eventually, every case must be decided on who the jury accepts as being the most honest. Re-creating a record or adding to an existing entry jeopardizes not only the integrity of the record but, more importantly, the integrity of the entire defense. Jurors tell us, with their verdicts, that altered records are the equivalent of a violation of a sacred trust. Standing in the shoes of patients, they consider that the medical chart records their communications with their physicians, issues that may not have been discussed with even spouses or family members. Where facts are changed or dates as to when entries are made, the entire record is viewed as an untrustworthy document and its author as the culprit who set out to deceive or conceal an error.

---

Consider a case in which a 38-year-old male presents to his internist's office with complaints consistent with an upper respiratory infection. The internist performs a throat culture and because of the patient's long-standing history of mitral valve prolapse orders a complete blood count and blood cultures.

The patient returns less than 48 hours later with continuing symptoms and is advised that his white blood count is 9,500 and that the cultures have not yet yielded any growth.

The following day, the physician notes in her chart that she called the patient and told him that the blood cultures yielded an organism usually found on the skin, but because of his history, she wanted an immediate echocardiogram and serial blood cultures.

---

The young internist later testified at a deposition, under oath, that this phone call took place on the same day that she wrote the note in the chart. The patient claimed that he never received a telephone call from his physician and that approximately three to four weeks later he developed a retinal embolus secondary to his untreated endocarditis.

Based on the negligence of the patient in failing to follow instructions, a decision was made to proceed to trial. The basis for the defense was that if the patient had followed the instructions, the proper diagnostic studies would have resulted in prompt and proper treatment.

At trial, the records of the subsequent treating physicians were subpoenaed. Those records included a copy of the office records of the defendant internist. To everyone's surprise, especially the defendant internist's, that copy of her records did not contain the entry about the phone call in which she recommended the echocardiogram and the serial blood cultures. Unbeknownst to the internist, her office staff had faxed a copy of her records to the subsequent treating physician—obviously before the addition to the records was made. My client was then faced with an unenviable choice: admit to falsifying a business record, perjury, or both. The case settled that day.

What made the result in this case even more troubling was that the patient's other medical records all demonstrated a long-standing pattern of noncompliance. Given that history, there is no doubt that a phone call was made to the plaintiff on the day that the internist said she did and that if the internist had merely written the note as "an addendum" and accurately dated the addendum for the date it was made, the legal result would have been much different.

Even more beneficial would have been a more proactive approach to this patient's care on the part of the internist. Having not heard from this patient who is known to be noncompliant and in the face of a dangerous diagnosis, we would expect to see escalated efforts on the part of the physician; another call or even a letter to the patient from the physician encouraging the patient's compliance would have been in order.

The lesson here is not to check every record sent out by your office to every subsequent treating physician or patient. If the records are accurately written at the time the care is rendered or the conversation held, then the physician will have no need to scrutinize them before they are provided to the person requesting them.

---

In another case, a 22-year-old female is referred to an oncologist by a pulmonologist after a bronchoscopy with biopsy. A CT scan confirms the presence of a mass consistent with lymphoma. At the time of the office visit, the patient gives a history consistent with Hodgkin's disease. The oncologist recommends that the patient returns in 1 week for the commencement of chemotherapy. When the patient returns the following week, chemotherapy is commenced for Hodgkin's disease. The office records indicate that the chemotherapy prescribed is based on the patient's history, exam, CT, and pathology findings.

Within the next three to four months, the oncologist refers the patient for further diagnostic studies. When those studies indicate that the lymphoma is not responding as he had expected, the oncologist refers the patient to another physician who requests that the original slides be reviewed. On further review, it is determined that the patient actually had non-Hodgkin's disease. Despite aggressive measures, the patient eventually expired. Her estate sued the pathologist who originally interpreted the specimen and the oncologist, alleging that the commencement of the chemotherapy precluded the use of first-line chemotherapy agents to treat the non-Hodgkin's disease effectively.

---

Although the oncologist would normally be able to defend this case based on his reliance on the pathology findings and the diagnosis, the pathology report was not available at the time the oncologist first saw the patient or the time that he started the chemotherapy. The original pathologist knew he was looking at a lymphoma but was unsure if it was Hodgkin's or non-Hodgkin's disease; therefore, he requested that the slides be sent to another laboratory for specialized staining and interpretation. The final pathology report was not even typed until two weeks after the chemotherapy had commenced. The only conclusion that could be drawn was that the entries in the chart were not made contemporaneously.

# Greed Causes Grief

Greed is a terrible vice. It causes nothing but grief and is rarely, if ever, worth the risk of whatever benefit a person believes he will derive.

---

A neurosurgeon is called to the emergency room to rule out an intracranial bleed in a 68-year-old trauma patient who was involved in a motor vehicle accident earlier that evening. The patient is simultaneously being evaluated by a general surgeon for a suspected ruptured spleen. The patient subsequently expired.

The family brought a claim centered on the delay in transfusing the patient and in operating on him. The chronology of events from the time the patient entered the emergency room until the time of his death was critical in determining which physician was aware of the decreasing hemoglobin and hematocrit. In reviewing the emergency room record, there are two notes from the neurosurgeon, one timed at 11:50 p.m. and one at approximately 2:30 a.m., shortly after his consultation was requested. The 11:50 p.m. note cannot be explained, nor can it be reconciled with any other note in the chart.

---

When confronted with this note, the neurosurgeon explained that because this was a Medicare patient, if the patient was seen on two separate calendar days, an additional consultation fee could be and was charged. When we finished discussing the criminal implication of his notes and billing and the potential for state licensing disciplinary action, the effect on the malpractice case became the least of this physician's problems.

The physician's license is certainly one of his or her most valuable assets. By charging for a procedure not performed or by claiming an expense as covered when it is not, the physician is committing fraud. Fraud is a crime that jeopardizes that license to practice as well as the physician's freedom.

# It's All About the Communication

We are often asked by physicians what is the hardest claim to defend. The answer surprises most of the inquirers. The most difficult claim does not involve the most intricate surgery or the most complex medical issue but, rather, the quality of the communication between the patient and the healthcare provider.

Under our legal system, in almost every circumstance other than an emergency, a patient's consent is required before a physician can treat that patient. This rule of law stems from the common law cause of action for battery, which simply means "an unauthorized touching." Over the years, most jurisdictions have made informed consent a statutory requirement.

Although most physicians are under the mistaken belief that a consent form signed by a patient and witnessed by a third person satisfies this requirement, those who have faced a claim of lack of informed consent know nothing can be further from the truth. The consent form merely provides proof that permission was given by the patient for a specific diagnostic test or procedure. The signing of the form normally satisfies the rules and regulations of the facility where the test or procedure is performed; however, a signed form does not defeat a claim for lack of informed consent.

Simply put, consent represents permission, whereas informed consent requires permission with knowledge. Consent is easy to prove with documentary evidence such as a form, properly signed and witnessed; informed consent requires much more.

The law of informed consent in almost every jurisdiction requires the provider to prove that he or she disclosed, in terms understandable to the patient, the reasonably foreseeable risks, alternatives and benefits of an invasive diagnostic test or procedure so that the patient could make an informed choice. If the provider fails to disclose properly such risks, alternatives, and benefits and the patient can prove that a reasonable person in the patient's position would not have undergone the test or procedure if those risks were disclosed, the patient can recover for monetary damages if the test or procedure caused the patient's injury; therefore, under the law of informed consent, even if the jury finds that there was no malpractice, the plaintiff can still receive the same amount of damages if he or she prevails on the lack of informed consent cause of action.

For example, assume a 35-year-old male patient with a strong family history of colon cancer is referred to a gastroenterologist for a colonoscopy. The patient, who has no symptoms suggestive of the disease, wants to have the procedure, given his family history. The gastroenterologist fails to disclose the risk of perforation to the patient in his discussion with him but does have him sign the consent form. During the course of the colonoscopy, the patient's colon is perforated, and the injury is quickly diagnosed and surgically corrected.

In our example, if a lawsuit were commenced, the most likely claims would include both a cause of action for medical malpractice and a cause of action for lack of informed consent. As long as the procedure was properly performed, most, if not all, of the claims for medical malpractice can be successfully defended on the grounds that a perforation is a generally accepted and recognized risk of a colonoscopy.

The claim for lack of informed consent poses different challenges. Even though the gastroenterologist could successfully demonstrate that a consent form was signed for the procedure, the form itself is proof only that permission was given to undertake the procedure. It should not come as a surprise that many patients say that they do not read the form or cannot read the form. Have you ever seen a physician or nurse ask a patient if they can read? In a document regarding informed consent, The American College of Obstetricians and Gynecologists discusses comprehension as a major element of informed consent. In this document, ACOG asserts, "Moreover, this information should be provided in language that is *understandable to the particular patient*, who may have linguistic or cognitive limitations" (emphasis added).[6] If the patient does not understand the information that forms the basis of his or her consent, it can hardly be said that such consent is indeed *informed*.

The critical issue when dealing with lack of informed consent is the qualitative sufficiency of the consent. The gastroenterologist must demonstrate that the risk of perforation was discussed in a way that this patient could understand the concept. Even if the risk was not discussed with the patient, the physician could still prevail if he or she can demonstrate that a reasonable person who was concerned about the increased chance of colon cancer would have undergone the procedure even if the risk were disclosed.

Informed consent really focuses on the art of communication. How the message is delivered and received is as important as the fact that it is transmitted; therefore, even when a practitioner performs the same procedure hundreds of times a year, the discussion needs to be specific to the patient's own clinical picture and social and educational limitations. If one patient is a migrant farm worker with limited understanding of the language or of basic anatomy, that discussion of the risks, alternatives, and benefits must and should differ greatly than if the patient is another gastroenterologist who regularly performs the procedure. Fay Rozovsky, in her book on informed consent, advises that "a certain amount of time must be set aside to communicate with patients to affect valid consents."[7]

As you might expect, the best proof of a discussion is a note in the chart simply stating the risks, alternatives, and benefits were discussed. Although there has been much debate over the years about whether the specific risks, alternatives, and benefits need to be documented, most trial attorneys are pleased simply to see that a note was written memorializing the conversation.

Because the controversy can easily become a dispute between the parties about what was actually discussed, anything that can be written in the note that will give the physician the ability to refresh his or her recollection of the conversation will surely bolster the chance of success. If the patient was accompanied by a family member or friend during the visit when the conversation took place, listing that person's name and relationship in the note will provide your attorney with the name of a key witness likely to be called by the plaintiff to refute your defense.

Over the years, I have found the most effective piece of evidence at trial to be the reason the patient wants to go forward with the procedure. I have often suggested to clients that for elective or cosmetic surgeries a line be added to the consent form that requires that the patient completes it, giving his or her reason, in his or her own words, for requesting the procedure (for example, "I would like to have this procedure performed because . . ."). If the patient later alleges a lack of informed consent, the patient's own words, especially in his or her own handwriting, can be enlarged to poster size to show the jury how strongly the patient felt about having the procedure.

Brochures given or diagrams drawn by the physician in an effort to educate the patient about the procedure further bolster the defense that the permission was obtained with knowledge on the patient's part. Although it is not necessary to copy the specific brochure and place it in each patient's chart, it is necessary to archive a copy of each piece of literature that you distribute to patients so that it is available for trial. By referencing the brochure or diagram in the note, it helps the physician's recollection at a later date and clearly establishes what was discussed.

The following is just one example of a note that succinctly summarizes the informed consent discussion for the patient undergoing the elective colonoscopy: A 35-year-old asymptomatic male with strong family history of colon cancer presents with his wife for elective colonoscopy. Risks, alternatives, and benefits discussed, and brochure given. Patient's questions answered.

The lesson, when dealing with informed consent, is that the information must be received in a way that is understandable and ultimately provable to a jury. Documentation that helps a physician to remember pertinent specifics about the patient will help to enhance credibility with the jury.

# Documentation Does Make a Difference

Often, physicians tell us that they don't have the time or the personnel to document adequately advice given or referrals made. We hear that it is too time consuming, that it takes away time from patients, and that this activity does not generate revenue. Occasionally, a physician will ask whether it really makes a difference in the outcome of a case.

The following case example is proof that documentation does work, and in the end, the savings in the cost of time spent preparing to defend a case, as well as other costs, clearly outweigh the time and effort needed to document and follow up on significant findings.

> An overweight prepubescent male presents to a pediatrician's office with complaints of hip pain. After an unremarkable physical exam, the pediatrician, who has an increased index of suspicion, recommends to the mother that the child be seen by a pediatric orthopedist and have a hip X-ray. The pediatrician gives the mother a referral written on a prescription pad and, as is his custom, places the duplicate copy of the referral in the patient's chart.
>
> The child is subsequently diagnosed with a slipped capital femoral epiphysis, goes on to have nonunion, and eventually has multiple surgeries. Suit was brought against the pediatrician. The plaintiff, at the time of trial, was an adult with a significant gait disturbance.

The case, which was tried by a partner at my former firm, proceeded to trial, with the plaintiff demanding a multimillion dollar settlement. The plaintiff's position, articulated by the mother and the patient, was that the physician never recommended a consultation. They denied ever being given a referral by the pediatrician.

After a month-long trial, the jury returned a verdict in favor of the pediatrician, finding his testimony and records more credible than the plaintiff's denial of a referral. Without the documentation, the case would have been far more difficult to defend.

Very important to the care of his patient, if the pediatrician in this case had maintained a referral log, tracking the receipt of consultation reports, the patient's condition would have surely been diagnosed sooner. The days are long gone where most legal actions stem from an interpretation of an X-ray or pathology specimen or the occasional risk attendant to surgery. We are facing more and more cases in which patients are lost to follow-up and fall between the myriad providers who make up the healthcare continuum.

Physicians and other providers, more than ever, represent links in a chain, and plaintiffs strive to prove that there was a gap but for which a diagnosis would have been made and the poor outcome averted. Technology offers today's medical practice many tools to help in recording and tracking contacts, recommendations, and referrals. If physicians avail themselves of these tools that can make a difference, the benefit to patient care will be well worth the effort and surely worth the expense.

Juries want to know that a conversation took place and that a referral was made. They need to have their verdict justified, especially when we ask them to deny compensation to a patient who has a verifiable and sometimes sympathetic injury. It is difficult to try a case without blaming the plaintiff for the outcome while, at the same time, showing the jury that the outcome would have been different if the doctor's advice was followed. Although this may be a subtle distinction, it helps a juror reconcile his or her decision without placing blame on any party.

# Where We Began

Our discussion ends where it began—with an understanding that a trial is so much more than a search for the truth. A trial is a stage. The parties and their attorneys are the players, and the facts and the documents are the script to be followed. Ultimately, the jurors are the critics who must determine whether the information presented by the parties, when applying their common sense principles to the applicable law, can be reconciled.

Although the law says that a defendant has no burden of proof and does not have to present any witnesses or any evidence, in practice, that is not always true. A physician facing a claim of professional negligence must explain why the result was less than hoped for, why a condition was not diagnosed earlier, or why treatment would not have made a difference in the outcome.

A much older, wiser trial attorney once told me that jurors must go home to their families at the end of a trial and explain, in the simplest of terms, why the jury rendered the verdict it did. It is that information that trial attorneys and their clients must convey to the jury throughout the trial, with their words and their records . . . until the words belong to the jury.

# REFERENCES

1. Aiken LH, Clarke SP, Sloane DM, Sochalski J, Silber JH. Hospital nurse staffing and patient mortality, nurse burnout, and job dissatisfaction. *JAMA*. 2002;288:1992.
2. Definitions of professional misconduct. *N.Y. Educ. Law* §6530(32).
3. Prosser RL. Alteration of medical records submitted for medicolegal review. *JAMA*. 1992;267:2630–2631.
4. *Matter of Jascalevich*, 182 N.J. Super. 455, 472, 442 A. 2d 635, 645 (N.J. Super A.D. Jan 27, 1982) (No. A-644-80-T4).
5. Berlin L. Alteration of medical records [Malpractice Issues in Radiology]. *Am J Roentgenol*. 1997;168:1407.
6. American College of Obstetricians and Gynecologists. Informed consent. In: *Ethics in Obstetrics and Gynecology*. 2nd ed. Washington, DC: American College of Obstetricians and Gynecologists; 2003–2004:10.
7. Rozovsky FA. *Consent to Treatment: A Practical Guide*. Boston, MA, and Toronto, ON, Canada: Little, Brown and Company; 1984:3.

# Chapter 14

# The Emotional Impact of Medical Errors

Stephen Deckoff and Geraldine M. Donohue

*. . . although patients are the first and obvious victims of medical mistakes, doctors are wounded by the same errors: they are the second victims.*

Albert Wu, MD

When I arrived in the emergency room, my patient had just been returned to his cubicle from the X-ray department. Mr. Feldner, a morbidly obese 55-year-old opera singer, had been operated on by me two months previously for a carcinoma of the splenic flexure of the colon. Surgery had been long and difficult, and I had been pleased at his uncomplicated postoperative course.

Now, however, he was clearly severely ill; all of the clinical signs and symptoms indicated an acute small bowel obstruction, probably strangulating, in all likelihood caused by adhesions from his previous surgery. Reassuring Mr. Feldner and his anxious wife that I would return in a moment, I stepped out to review the plain films of the abdomen that the resident was just putting up on the viewing screen. Suddenly, I was completely paralyzed; my feet seemed nailed to the floor and a pressure within my chest rose and intensified with each heartbeat. There before me on the screen, standing out starkly, amidst distended small bowel loops, was the ring of a retained laparotomy pad.[1]

Examination of an already failing healthcare system intensified in 1999, with the emergence of the Institute of Medicine's *To Err Is Human: Building a Safer Health System*.[2] This report indicated that thousands of patients had lost their lives to medical errors and hundreds of thousands more had incurred injury. An explosion of attention and interventions aimed at reducing these medical errors followed almost immediately and created the climate soon known as the patient-safety movement.[3]

Society places enormous expectations on physicians. With the advent of the most technologically sophisticated diagnostic tests and treatments that the profession of medicine has ever known, it is no wonder that patients and families alike have come to expect nothing short of perfection from their doctors.

With this standard of perfection in place, what is the impact of these errors on our nation's physicians? This is an area that has been sorely under examined. As Wu wisely acknowledges, the physician truly is the second victim.[4]

# A Shattering World

In this retained object case, the surgeon suffered a terrifying sensation that overwhelmed him. For the first time in 20 years of clinical practice, he had unquestionably harmed his patient. Under these circumstances, most physicians would probably react similarly. Guilt—real and justified—was only one of the gamut of emotions that swept over him, invading him to the core. In an instant, his life had changed completely.

In his words:

> I was so ashamed . . . such shame and humiliation. . . . It was an anguish that sickened me and I could barely stand upright . . . and then I had to tell my patient and his wife . . . tell them that I made a mistake that was the cause of my patient's great suffering.[1]

The realization that he has made an error can set in motion a crisis state. The physician is filled with dread and uncertainty and does not know in which direction to turn. The environment in which he once felt so comfortable now seems alien. The enormity of the situation paralyzes him. A crisis reaction has the power to change the way he feels emotionally and physically, the way he perceives the events around him and the way he behaves.[5] The physician's own words confirm the truth of these observations:

> My mind was flooded with questions that I could barely keep up with. He'd have to undergo immediate surgery, but by whom? Surely he would not trust me, or would he? If he did want me to do the surgery, should I? Would I? Could I? I needed to talk with someone, to do something, to do what's right . . . but I couldn't entirely grasp it all. . . . I remember my heart suddenly beating

faster than I had ever known, I felt like I was losing control and really just didn't know what to do next.[1]

Depending on the severity of the error, physicians may question whether they are good doctors and may even contemplate withdrawing from practice. When anguish and torment penetrate so deeply, time may never completely relieve them, and physicians have been known to abandon their careers and flee the area in an attempt to re-establish their lives elsewhere.

> One physician left a now paralyzed adolescent patient in the recovery room and disappeared. It is believed that she could not face the parents and tell him something went terribly wrong during the neurosurgery. People were frantic looking for her. She surfaced again weeks later. Most were angry that she had abandoned her patient and family in their time of greatest need. Some thought that she was contemplating leaving this world permanently, because she could not live with her mistake.[6]

Crisis theory refers to this as the "fight or flight" response.[5] It is a physiological response within all human beings, intended to be used for survival. Some doctors feel they have no choice but to escape in order to survive the pain of harming someone that they hoped to heal. Fortunately, the overwhelming majority of physicians have the character, courage, and stamina to resist the desire to run.

A psychiatrist, early in her career, experienced the loss of her patient and explained the impact it had on her:

> My patient was a female doctor; everyone was very pleased with her progress. I was the last one to see her that morning. I discharged her, gave her prescriptions, and within 24 hours received the news of her death . . . by hanging. I could not get her voice, her face, her expression, her walk, her very least mannerism out of my head. I would be talking to someone, and it would look as if I was having a normal conversation—but I wasn't. I was completely distracted and preoccupied with my former patient, every waking moment.[7]

Diagnosed with a chemical imbalance, this patient had been informed that she would probably be on lifelong medication. This treating psychiatrist tried to recall in minute detail each session they had together, now questioning her capability to assess and help her patient.

> Her prognosis was likely far harder news for her to hear than I certainly appreciated. Now, I was filled with blame . . . and with a shame and an embarrassment I didn't think I could bear. I replayed over and over and over again in my head every conver-

sation. Was there some cue or clue she gave off to me that I had obviously missed? Someone else would have seen this coming. I questioned everything . . . my intuition . . . my abilities and my competence as a physician.[7]

The shock and pain of her patient's death took over her life:

When I turned out the light at night, she was my last thought before going to sleep. My patient was gone, dead, killed herself, and I couldn't save her. If I slept at all, as soon as I awakened she was my first thought.[7]

A near identical reaction to the news of a patient's unexpected death occurred in a medical setting. An excerpt of the physician's interview revealed this:

I certainly ruminated . . . trying to visualize mentally exactly what this fellow looked like, how easy he got in and out of the bedside, on and off the table, and out of my office, got his clothes on and off. What was his breath like? What did he smell like? Was he well kept? All those kinds of little things where you might have missed some sign that this fellow needed to have more care than what you provided.[8]

When such events occur, physicians experience an injury to their dignity and to their self-respect. They have been taught to a standard of perfection. Errors should not occur, and if they do, they may reflect a defect in one's character. They have seen their colleagues' errors paraded before them at numerous conferences and meetings, and even though many would deny a feeling of *schadenfreude* ("the enjoyment obtained from the troubles of others"[9]) on such occasions, many do believe that such things could never happen to them.

Does the world shatter for all physicians when a mistake has been made? In most instances, yes, it does, at least in the short term, but such is not the case for all physicians. In Paget's research, one physician described his experience when asked about the meaning of making a mistake:

If I've made a mistake which is a rational sort of mistake, understandable. . . . I don't find it extremely difficult to cope with it . . . like, do I lie awake nights? No. You know, I think I can live with my mistakes primarily because I usually try to be very conscientious and to do the best I am able. If I made a mistake because of ignorance . . . that would be very upsetting, but when I make a mistake and I feel it is a legitimate one, it's not hard to live with.[10]

An intriguing question is raised as to what constitutes a "legitimate" mistake from any other mistake. In Paget's research, she examines the phrase "it was an honest mistake."[11]

> Saying "it was an honest mistake" not only disclaims blame but implies something else—the possibility of being both mistaken and unblameworthy.[11]

In this description, there is a distance both from the patient and from responsibility for the mistake. If a physician believes that because he is "conscientious" and "does the best he can for his patients" any errors that are made are "honest" ones for which he bears no responsibility, then he is always defended against feelings of guilt, should a mistake occur. Can an "honest" physician really believe this, however? Although understandable, such a belief can stem from overconfidence, and at times even overbearing pride. Not only is it false, but it is dangerous; unless an error is discussed and responsibility for it admitted, it cannot be used as a learning experience, and similar mistakes are more likely to recur in the future.

What is the aftermath for both physician and patient if the mistake is not emotionally acknowledged? There is no right or wrong way to experience the emotional impact of having made a medical error; however, there are some coping responses that will be more useful than others. Responses that leave the physician remote or cut off from the experience may block healing from occurring at all. Being able to look objectively at one's mistake from its very onset is a characteristic very few possess. As Hilfiker wrote:

> My initial response to the mistakes I did make was to question my competence. Perhaps I just didn't have the necessary intelligence, judgment, and discipline to be a physician. But was I really incompetent? . . . When I looked at it objectively, my competence was not the issue. I would have to learn to live with my mistakes.[12]

Does a physician learn to live with his mistakes? He has just injured a patient or perhaps caused a patient's life to end prematurely. Most feel their world is shattering in front of them. There is a threat to his own value both as a physician and as a person, a threat to his competence, and a threat to his concentration, being now unable to focus on little else but the mistake and the patient who he has injured. The environment in which he once felt very much in control has radically changed; he now feels on exhibit, is anxious, and now acutely senses a loss of control and, significantly, the feeling of a loss of belonging. How does one learn to live with one's mistakes? One must begin an arduous journey.

# An Absence of Outlets: Unspoken Grief

Ingrained in physicians, from the start of medical training, is the need to be compulsive and to be devoted to patients and society before all else. This harks back to the teachings of Sir William Osler. The following is a quotation from Osler's address "The Student's Life":

> What about the wife and babies if you have them? Leave them! Heavy are your responsibilities to yourself, to the profession and to the public.[13]

The ideal expertise and conduct demanded of the physician accounts for the need for compulsivity and responsibility in the medical profession. Gabbard, in his well-regarded understanding of the role compulsiveness plays in the makeup of nearly all physicians, wrote the following:

> Herein lies the grand paradox: compulsiveness and excessive conscientiousness are character traits that are socially valuable, but personally expensive. Society's meat is the physician's poison.[14]

Gabbard suggests that it is the compulsive individual who is initially drawn to the profession of medicine.[15] Gabbard notes that physicians, at the expense of their personal lives, stay steadfastly by their patients' side making certain all has been done to prevent any deterioration in the patient's condition. They check and recheck laboratory data to be certain nothing has been overlooked. They "run the extra mile"[14] to be sure a rare disease is not behind a puzzling presentation. They work disproportionately long hours and then continue compulsively to read the all-pervading stacks of journals, making every possible effort to keep current with the literature.[14] This compulsivity of reading is a means to ameliorate the physician's anxiety that he cannot know everything.[16] This correlates well with an excerpt from a physician interview by Christensen's research team:

> As I think about it, there is this element of control and responsibility that's infinite. There is no point at which you can say comfortably, "Yeah, I did as much as I can and I couldn't do any more." You never reach that point.[17]

As a result, as human beings, physicians will make mistakes. There is no avoiding the feeling of loss when a medical error has occurred. The magnitude of loss will be greater for some physicians than for others. The physician has lost "himself" or his former image of himself. His feelings of pride and competence in his work and confidence in his ability to successfully treat his patients—all seem to have been lost.

Such devastation brings a multitude of losses into the physician's emotional world. How does a physician's grief compare with the grief of others?

Individuals react to loss in their own unique and personal way. The sorrow and grief that follow are generally shared with others. People customarily surround the suffering individual, offering supportive gestures, care and concern, understanding, and consolation. The grieving person feels less alone. The encircling support brings relief from the inordinate strain, but this sharply contrasts with the experience of the grieving physician.

> There is no process to evaluate supportively the circumstances of a mistake, and there exists no method to care for the fallible physician, whose feelings most frequently are kept in the dark.[18]

This experience of loss for the physician who has made a mistake has been compared with the stages of death and dying, described by Kübler-Ross, in her distinguished and breakthrough work.[19,20] Although best known for identifying the stages of denial and isolation, anger, bargaining, depression, and acceptance, Kübler-Ross also investigated fear of and attitudes toward death. Again, her work mirrors the fear and attitudes toward the medical mistake.[20] Words that are fitting for both, through society's eyes, include "regret," "distasteful," "fear," and "anguish."[21]

> . . . many of the old customs and rituals which have lasted over the centuries and whose purpose is to diminish the anger at the gods or the people . . . thus decreasing the anticipated punishment. I am thinking of the ashes, the torn clothes, the veil . . . they are all means to ask you to take pity on them, the mourners, and are expressions of sorrow, grief, and shame. . . . If someone grieves, beats his chest, tears his hair, or refuses to eat, it is an attempt at self-punishment to avoid or reduce the anticipated punishment for the blame that he takes on.[22]

A physician's reaction to his or her mistake is unlike any other grief reaction. What is different? Shame and embarrassment will often inhibit the physician from discussing the mistake. Ordinarily, the sanctuary of home with loved ones would be thought of as a place of safety to speak about the mistake. This, however, is not always the case.

The psychiatrist whose patient committed suicide eventually went home that evening:

> I had to tell my husband. . . . He knew just by looking at me something was wrong. And in my . . . my devastation . . . I still clearly remember my first words were "don't tell anyone." Not my family, not our children, not our friends. I felt an excruciating

humiliation. . . . I needed to maintain the secrecy for as long as I could. I wish I didn't even have to tell him.[7]

Frequently, a discussion of the mistake, even with one's spouse, is completely avoided. One yearns for support from those closest and from one's colleagues, but discussing medical mistakes may itself trigger feelings of guilt, doubt, shame, self-blame; isolation may seem preferable.

> Shame can creep into the very core of our experience of ourselves and thus constitutes the essential pain, the fundamental disquieting judgment that we make about ourselves as failing, flawed, inferior to someone else, unworthy of the praise or love of another, or falling short of a cherished ideal.[23]

Researchers examining the perceived effects of a medical mistake on collegial relationships reported that in most cases physicians focus on the problem and avoid any conversation about feelings.[24]

> You know, it's interesting how people seldom will call each other and say that there's been a mistake. But, you know, I listen to people kind of talk about each other and . . . I guess I judge the way I hear somebody talk about other doctors. I figure that behind my back they'll probably say the same kinds of things about me.[8]

Doctors may admit a mistake in private, but it is the rare situation when they will humble themselves and admit to their failings professionally.[25] The physician is more likely to turn emotionally inward. He or she becomes quiet, avoidant, withdrawn, and isolative. Because of the shame that comes with making a medical mistake, particularly in an environment that does not allow for mistakes, he or she is left alone at a time when he or she is most in need of others. That aloneness penetrates both his or her personal as well as professional life. If the profession of medicine has no room for mistakes, society does not as well.[26]

As crusading physician advocate, Wu reports this:

> We live in an age in which the only universally acceptable cause of death is decapitation—all else is considered reparable. Patients have an understandable need to consider their physicians infallible, but the medical profession has colluded with them to deny the existence of error.[4]

Bennet, surgeon turned psychiatrist, calls the physician "the wounded healer."[27] He provides instances in which the clinical mistake may be experienced by the physician as a personal failure, even when errors have involved judgment, rather than actual negligence. Examples may include a surgeon's injuring the common bile duct when removing the gall bladder or a family practitioner's misdiagnosing a child as suffering from influenza who later dies from meningitis or an overworked doctor who, too tired to get out of bed, gives advice over the telephone that ultimately leads to the patient's death.

Bennet believes that in order to heal, one most recognize and accept one's own frailty and one's own weakness.[28] When physicians do not discuss their weaknesses, they are at risk for entering into a period of disillusionment and depression.[29]

Physicians are often unable to cope, and their vulnerabilities manifest themselves in ways such as separation, divorce, and stopping medical practice. Suicide, alcoholism, and drug addiction are known to occur all too commonly. Adding to their problems, with each passing day, the medical profession is increasingly subject to drastic and overwhelming changes. An inadequate healthcare system, increasing malpractice premiums, and decreasing third-party reimbursements are just a few of the major stressors physi-cians are facing. Personal conflicts and genetic predispositions may also often be implicated.

With so many variables in place, it is difficult to ascribe a physician's error to any single vulnerability. What can be concluded, however, is that the medical mistake itself is a source of inner conflict that leads to stress that, if not addressed, may lead physicians to rely on dysfunctional methods in order to cope. Tempted to suppress these feelings of internal conflict, physicians may try to avoid them by overwork, isolation, and withdrawal. When conflict goes unexamined, it will surface in another way. This may threaten the physician's own emotional and physical health as well as his or her relationships with others.

> Safeguards might include the provision of discreet and confiden-
> tial access to psychotherapy and an open discussion of the stress
> encountered in a medical career. The barriers that may prevent
> physicians from seeking help for mental disorders (such as the
> threat of losing their medical license) must also be addressed. . . .
> In time, perhaps these and other measures will help doctors to do
> what they do best: save lives, beginning with their own.[30]

Although there are exceptions, most physicians, like other people, do not readily seek psychiatric assistance, but the physician who has erred needs a changed environment—one where mistakes can be openly discussed. These outlets are essential, for healing cannot take place in a world of silence; the grief must be spoken. Full discussion of the occurrence can lead to positive changes. Thoroughly examining the events leading to the error may lead to the discovery of actions or systems changes necessary to avoid future mishaps.

The emotional impact of a medical mistake is devastating, but what can be controlled is the method of management of these paralyzing feelings. A confidant is absolutely essential: a trusted person that will allow one to unburden oneself of the myriad emotions being experienced. The more outlets one develops, the more rapidly one is able to gain a perspective on the error and to learn to live with it.

> Mistakes are an inevitable part of everyone's life. They happen; they hurt—ourselves and others. They demonstrate our fallibility. Shown our mistakes and forgiven them, we can grow, perhaps in some small way, become better people. Mistakes, understood this way, are a process—a way to connect with one another and with our deepest selves.[31]

# Facing Your Fears

> This is probably the only patient where I feel like I totally blew it. It was while I was working on a tropical island. She was almost 16 years old. She had diarrhea for a week, a real bad headache, and a fever of 104°F. She had a fairly benign, but slightly diffusely tender abdomen. She had an elevated white count. I worked her up for different causes of diarrhea, treated her for malaria, and gave her Septra. Didn't really know what the cause was. I kept her on the ward overnight. The next morning she died. She had typhoid fever. . . . If I had been on top of it and made the right choice in the first place, she probably wouldn't have died.
>
> I was frightened of what other people would think of me. I was afraid of what my peers would think. There are no secrets there. It was extremely depressing. I had before developed the idea that I was a better than average physician, and suddenly, it was whether I was even an average physician. I didn't discuss my underlying feelings. I don't normally disclose my feelings to my colleagues. . . . I needed someone, a peer, to put their hand on my shoulder, to tell me it wasn't my fault.[32]

Fear of being sued is not offered in this excerpt of an interview with a physician participating in Newman's research on the emotional impact of mistakes on family physicians. There are likely many reasons that fear of litigation was not mentioned, most probably because it was a nonlitigious society where this young doctor was practicing. It is striking, however, that the feelings that this physician expressed mirrored the experiences of physicians working in highly litigious environments.

The pain a physician feels when he or she has harmed his or her patient in error is extraordinary and shattering, and myriad fears are faced. The physician experiences a fear of shame and humiliation before his or her colleagues and patients, friends, and neighbors, should the event become public; fear that hospital privileges will be lost; fear that he or she will be sued for medical malpractice; fear of loss of malpractice insurance along with fear of financial ruin should a jury return a verdict above his or her policy limits; fear that state authorities may rescind his or her license to practice medicine; and the ultimate fear—that one's professional career is over.

It is no wonder that the esteemed physician crusader Sara Charles has written, "Self-consciously, we feel compelled to save ourselves rather than serve our patients self-forgetfully, and thus, we find that protecting ourselves from legal actions may supersede healing our patients of their ills."[33]

Some of these fears are real and justified; others are not. Although a lawsuit may indeed eventuate when a medical mistake or adverse outcome has occurred, statistics across the country show that the physician prevails in the vast majority of lawsuits. According to the Physicians Insurers Association of America Risk Management Review, the likelihood that a malpractice lawsuit will result in a payment to the plaintiff is about one in four.[34] Charles cautions physicians that it is prudent to be protective of one's financial assets should a financially exhaustive outcome occur for the physician.[35] Know, however, that such outcomes are exceptionally rare.

When the physician is faced with a lawsuit, he or she is thrust into the unfamiliar world of the legal environment. The legal environment is as foreign to the physician as the medical world is to his or her patients. One very distinct difference is in the "breaking of bad news." When a physician must tell a patient something that is difficult to hear, attention should be paid to the setting for the meeting and to the words selected so that the patient can absorb the news to the best of his or her ability. In the legal world, plaintiff's attorneys do their best to make the physician feel defeated from the onset of the lawsuit, beginning with the delivery of the original documents, known as the Summons and Complaint. This customarily happens in the physician's private office, where humiliation in front of colleagues, staff, and patients, and distraction from his or her work begins.

One physician reported the following:

> I was seeing patients in the morning, moving from one examination room to another, with patients in the waiting room when I was called to the reception area because I was being delivered legal

papers. In fact, I was being sued. It happened to be my birthday, and I couldn't help but think that the attorney was behind the decision to serve the papers on this particular day . . . not the day previous, nor the day following . . . but on the birthday. Some may say coincidence, but I am certain it was a ploy . . . just the start of further indignities to follow. Attorneys have no idea what it is like to be treated with such little disregard.[36]

Anguish is a part of the emotional experience of the physician from the moment a medical error or adverse outcome occurs to the lawsuit that may ultimately eventuate. If the situation results in litigation, what he or she may feel from the moment a process server delivers the legal documents is that he or she intentionally wronged someone. When faced with further legal papers, known as the Bill of Particulars, it will be difficult not to personalize the allegations. The now defendant physician will be confronted with such language as this:

Defendant Doctor, by his agents, servants, and/or employees was careless, reckless, and negligent in causing, permitting and/or allowing acts of professional negligence to occur; in failing and neglecting to properly and promptly treat, care for and diagnose the condition of the plaintiff, particularly with regard to. . . .

In lacking that degree of skill, care and competence which defendant held himself out as to possessing and upon which the plaintiff relied.[37]

Medicine is an art and a science; where human beings are involved, errors will happen. It is hoped that medical errors can be appreciably reduced and, ideally, recognized and corrected before they harm a patient. The statistics of medical mistakes occurring on an annual basis is staggering and tragic, but does this justify the demonization of our physicians, almost all of whom are devoted members of an honorable profession? Physicians regularly report that their fear of litigation is eroding the current state of the physician–patient relationship. Society cannot function without doctors; physicians are essential for the maintenance of each and every individual's health and to battle illness that may surface.[35]

Let us consider two cases in which a legal action for medical malpractice was instituted. This chapter opened with the first case, involving the retained foreign body, where a negligent error had undoubtedly occurred. In our second case, the physician believed that no error had been committed and that the undesirable outcome was the result of the natural course of the patient's illness.

The surgeon in the retained foreign body case, prior to any legal action occurring, commented:

I know that once an action is instituted against a physician, the legal advice is to not discuss the case with anyone, especially the patient; however, when an obvious error has been committed, before there is any legal involvement, in the immediate aftermath of the event, it is the physician's duty to inform the patient of the facts and to admit the error. An apology and most sincere expression of regret is appropriate, but a mea culpa should be avoided. We ought not additionally burden the patient with our own guilt.[1]

The surgeon reported that in the case of Mr. Feldner both the patient and family were understanding and forgiving, saying, "We know you did the best you could." There was anger directed at the nurses for the incorrect count. As the leader of that operating room team, the surgeon felt uncomfortable with the blame's being placed entirely on the nurses:

Multiple backup systems are required for the delivery of safe care. A surgeon cannot become solely reliant on a correct count. Before closing, regardless of the count, standard, accepted good surgical practice requires that a thorough examination of the abdominal cavity (sometimes with X-ray assistance) be performed. When combined with the nurses' count, the possibility of a retained foreign body should be eliminated, and if such an event occurs, it represents a truly preventable error.[1]

The surgeon advised that Mr. Feldner be re-operated on at once, and both the patient and his family wanted him to perform the surgery. At laparotomy, a gangrenous loop of jejunum was found herniated through the ring of the retained laparotomy pad.

The physician continued:

Unfortunately, his course was long and complicated. . . . Three additional surgeries were required . . . including a tracheostomy. . . . he was hospitalized for months. A medical malpractice action was instituted against me, and as stinging as that was . . . and it hurts all these years later to discuss it, I think it is understandable to agree that this patient deserved compensation. The case settled in the moderate range.

Charles believes that the tort system is about compensation, not competence.[35] In the retained foreign body case, the surgeon believed that his patient certainly deserved compensation:

My patient endured unimaginable suffering, really at my hands, and fairly compensating him was the right thing to do. The lawsuit did hurt . . . another blow to take when I didn't think I could feel much worse about his pain . . . and about the complete and total upheaval to his life. I really have to say I tried not to personalize this lawsuit. Recognizing that he deserved compensation and not to be victimized any further . . . helped me to feel less of a victim as well.[1]

The second case involves a pediatric surgeon. He described that after enduring six years of torment his lawsuit culminated in a two-week trial. The physician and his defense team had confidence that the case would be won. What he faced was a trial filled with confusion, showmanship, and persuasiveness to a lay jury that he believed understood little or nothing about this rare, complicated case of a child born with congenital anomalies of the gastrointestinal tract.[38]

> It was the most frustrating experience in the court in which the decision and impression that the jury got was somewhat biased and influenced by the overwhelming personality, drive, and charisma of the plaintiff's attorney. I believe the way he conducted the case was very efficient; I don't believe it was clinically and scientifically accurate . . . but I was told many times by the attorneys this is not a matter of the truth but a matter of perception. This disturbed me tremendously.[38]

Charles reports that there are multiple perspectives, from physicians and attorneys, of the same situation, in every lawsuit.[35] She shares wisdom that has been passed onto her that very good attorneys warn "the truth may or may not eventually come out" in each claim.[39] A difficult concept to hear and likely harder for Charles to voice follows: "For those of us who have read depositions and have been on trial, one of the most disappointing, and sometimes shocking, discoveries comes from the participants who, from our perspective, under oath, distort or completely violate the truth. It is more philosophical than cynical to face the hard reality that as much as we want and need the full truth to surface we may have to settle for less than that."[39]

The physician went on to describe his experience:

> It was with great drama that the small child was brought into the courtroom, shirt ripped off to display, for all to see, the abdominal disfigurement. An inescapable reminder of a surgery intended to heal the youngster, but to the jury, this sympathetic suffering little figure triggered a response that someone would need to pay. Yes, that someone would be the surgeon.
>
> The plaintiff's attorney, in my case, was denigrating and looked for every possible kink in one's armor . . . to really insult one from

beginning to end, not really giving one the opportunity to answer. It was really the most frustrating situation that one could imagine.[38]

He went on to say this:

> It overtook every minute of my thinking process. It was very dis-
> ruptive. It had a tremendous impact on one's confidence, one's sur-
> gery . . . in one's self. My every waking moment, my every thought
> was about this case. The frustration was enormous. I haven't got-
> ten back on track yet. Everything was put on hold, postponed until
> there was some resolve to it all. Settlement, not vindication, was
> the resolution, but it was either settle or gamble on the jury com-
> ing back with a verdict fifteen times the amount of the settlement.
> Who can afford to take that kind of risk? So we settled.[38]

Returning to one of the many fundamental truths proposed by Charles, is it that the tort system is about compensation, not competence? What about when competent care was rendered and compensation is still sought? "The goal of any lawsuit is to obtain compensation, and in many cases the hope of the plaintiff's attorney is that the outcome is so tragic, that the events that lead to the outcome are sufficiently murky or complex, or that the jury becomes so sympathetic to the insured patient that, regardless of the facts, the provision of compensation will seem inevitable and irresistible. This understanding of the real world purpose of tort law allows many physicians to interpret their involvement in litigation as just part of doing business."[39]

Why must you have to settle at all? At this point, the tort system is the only system that physicians have when they are faced with a medical malpractice lawsuit. It may be a system that physicians believe does not seem to work fairly, that justice has not been served, and that the physician is left feeling exposed without having been given "his or her day in court." The physician feels that his or her reputation remains clouded by the experience and that the obsessiveness so ever present throughout the entire litigation process seems to know no end.

There has been much written about the anatomy of a lawsuit and prepar-ing for litigation, and it will be necessary for the physician faced with a law-suit, with the guidance of his or her attorney, to become well versed in this area. This is where any perfectionistic tendencies the physician may possess will be most useful in the preparation for the legal process ahead.

The lifespan of a lawsuit ranges over multiple years. As was described in the pediatric case, the physician's "torment" lasted six years. Physicians can be lulled into a sense of false security during extended periods of silence; with activity in the suit, there can be a rush of emotion, as if the physician had just been sued that very day. Regardless of whether the physician's suit is dismissed, settled, or goes to trial, there is no escaping the pain of being sued. One physician on winning a suit after a 3-week trial exclaimed, "It was not a victorious feeling, and somehow I thought it would be."

The final section of this chapter explores how to handle the disturbing emotions erupted by litigation and how to continue to manage one's life when faced with a lawsuit. According to Charles, being named in a lawsuit can result in a plethora of feelings; it can become a rage that feels hard to contain—directed at all involved—from the patient to the attorneys to the system itself.[35] She cautions physicians, however, not to allow the rage to become all consuming and drain the physician of his energies and multitude of strengths.[35] A final comment from our pediatric surgeon:

> I was in a stadium once and looked out at the thousands of people around me and thought to myself I have operated on about this many people during my career. That is how I have spent my life. I have had a wonderful career of taking sick babies and sick children and making them well. This horrendous lawsuit and court experience will not knock me down.
>
> But really it isn't "how you fall that matters but how you get up." And that is the position I am in now. This will actually change me. I thought I had always been an extremely cautious and careful physician, but from now on, I will have to be even more so.[38]

# The Hope of a Just Culture

Harking back to the words of Sara Charles, "We find that protecting ourselves from legal actions may supersede healing our patients of their ills."[40] This suggestion emphasizes the need for a "just culture" in the practice of medicine and in the delivery of health care today. Marx, an engineer and human error management expert, is a leader today in the movement to change the culture in health care from a system that has historically blamed the individual when a patient has been harmed to one where errors can be freely discussed and examined and a just culture created. Removing the fear of punishment would prevent the concealment of errors and allow for their intensive investigation to prevent future recurrence.[41] We want to move away from a culture that prohibits human error to one that promotes learning from mistakes through a thorough, open examination of the causes of the error.[41]

Levinson and Dunn have noted in their article *Coping with Fallibility* that physicians are trained to analyze the medical components of a problem, finding out what went wrong.[42] Physicians have not been trained to investigate why errors happen just as they have not been prepared for the emotional impact mistakes will leave on them.

How are medical errors made? In his classic article, *Error in Medicine*, Leape, a pioneer in giving a voice to the long-avoided subject of medical error, addresses the multitude of reasons why errors occur.[43] Leape, in addressing the work of James Reason, a leading expert on error management, began to expose to the medical community the defects in cognitive processes humans share that allow errors to occur.

"Slips" and "mistakes" are specifically examined. Slips are "unconscious glitches" and mistakes result from "conscious thought."[44] Slips and mistakes are a part of life for all human beings, but they differ in their origin. Slips are attributed to both physiological and psychological reasons such as fatigue, busyness, insomnia, illness, stress, boredom, and myriad emotional states.[43]

Mistakes result from a lack of knowledge and are far more complex in their evolution. According to Leape, "Slips are most common, since much of our mental functioning is automatic, but the rate of error in knowledge-based processes [mistakes] is higher."[45]

> An automobile can be used as an example to illustrate the difference. If a person enters the car with the intention of stopping at the bank and then heading on to work and suddenly arrives at the office with the errand left undone, this would be a "slip" of consciousness. Contrast this with a car that will not start. The driver believes the battery to be dead, obtains some assistance, jumps the car, and it still does not start. Puzzled, the driver investigates further to discover an empty gas tank. Conscious thought in decision making was taking place in approaching the problem. This is a "mistake."

Leape addresses the many biases that exist that allow mistakes to occur— for example, the "confirmation bias," where one seeks out opinions of others only to confirm one's original impression and filters out that which does not fit the working hypothesis. Similar to the confirmation bias is the use of the "availability heuristic," which is the tendency to grab onto the first impression that comes to mind. Another hazard is the "memory bias," which allows decisions to be made based only from what is in one's memory.[43] The memory, however, is biased. If a physician has never seen a rare or atypical presentation of a disease, relying on memory will bring danger for both patient and doctor. Troublesome, the memory bias is supported by the old adage used in medical training: "If you hear hoof beats, don't look for zebras." Unrecognized, these biases result in faulty diagnoses.

The body of literature on why errors happen continues to grow. The absence of systems in place to stop an error from reaching the patient has gained much attention, and great successes can be achieved by attending to what Reason calls "the system approach."[46] Lessons can be drawn from the safe operation of "high reliability organizations" like aviation, aeronautics, and nuclear plants, where "The system approach concentrates on the conditions under which individuals work and tries to build defenses to avert errors or mitigate their effects."[46]

Successful teamwork is also associated with enhancing patient safety.[47] Although it is recognized that all members of the healthcare team must clearly communicate for the delivery of safe patient care, healthcare teams do not always function effectively.

To quote Salas and his research team:

> Although each clinician has extensive skills in his or her own specialization, it is the coordination among those skills that make the quality of the patient's treatment a seamless success. Communication across multiple units, physicians, nurses, and others becomes vital to ensuring that accurate and complete information is available, properly exchanged, and regularly updated.[48]

Revisiting the concept of "just culture," within the healthcare team, there needs to be openness for the discussion of errors that occur and a nonblaming environment that supports investigating such errors to diminish the chance of recurrence. Managing medical errors in a nonpunitive environment will both improve patient safety and diminish the emotional trauma for physicians should an error occur.

# Return to Normalcy

Although seemingly unimaginable at the time, after a medical error, the life of the physician will once again resume a state of normalcy. The devastating emotions initially experienced will fade as the physician begins to regain his or her lost confidence. How does this happen? The physician must:

> Remember, you are a member of an ancient and honorable profession and have worked hard to be a worthy member of that profession.[49]

It is within himself or herself that the distraught physician must find the answers to the emotional crisis that erupts when faced with a medical error. Physicians must have a strong conscience—born out of an emotional maturity and an awareness of the realities of medical practice. Most physicians decide early in their lives that they wish to join the "noble profession" of medicine. They want to help people, and they believe that if they are conscientious and diligent they will be able to do so. During medical training, however, no mentor ever warns them that they are human beings, that systems are not perfect, and that one day they will suffer the tortures of the damned as they make mistakes and harm those they meant to heal. Certainly such a warning would not deter many from their chosen path. They believe that they will not err, and should they do so, they will be strong enough to face the consequences of their actions. It is heartening for society that there are so many optimistic young men and women who are not deterred by the likely torments of medical practice. Enrollment in medical education continues to be strong—fortunately, or there would be no physicians.

An effective support system is needed to allow the physician's life to resume a rhythm of normalcy. If the physician is doubtful that the support in his or her life is adequate, more supportive outlets must be established. For some physicians, this is met within the home with the support of a loving spouse and family; for others, this may mean turning to trusted friends or just that one essential confidant. The compassion and understanding of trusted others are of incomparable value.

In order to maintain a healthy perspective, a balance must be sustained in the physician's life. To quote Freud: Love and work are the cornerstones of our humanness. When a professional problem, such as a medical error, has pierced the physician to his or her very soul, then the love of family, friends, interests, and life becomes crucial.

A spiritual healing process must occur, and confidential discussions with leaders of one's faith may bring immeasurable relief.

Availing oneself of the emotional support offered by a professional therapist may bring relief to the physician and ease his or her suffering. Cognitive therapy is particularly advantageous in assisting the physician to examine how he or she perceives the event. A doomed perception that "the sky is falling" will lead to a depressed mood; learning to give less power to the emotional impact of the error as taking over the physician's life will result in an improved state of mind.

Discussions of errors and their consequences with colleagues frequently offer some consolation. They may often admit to having made such errors themselves or just barely to have avoided them. They can reassure the physician of his or her value and that they would not hesitate to have him or her care for them and their families.

In situations in which the error has resulted in legal action against the physician, a defense attorney will be another source of support for the physician. The attorney is there to prepare the physician's defense, to help the doctor navigate through the legal system, and to be his or her confidant.

The reality is that there are many hundreds of patients who are helped for each one who is inadvertently harmed. When placed on the balance beam, the good that physicians do so heavily outweighs unintended harmful actions that there is certainly no contest. This is the answer to the need to atone, to be forgiven, and especially to make restitution. How can restitution be made for the patient who has been injured? The monetary compensations afforded by the law help, but little.

The real restitution must be made by caring for the thousands of sick people who need medical care, and the true tragedy would be to give up the practice of medicine and walk away. It is highly likely that other mistakes will occur, and the guilt that the physician will feel for the consequences of his or her actions may remain with him or her to the end of his or her days. It is a heavy burden that physicians must bear, but after all, that is why medicine is a noble profession.

## REFERENCES

1. Anonymous. Interview with the author (GMD). June 26, 2007.
2. Kohn LT, Corrigan JM, Donaldson MS, eds. Institute of Medicine. *To Err Is Human: Building a Safer Health System.* Washington, DC: National Academics Press; 1999.
3. Leape LL, Berwick DM. Five years after to err is human: what have we learned? *JAMA.* 2005;293(19):2384.
4. Wu AW. Medical error: the second victim. *BMJ.* 2000;320(7237):726.
5. Aguilera, DC. *Crisis Intervention: Theory and Methodology.* 8th ed. St. Louis, MO: Mosby; 1998.
6. Composite case derived from closed PRI medical malpractice case.
7. Anonymous. Interview with the author (GMD). July 1, 2007.
8. Christensen JF, Levinson W, Dunn PM. The heart of darkness: the impact of perceived mistakes on physicians. *J Gen Intern Med.* 1992;7(4):427.
9. Merriam-Webster Online Dictionary. Available at: http://www.merriam-webster.com, accessed October 23, 2007.
10. Paget MA. *The Unity of Mistakes: A Phenomenological Interpretation of Medical Work.* Philadelphia, PA: Temple University Press; 2004:3–4.
11. Paget MA. *The Unity of Mistakes: A Phenomenological Interpretation of Medical Work.* Philadelphia, PA: Temple University Press; 2004:12.
12. Hilfiker D. *Healing the Wounds: A Physician Looks at His Work.* New York, NY: Pantheon Books; 1985:82–83.
13. Blackwell B. Physician lifestyle and medical marriages. *Wis Med J.* 1982;81:23.
14. Gabbard GO. The role of compulsiveness in the normal physician. *JAMA.* 1985: 254(20):2927.
15. Gabbard GO. The role of compulsiveness in the normal physician. *JAMA.* 1985: 254(20):2926–2929.
16. Gabbard GO. The role of compulsiveness in the normal physician. *JAMA.* 1985: 254(20):2929.
17. Christensen JF, Levinson W, Dunn PM. The heart of darkness: the impact of perceived mistakes on physicians. *J Gen Intern Med.* 1992;7(4):426.
18. Christensen JF, Levinson W, Dunn PM. The heart of darkness: the impact of perceived mistakes on physicians. *J Gen Intern Med.* 1992;7(4):424.

19. Kennedy EM, Heard SR. Making mistakes in practice: developing a consensus statement. *Aust Fam Physician.* 2001;30(3):295–299.
20. Kübler-Ross E. *On Death and Dying: What the Dying Have to Teach Doctors, Nurses, Clergy and Their Own Families.* New York, NY: Scribner; 2003.
21. Kübler-Ross E. *On Death and Dying: What the Dying Have to Teach Doctors, Nurses, Clergy and Their Own Families.* New York, NY: Scribner; 2003:16–18.
22. Kübler-Ross E. *On Death and Dying: What the Dying Have to Teach Doctors, Nurses, Clergy and Their Own Families.* New York, NY: Scribner; 2003:18.
23. Lansky MR, Morrison AP, eds. *The Widening Scope of Shame.* Hillsdale, NJ: The Analytic Press; 1997:82.
24. Christensen JF, Levinson W, Dunn PM. The heart of darkness: the impact of perceived mistakes on physicians. *J Gen Intern Med.* 1992;7(4):424–431.
25. Bennet G. *The Wound and the Doctor: Healing, Technology and Power in Modern Medicine.* London, England: Secker & Warburg; 1987.
26. Hilfiker D. *Healing the Wounds: A Physician Looks at His Work.* New York, NY: Pantheon Books; 1985.
27. Bennet G. *The Wound and the Doctor: Healing, Technology and Power in Modern Medicine.* London, England: Secker & Warburg; 1987:206.
28. Bennet G. *The Wound and the Doctor: Healing, Technology and Power in Modern Medicine.* London, England: Secker & Warburg; 1987:219.
29. Bennet G. *The Wound and the Doctor: Healing, Technology and Power in Modern Medicine.* London, England: Secker & Warburg; 1987:220.
30. Schernhammer E. Taking their own lives: the high rate of physician suicide. *N Engl J Med.* 2005;352(24):2473–2476.
31. Hilfiker D. *Healing the Wounds: A Physician Looks at His Work.* New York, NY: Pantheon Books; 1985:76.
32. Newman MC. The emotional impact of mistakes on family physicians. *Arch Fam Med.* 1996;5(2):71–72.
33. Charles SC, Frisch PR. *Adverse Events, Stress, and Litigation: A Physician's Guide.* New York, NY: Oxford University Press; 2005:211.
34. Physician Insurers Association of America. *Risk Management Review: Comparative Claim Payment Analysis. Claims closed in 2005.* Rockville, MD: PIAA; 2005: Exhibit 3.
35. Charles SC, Frisch PR. *Adverse Events, Stress, and Litigation: A Physician's Guide.* New York, NY: Oxford University Press; 2005.
36. Anonymous. Interview with the author (GMD). May 4, 2007.
37. Excerpt from a Bill of Particulars from a closed PRI medical malpractice case.
38. Anonymous. Interview with the author (GMD). August 3, 2007.
39. Charles SC, Frisch PR. *Adverse Events, Stress, and Litigation: A Physician's Guide.* New York, NY: Oxford University Press; 2005:134.
40. Charles SC, Frisch PR. *Adverse Events, Stress, and Litigation: A Physician's Guide.* New York, NY: Oxford University Press; 2005:211.
41. Marx D. *Patient Safety and the "Just Culture": A Primer for Health Care Executives.* New York, NY: Trustees of Columbia University; 2001. Available at: http://www.mers-tm.net/support/marx_primer.pdf, accessed October 23, 2007.
42. Levinson W, Dunn PM. A piece of my mind: coping with fallibility. *JAMA.* 1989;261(15):2252.

43. Leape LL. Error in medicine. *JAMA*. 1994;272(23):1851–1857.

44. Leape LL. Error in medicine. *JAMA*. 1994;272(23):1853.

45. Leape LL. Error in medicine. *JAMA*. 1994;272(23):1854.

46. Reason J. Human error: models and management. *BMJ*. 2000;320:768.

47. Sales E, Sims D, Burke S. Can teamwork enhance patient safety? *Forum-Risk Manage Found Harv Med Inst*. 2003;23(3):5–9.

48. Sales E, Sims D, Burke S. Can teamwork enhance patient safety? *Forum-Risk Management Foundation of the Harvard Medical Institutions*. 2003;23(3):5.

49. McCandless HC. A survival kit for physicians: back to the basics. *Postgrad Med*. 1994;96(7):62.

# Chapter 15

# Narrative Medicine: Healing the Divides

Rita Charon

*Bearing witness to a trauma is, in fact, a process that includes the listener. For the tesimonial process to take place, there needs to be a bonding, the intimate and total presence of an* other—*in the position of one who hears. Testimonies are not monologues; they cannot take place in solitude. The [patients] are talking to* somebody, *to somebody they have been waiting for a long time.*

Dori Laub, MD

A giant bouquet of red and yellow flowers greeted me in the clinic. The card read, "A million thanks for all you've done for me." My patient had come the week before, on my invitation, to present to a group of healthcare executives who wanted to learn about patient education. An hour early she had arrived (her nerves were terrible, she told me), dressed beautifully in a black dress and stockings and heels. She had presided at this high-powered executive conference, telling eloquently of her struggles against asthma and arthritis and diabetes, her son's violent death on the streets as a young man, her daughter's trouble with the law, her raising her grandchildren on her own, and then with great dignity and pride, she told of getting off welfare into job training and finally into a responsible full-time position as a security officer in a big municipal concern. Did I ever feel proud as she explained how not only does she manage her own diabetes, but glucometer in hand, she monitors the sugars and diets of half her security co-workers.

How did we get here, I mused as I gazed at the roses and lilies, to be able to receive so much from one another? I only watched with awe as she surmounted challenge after challenge; then she says how much, all of this time, it meant for her to feel me right there beside her. *This* is what the life is for. This is what *life* is for.

L ives of doctors and their patients are unusually and brazenly intertwined. Little do patients know how their doctors brood about them, dream about them, take sustenance from their triumphs, and despair from their inevitable declines, and little do doctors know what space they occupy in the lives of their patients. Doctors expect that detachment—or at best, *aequanimitas*—will govern their relationships with patients. They are cautioned in medical school against getting overattached to patients. "I was told I spend too much time talking with patients," says gifted student after gifted student, warned against the very actions that may well lead to sturdy therapeutic alliances and effective care. Nevertheless, patients describe these doctors who take the time to talk and listen as the trusted ones, the helpful ones, the ones who make a difference in illness, whereas those who stand apart are seen as, at best, absent and, at worst, offensive.[1]

Doctors and patients are thrown by illness into unimaginable intimacies. We touch people physically, of course, in ways that no one else but their parents or lovers have permission to do. We hear their secrets and have to learn what to do with them. Those of us who make house calls enjoy the peculiar familiarity of being a guest in the patient's home, of seeing the patterns of life and heart visible in the clutter in the kitchen or the photos on the piano. At times of birth or loss or death, we are allowed entrance into dramas of unutterable gravity and privacy. Never simply passive observers, we are assigned purposeful and consequential roles in these dramas, our own power and significance in others' lives often overwhelming and always deeply meaningful to us.

My vignette seems to be a modest enough story—a young woman with chronic illnesses and a difficult social situation somehow betters her life with education and hard work. As her doctor, I feel privileged to witness these changes in her life and to have felt a part of them. Those who are not doctors might have a hard time understanding how the primary care internist can derive such joy and satisfaction in caring for this patient—none of her progress was my doing, for sure, and my every-few-month visits with her to manage her chronic illnesses could not have been too significant in her choices and successes. Nonetheless, such steady revolutions in individuals' lives are thrilling to us. As quiet but at times powerful companions in our patients' lives, the doctors get a profound view, an insider's view, of the matter of life. Even in the absence of dramatic cures or drastic changes in health, these medical companionships that see patients through the long haul of life are the nourishing and vitalizing and dazzling gifts we cherish.

The doctor I am for the woman I described previously here is the doctor I hope to be for all my patients—faithful, skillful, optimistic, available, supportive, and effective. As I wonder to myself how we got to be a good pair, I see that we are transparent to each other. We need not hide fears or disappointments or pressure from each other, knowing we can tolerate each other's feelings. She gets mad at me sometimes when it takes me too long to return her phone calls, for example, and our relationship can weather her anger. We are curious about each other and find each other interesting. I once requisitioned all volumes of her Presbyterian Hospital medical chart so as to see fully her health trajectory. When my handwriting appeared in the chart in the early 1980s, I was reminded of myself as a naïve trainee, so green, so clueless, and yet quite impressionable and, therefore, available to her as partner. We *moved* together through the years, which is to say, something happened between us. St. Augustine describes his conversations as building a tactile bridge between himself and his listeners: "The word in my mind exists before it is put into language. I search for the right sound to carry it abroad. I need a way for it to reach you without leaving me. And even now you are hearing what I have in my heart, and it is in yours. It is in both of us, and you are now possessing it without my losing it."[2] My relationship with this patient feels palpable to me in this way, as if we are attached somehow, not only on the same wavelength but *tied* to each other permanently. Our relationship changes with time, and as it accrues history, it deepens and develops fresh meaning. We both feel beholden to and dutiful toward each other, as she helps me in my teaching and I help her in managing her medical conditions.

# Routine Practice

All dutiful doctors reach toward effective care in practice, accruing CME, attending clinical rounds, scouring cyberspace for data that will help us to reach good clinical decisions for each patient. We base our actions on evidence, knowing full well how little we know about health and illness. We dream, often with terror, about our patients, aware as nondoctors are not of how badly things can go in a body, how unthinkably bad the suffering can be of end-stage pancreatic cancer or the pulmonary death. Because we have been dutiful students of our sciences, we have taken the measure of the uncertainty that surrounds the simplest medical treatments, the risks they entail, the modesty of their capacity to help. We have taken the measure of the savagery of disease—the random unfair occurrence of leukemia in the bloom of a young father's life, the dementia come early to the scholar whose book will lie unfinished, the pulmonary fibrosis that outpaces our efforts to transplant the damaged lungs.

Doctors, by definition, *know* more about the illness and its future than do the patients. There is, therefore, a chasm between what the doctor can envision and what the patient can envision as they stand at the threshold of a serious illness. It is a chasm dictated by the difference between them in health, knowledge, experience, and responsibility. One of the two is sick, and one of the two is well. One of the two is blind to the future, and one of the two can see it whole. One of the two will suffer pain and illness, and one of the two will suffer uncertainty and defeat. These dual sufferings usually unfold in parallel, one encapsulated away from the other. Indeed, it would be seen as a professional lapse, would it not, for the physician to confess to the patient how much he or she suffers the illness of the patient?

We feel the tension between supportive optimism and the need to disclose what the road to be traveled might be like—the pain of end-stage prostate cancer, the exhaustion of chemotherapy and radiation, the toll of long-term dialysis, the nihilism of dementia. In addition, because we are the ones, often, discovering and *telling* the patient the horrible news, we are gripped by our own sense of culpability. Should I have done an abdominal CT scan when he first developed that belly ache? Why didn't I send her to the cardiologist when she first felt dizzy instead of waiting to get the Holter? We never feel *in* the situation with the patient because of how much more we know than he or she does and how much less we know than we would wish.

We are usually separated from our patients by the roles we must play, and we are certainly not equipped by our training to imagine patients' situations or to try to experience their illnesses from their side of the chasm. Instead, we are encouraged to *stay* on our side of the chasm—exerting our professional authority, our decorum, our effacement in the face of their suffering. The intern writes in the chart, "80 mg of lasix was pushed" and not "I gave her 80 mg of lasix IV." We grow up in medicine thinking there is something forbidden in this world about the "I." The students who are admonished not to get too close to their patients are absorbing the received wisdom of centuries of clinical practice. "The patient," as it is written in Law Number IV of the House of God, "is the one with the disease."[3]

Nevertheless, we all know how we suffer the illnesses of our patients. Reading Sir William Osler's "Aequanimitas" over and over will not convince a doctor that he or she must always practice, as Osler suggests, with imperturbability. "Imperturbability means coolness and presence of mind under all circumstances, calmness amid storm, clearness of judgment in moments of grave peril, immobility, impassiveness, or, to use an old and expressive word, *phlegm*. It is the quality that is most appreciated by the laity though often misunderstood by them."[4]

There are many times when exactly this quality of mind is called for in the practice of a doctor; there are also many times when its opposite is called for. The current emphasis in medical practice and education on humanism, communication, and professionalism highlights the importance of mutual and supportive relationships within health care.[5] Patients and their doctors are joining to call for engaged practice, empathic care, and individualized recognition of one another's plight.[6] This kind of practice may indeed become not only more effective for patients and more rewarding for physicians; it may also prove to be a protective practice, able to guard physicians against unwarranted malpractice suits. If patients desire this kind of connection with their doctors *even in the face of medical error*, then it becomes urgent for us to know how to form these connections with patients, how to imagine what our patients endure in illness, how to express our investment in their future, and how to accompany them through all that sickness brings. These clinical skills are essential both to practice effectively and to avoid being sued and can be developed with the methods of narrative medicine.

# The Nature of Narrative Medicine

The features of my work with my patient described previously here—transparency, singularity, curiosity, development in time, mutuality, duty—are aspects of what I have come to call narrative medicine.[7] Early in my practice, I realized that I was being paid by my patients to be a skilled listener and interpreter of their stories. I knew somehow that such aspects of life and relationships as transparency and singularity and development in time—aspects of my budding relationships with these patients newly in my clinical hands—were the backbone of and maybe the *reason* for the telling of stories. Knowing little of how stories are actually structured or what happens when one tells or listens to one, I went timidly to the English department to see whether they could help me learn about them. What I learned about how narratives work indeed, I believe, has made me a better doctor.

Stories, I now understand, are complex structures with many discoverable levels of meaning built into their words and forms and allusions and images. I learned not only how stories are built but how their tellers and listeners become engaged with one another in the processes of narrating. As I have gotten to be a better reader of literary texts, I have, by virtue of the same skills, gotten to be a better listener to the stories of illness my patients tell me in the office. I think I have begun to learn how to *honor* my patient's stories, that is to say, how to get the news from their stories; how to absorb all that they convey in words, actions, silences, gestures, tones of voice, and facial expressions; how to imagine the tellers' situation from their point of view; and how to participate fully in the processes of narrating that hold members of a story together. Perhaps what I am learning is how, like Augustine's listeners, to walk across the bridges my tellers construct with their words.

My colleagues and I define narrative medicine as medicine practiced with narrative competence—the capacities to recognize, absorb, metabolize, and interpret stories and to be moved to action by them on behalf of their tellers.[8] Narrative competence lets doctors *hear* patients, not only the words they say but the messages they convey. The narratively trained doctor has an awakened imagination, and he or she can use it to picture the situation of the patient—who is with the patient at home? What pressures besides health problems are on his or her mind? What might interfere with the patient taking medication or showing up for treatment? What is at stake in this situation? Why does this health problem *matter* for the patient? What can I do to help this person? Because it is based on a wider base of attention, narrative medicine captures many aspects of life altered by sickness, both in the patients' lives and in the doctors' lives. This heightened attention gives power to the doctor and the patient because they come to recognize and embrace all that being sick means and all that taking care of the sick might call for. Narrative methods help the doctor and patient to understand themselves as a dyad. Like the example from my practice described previously here, the doctor and patient can say to each other: What is she to me? What might I be to her? These questions set the stage for honest appraisal and then powerful *use* of the healing connections between human beings.

Medical schools, nursing and social work schools, hospitals, managed care plans, and even healthcare corporations are adopting our theories and practices as useful ways to teach the very hard-to-learn skills of practice—attention, recognition, empathy, respect, and affiliation. By teaching clinicians and students the narrative skills of close reading, reflective writing, and attentive listening, we are able to help them to develop such skills as cultural sensitivity, ethical discernment, conflict mediation, and engaged and reflective practice.[9] More simply put, narrative training can help doctors to imagine what their patients go through, revealing to them until then unimaginable means to be of help.

Narratively competent practice reveals what clinicians experience in caring for the ill, as well as what their patients endure. Writing about practice enables clinicians to express and accept their own deep suffering as they witness decline and death of patients in what feels like chronic defeat. Doctors live their lives around sadness and loss, and genuine practice opens the doctor to painful and chronic feelings of grief and guilt and sorrow (as well as other damaging feelings such as rage, boredom, revulsion, or the exhaustion of feeling altogether). By accepting these deep feelings instead of trying to shield against them, doctors can come near to their own patients, for the feelings of sorrow and loss can be bridges that join these two suffering human beings. Recall the notion of parallel play from child psychology, in which infants who are too immature to relate to one another play side-by-side in unconnected play. As they mature, they accrue the relational skills to allow genuine, shared play. It is the same for doctors and patients. We engage in parallel suffering, isolated from one another by a lack of skill to connect but suffering terribly on our own. With the skill to reach each other, doctor and patient need not suffer alone in parallel. Instead, after the suffering is joined—by words, by acknowledgment, by recognition—the total amount of suffering declines.

By now, our narrative medicine training workshops have attracted doctors of many specialties, nurses, social workers, chaplains, psychoanalysts, physical therapists, literary scholars, and writers from the United States, Canada, Europe, Asia, Australia, the United Kingdom, and South America. New programs in narrative medicine bloom when our trainees return to their home institutions, giving us reason to believe that these methods and theories speak to *lacks* currently experienced in clinical training and healthcare practice worldwide.

Clinicians who have worked with us at our Narrative Medicine workshops have come to practice their medicine or surgery differently as a result of this new discipline. Obstetrician-gynecologist Lori Linell Hall gave up her practice of reproductive medicine at a prominent academic medical center in the Southeast. She describes the debilitating burnout that forced her from practice: "I longed to lead a normal life, to not be on call and carry a pager, but have every weekend off . . . to not have to think about or worry about being sued, to not have to deliver bad news to patients . . . or to be attacked and lied about in a deposition."[10] Dr. Hall found that reading literature and writing poetry enabled her to return to her love for medical practice and her resumption of an obstetrics and gynecology practice. She was grateful to have found the narrative medicine community of healthcare professionals who, like her, had discovered the restorative and centering powers of a narrative practice. Emotional scars such as Dr. Hall's are evident throughout medical practice, for both doctors and patients. Israeli family physician Shmuel Reis writes about how the scars he shares with his patients, from their experiences of the Holocaust, join them in the act of bearing witness to suffering. When he attended our workshop, he helped all of us to understand the place of mutually witnessing and receiving testimony of trauma in our practices, whether our patients had suffered cataclysmic traumas or more private ones.[11]

Pediatrician Sayantani DasGupta, a member of the Core Faculty in Narrative Medicine at Columbia, has written eloquently about the goals of mindful and reflective practice, introducing the concept of "narrative humility" achieved through narrative means.[12] DasGupta finds that the care of children in particular requires these narrative approaches so as to *hear* even the child who cannot yet talk and, by extension, all our patients who, because of disease or disability, are prevented from voicing their concerns directly. Not only patients but clinicians need help in articulating their thoughts and needs. A team of clinicians and educators from Summa Health Systems in Ohio, including a social scientist, a nurse, an educator, and a physician/executive, are publishing a book entitled *Narrative in Health Care: Healing Patients, Practitioners, Profession and Community* that brings the concepts and methods of narrative forms of clinical practice to a broad audience of healthcare professionals in the United States and abroad.[13] When they studied with us, they modeled the teamwork essential for narrative practice, enacting the dividends of interdisciplinary collaboration as co-authors and also as colleagues who can *hear* one another out as they accompany one another on a search for meaning in practice.

These four examples can represent the collective professional experiences of clinicians and educators who are developing the methods of narrative medicine. Together, we are learning what skills clinicians need in order to reach patients, to understand their situations, and to provide health care leavened with respect and tendered with engagement. We are also learning how to equip clinicians with the skills to trace systematically and bravely their own personal development, for representing their interior experiences as they care for the sick enables them to tolerate and then to invite engagement with their patients. Across these disciplinary and geographic boundaries, healthcare professionals from all over the world are using narrative methods to form muscular and powerful clinical relationships that recognize patients and nourish clinicians.

# Narrative Medicine and Medical Error

How can these sturdy clinical relationships protect doctors from being sued or help after legal action has been inaugurated? I do not wish to focus here on egregious examples of negligence, which indeed *ought* to be litigated, but instead on the situations of unforeseen injury, or situations in which patients blame their doctors for inevitable disease. Patients seem to expect medicine to be more powerful than it is, and doctors automatically blame themselves when their patients get sick. The result, as this book outlines, is a rise in malpractice suits even in the absence of documentable negligence or mistreatment. We know by now that the most common reasons that patients sue their primary care physicians are not doctors' technical lapses but their interpersonal lapses.[14] Even in the face of serious injury, patients value disclosures from their doctors about what happened, why it happened, what the consequences of the error are, and how recurrences can be prevented. In addition, they seek emotional support from their physicians in the context of error, including, but not limited to, apology for the error.[15]

Narratively competent practice—a practice marked by attention, reflection, engagement, and the ability to adopt the perspective of patients and their families—is coming into view as not only effective but also protective practice. The literature suggests that patients want their doctors to listen to them, to recognize them individually, to show some investment in their well-being, and to value working with them.[16] When injury or error has occurred, patients suffer abandonment and isolation as doctors and nurses turn away from them defensively. Patients and their families, like the clinicians, experience profound feelings of guilt when care goes wrong. Those who suffer the injury not only value honesty and truth telling but also yearn for the deep elements of authentic connection—recognition, shared understanding, and forgiveness.[17] The suffering that occurs around medical error or injury is no different from the suffering that surrounds sickness in general. Both patients and their doctors suffer terribly, but they suffer apart. If doctors and patients can escape the isolating parallel suffering they endure, in the face of injury and error as well as in routine practice, they can join in mutual disclosure and forgiveness, reawakening trust and again being able to heal.

I am suggesting deep changes in practice, as I hope is clear. To replace isolating and blaming parallel suffering with shared sorrow is not something one does after one's lawyer calls with bad news. Instead, these narrative methods are fundamental to ongoing practice. These are not little post hoc solutions to be applied to messy situations after a patient has sued a doctor or after an injury has occurred. By then, there is little to be done to sustain or to strengthen the medical relationship so that it can weather the attack of legal action. Pressors won't work in the absence of volume; similarly, narrative methods won't fix a medical relationship savaged by a malpractice claim unless there is an underlying alliance to be acted on. However, a narrative practice can lead to long-term tonic and tectonic shifts in the ground of the relationships we develop and maintain with patients so that, should a claim be made, the doctor and the patient have the substrate of knowledge, trust, and regard between them to see them both through the ordeal.

# Narrative Bridges Between Doctor and Patient

Narrative methods of practice enable us to bridge the chasms between doctors and their patients. Fundamental and long-term changes in office and hospital routines can illuminate the patient's situation for the doctor so that the doctor is not in the dark about the patient's own form of suffering. These methods can also illuminate the doctor's interior, making visible and audible powerful but otherwise inaccessible stores of knowledge and affect that can help the relationships to succeed. Shmuel Reis's discovery of how trauma saturates his medical practice in Israel reminds all of us of our duty to bear witness to the suffering in our patients' lives, not only to fix certain aspects of the fixable but to confirm suffering's presence, to add our own sorrow to its inevitability, to mark the gravity, for the patient, of his or her losses and sorrows and scars. The following litany of narrative changes in my own practice of general internal medicine suggests, I hope, the kinds of alterations one might make in the day-in, day-out practice so that doctor and patient are neither strangers to each other nor strangers to themselves.

When I meet a new patient in the office these days, instead of launching into all of the questions of the History of Present Illness and the Past Medical History and the Social History, Family History, and Review of Systems, I say these two sentences: "I will be your doctor, and so I need to know a great deal about your body and your health and your life. Please tell me what you think I should know about your situation." I have learned to sit still after I say these two sentences, not to write or type, but to absorb all that the patient might emit. In words, silences, gestures, facial expressions, and tears, patients utter to me profound accounts of complex experiences. It is always a unique and singular blend of description of physical symptoms, prior medical care, family events, emotional states, childhood history, life background, work situation, loves, losses, fears, and triumphs.

I sit amazed to be privileged to be the witness of such moving and authentic narratives of self. I don't know how I practiced general internal medicine before having developed this routine. Instead of hearing fragmented bits of data solicited by my often disconnected questions, I hear a unified, eloquent statement of the events of illness framed within the events of life. As I listen to my patients tell of their situations, I can take in not only what has gone wrong with their bodies but how they live, who is meaningful to them, what gives them pleasure, what they look forward to, what they have lost, and what they could not live without. I write down a transcript of this account when the patient comes to a close (usually within 15 minutes of starting), not turning it into a medical write-up but trying my best to represent what was said. At the close of the medical visit, I give the patient a copy of the entire note, including this account. In this way, I can get a confirmation from the patient that I heard him or her accurately, and if I did not, I have the opportunity to correct the account destined for the medical chart.

This routine has led to other novel practices. I now give each patient his or her own "Patient-Held Medical Record." These records are sturdy, attractive binders of the same dimensions as a medical chart, within which patients keep all the notes I write about them and any laboratory results or radiology reports the patient might want to see. They often tuck into one of the pockets in the binder their logs of home glucose monitoring, blood pressure readings, or notes written to me by the visiting nurse or other physicians. Every time my patient comes in to see me, he or she will bring the Patient-Held Medical Record, which contains not only what I have written about the patient but also what the patient has written for me. For more and more of my patients now write about their situation for me—their actual experiences of a migraine headache, for example, or of a panic attack or an episode of insomnia.

One patient last week wrote a satirical account of getting her bone density scan. Called "Mr. White Coat," the story poked fun at the radiology technician who administered the scan. He apparently had acted brusquely and self-importantly, and by writing a cutting farce about the experience, my patient not only got the unpleasant experience off her chest but also had a pleasurable creative experience and entertained my colleagues and me in the process. She next wrote a very serious examination of family dynamics as grandparents age and find themselves more and more dependent on children and grandchildren. Such writing about health problems not only helps me to understand the patient/writer fully but also, independently, seems to help the patient to reflect on and therefore develop perspective on complex situations.

These narrative practices led me to realize how much goes on in the office and how little of it I am able to perceive and capture during any office visit. Thus, I initiated a Witness Project in my practice, inviting good observers to sit in with my patients and me in the office (of course, with the patient's permission) to represent what occurs in the visit. I explain to the patient that I cannot see and hear everything that happens in our office visit, and therefore, my witness will join us to take notes and share the notes with me. The notes my witnesses write are striking. Because I choose witnesses who are fine perceivers and able writers but not very experienced clinically (English major premedical students are ideal), the notes they write capture the human dimensions of our interactions without getting waylaid by clinical concerns. Reading the notes does two things for me: It reveals aspects of the patient that had escaped me, and it shows me things about my own behavior in the office that surprise me. In the witness notes, I see myself looking bored, acting rushed, taking calls or interruptions in the middle of visits, getting irritated at the patient (or at the computer!). All of these elements of the visit influence the work my patient and I are able to do together. Although humbled by many of the notes, I am deeply grateful for the vision and honesty of my witnesses, for on the basis of them, I have already significantly improved my practice routines.

Here are the notes written by my witness after a recent visit from the patient whose description begins this chapter. As the internist in this conversation, I had a somewhat different understanding of the proceedings, demonstrated by my scheduling a stress-thal at the close of the visit (which was completely normal):

> She holds herself with a regal bearing. . . . As she sits, she hugs herself around the belly with her arms, but then raises up her arms to stab the air with an index finger, marking her statements with a jab of emphasis. She has been taking care of herself, and Dr. Charon is clearly proud of her and mentions to me that the patient is managing the diabetes of half of her coworkers in the— security department. And she is not just a security guard—now she is an officer. She is planning on taking the sergeant's test soon. The only worrisome problem was a pain she was getting in her chest, near her shoulder. She has joined Curves and enjoys using the machines. . . . [W]e converse animatedly for a while about the benefits of a women-only gym. It's just not her style to go to those gyms that are like meat markets, with the girls all dressed in next-to-nothing. Curves is evidently treating her right—she radiates confidence as she says that she's eating less; when she comes home from the gym she is so pumped up and full of energy (even after working) that she is hardly hungry. The goal is to get to her officer's test weight, right? asks Dr. Charon, and the patient agrees with a grin. They are like an athlete and a coach, motivating and energizing each other, and it is heartening to see both a patient doing so well as well as a physician so cheered by her progress.

I appreciate the chance to see my patient in my office in this focus—not on the potential pathophysiology but on her vitality and our partnership. That my witness doesn't even mention the stress test interests me too, for I can see that I must have very much downplayed my own concerns about the significance of the chest pain—in this obese, hypertensive, diabetic! It may be that the witness experiences the visit more in line with the patient's perspective than the doctor's, and therefore, my dividend is not only to see the visit whole but to see it from closer to the patient's point of view than I would be able to attain on my own.

These are a few concrete examples of how narrative medicine has influenced my own practice. Clinicians who have joined us for narrative training have developed their own methods, within diverse practices, for harnessing narrative knowledge of their patients. Neonatologists in the NICU or geriatricians in long-term care facilities will develop different methods to reach their patients and the patients' families with narrative knowledge. Emergency medicine physicians or hospitalists will employ methods of different tempos for establishing narratively rich connections with strangers who are bound to endure dramatic and intense events in telescoped time periods. Rural physicians who know all of their patients in "real" life in a small town will have a different ground of intimacy with persons in their care and will require methods tailored to their situation. I hope that my short description of changes within my hospital-based office practice of urban internal medicine suggests to readers some aspects of practice that are amenable to change within the realms of narrative practice.

Narrative practice also brings the doctor in closer relationship to his or her self. Unlike the changes within diverse practices, we find that the methods narrative medicine has developed to reveal doctors' interior knowledge and feelings toward patients are enduring and constant. The simple exercise of writing about one's practice and having readers with whom to share the writing has led consistently to deep levels of change within the self of the clinician. Many participants in narrative medicine training sessions develop deep commitments to *examining* their practice by writing about it and then reading aloud to colleagues what they have written and find ways to sustain this commitment over time. At Columbia, we have a growing number of writing seminars that meet in inpatient or outpatient settings regularly. On the adult inpatient oncology unit, the pediatric oncology unit, the AIDS/HIV clinic, the social work department, the family medicine inpatient service, even the pastoral care department, we meet with healthcare professionals to let them read aloud to one another what they have written about their practice.

The writing is always grave; the situations represented are always complex. I am no longer surprised to find the quality of the writing elevated and powerful. In responding to the writing as it is read aloud, I make sure to comment first on the textual aspects of the writing—a striking metaphor, the form of the writing, the similarity or dissimilarity to something written in the past by the same writer. What we are *after* in this kind of teaching is to equip the healthcare professionals with the tools of writing—the perceiving, representing, composing, and reflecting that go into any serious piece of writing. I do not care that they publish what they write or even become better as writers; what I care deeply about is that their process of representing clinical events helps them to perceive the events all the more strongly and completely.

The stories they write are, at one level, about their patients. They are also about themselves. Healthcare professionals have, of course, their mirroring stories to tell—of what they witness patients to endure in illness and of what they themselves go through in the care of the sick. After the healthcare professionals begin to tell seriously to one another—and to themselves—their own interior experiences of caring for the sick, they can genuinely undergo these complex experiences, metabolize them, let them become part of self. In the cultures of medicine, doctors' suffering seems relegated to sardonic humor stories or private psychotherapy sessions. Except for the few who join Balint groups, in which doctors talk with one another about their difficult cases, and except for the rushed dinnertime conversations about those parts of the day that simply cannot be suppressed ("my guy in the unit bled out"), we doctors withhold our own narratives, knowing neither the benefits of expressing them nor to whom and how to tell them. Here is a description, written by a teacher of family medicine, about a narrative medicine teaching session in the South:

> At a recent conference in Family Medicine, a colleague and I presented a seminar on narrative medicine. . . . Dr. Irvine and I gave the participants [these directions] during our seminar: "Write about a patient whose suffering has moved you. You will have 15 minutes to write." A young physician raised her hand. "I really can't think of any patient to write about. I've been working in a nursing home for awhile. My patients are barely conscious. I don't even know them. And anyway, you know, I don't get that involved with patients." Irvine responded, "That's okay. Just write what comes to mind." She and the rest of the group began writing. Within minutes, we heard someone crying. We looked around and found that the someone was the young, unmovable physician. When she later took her turn to read her story, it centered on the still-rosy cheeks of one of the comatose old people in her care.[18]

By becoming not only more conscious of but more moved by the stories of illness, doctors and their colleagues in other healthcare professions are equipped to reach patients in their own suffering. This young physician caring for older comatose patients has made contact with her own sadness and sense of loss for these patients. Mightn't she now shift her position in her professional duties toward, perhaps, a more authentic contact with these persons and their families? Mightn't she make more room within herself for the human feelings of grieving or even of valuing what is still alive in these irrevocably ill patients? And mightn't she discover opportunities for benevolence that she, now, can perform on behalf of her charges, benevolence that may not cost much time but require from her this new, narratively informed frame of mind? Secondarily, mightn't she be spared some of the errors of inattention that she would have risked in her former state of inattention?

In the frontier work on errors and medical malpractice represented in this book, the practices of narrative medicine come to the fore as methods of repositioning ourselves vis-à-vis our patients and their families. Other methods may share our goals of global repositioning—mindful practice, relationship-centered care, and patient-centered care are all names for neighboring efforts in health care. What these methods share are means for doctors and patients to cross the damaging divides in health care to achieve contact, to reach one another, to hear one another out, to adopt one another's perspectives, to acknowledge the sadness and rage and love within their daily lives together. Revolutionary, this contact between doctor and patient can itself begin to perform what is now sadly lacking—the acknowledgment of one another's losses, the confirmation of worth so desired by all who suffer, the *mutuality* of fortitude and need heightened in times of illness, and the deep desire, all around, to be of help. Instead of parallel suffering, in which patients suffer unheard pain and doctors suffer untold defeats, we are approaching a state of affairs where we humans are united in the face of inevitable human losses and do our best to endure the pain and to carry on.

# A Narrative Life

There is a levitating quality about the form of medicine that connects doctor with patient, that includes mutual recognition, that bears witness to the many forms of suffering beheld. It has the power to lift you, to transfigure you, to inhabit you with almost eerie knowledge of self and other. You sit in your office with a sick person, open to her story, able to think quickly through her medical problem while you *join* her in her pain, putting yourself at her disposal. You find yourself saying things that help her, not because you follow a drill, but because you have developed the skill to enter her world. It is hard to find the words to talk about such encounters. We become transparent to each other, doctor and patient, united in considering the patient's ordeal. Not ghostly or goofy, this state of attentive presence is summoned in the doctor by the patient's authentic call. The self who is summoned by the call of the patient is the authentic self.

Answering our patients' calls, we are better than we otherwise would be.

Reflecting on the desire to practice protective medicine helps us to position medicine within the wide frame of human relationships. It is not only in medical practice that one person undergoes pain or suffering and the other tries to help. Such duty is not limited to health care but extends to situations like natural disasters, family discord, or wartime in which suffering descends on a person—sometimes caused by an individual and sometimes not—and others who surround the suffering feel sad, often feel guilty or somehow to blame for the misfortune, and have the desire to apologize or to seek forgiveness for their part in the situation. Not only, that is, in medical practice does one human being feel he or she has been wronged. Not only in medicine does one human being worry that he or she has wronged another and should apologize. In realms far away from medicine, apology and reparation are powerful means to deal with suffering. In his book *On Apology*, psychiatrist Aaron Lazare frames medical error within this vast tapestry of human relationship, showing us how medicine is but a subset of human living in which persons are connected by their actions and their fidelity, their relationships ruptured by accident or folly, and their yearning for repair and reconciliation an important and often overlooked aspect of their growth and integrity.[19] This recognition helps us to accept that in caring for our patients, even in the face of error, we are enacting not only our medical duties toward patients but our human responsibilities to heal.

## REFERENCES

1. See the many pathographies, or illness narratives, in print of late that describe characteristics of helpful and unhelpful physicians, for example, *Leukemia for Chickens* by Roger Madoff (New York, NY: Jennifer Madoff, 2007) and *Ordinary Life: A Memoir of Healing* by Kathy Conway (New York, NY: W.H. Freeman, 1997).
2. Wills G. *Saint Augustine*. New York, NY: Penguin Books; 2005:69. I thank Dr. Clayton Baker for pointing me to this breath-taking utterance by Augustine.
3. Shem S. *The House of God*. New York, NY: Dell; 1978.
4. Osler W. "Aequanimitas." In: *Aequanimitas, With Other Addresses to Medical Students, Nurses and Practitioners of Medicine*. 3rd ed. New York, NY: McGraw-Hill; 1932:3–11. (Valedictory Address, University of Pennsylvania, 1889.)
5. Beach MC, Inui T. Relationship-centered care: a constructive reframing. *J Gen Intern Med*. 2006;21(suppl 1):S3–S8.
6. Halpern J. *From Detached Concern to Empathy: Humanizing Medical Practice*. New York, NY: Oxford University Press; 2001.
7. Charon R. *Narrative Medicine: Honoring the Stories of Illness*. New York, NY: Oxford University Press; 2006.
8. Charon R. Narrative medicine: attention, representation, affiliation. *Narrative*. 2005; 13:61–70.
9. DasGupta S. Teaching cultural competence through narrative medicine: intersections of classroom and community. *Teach Learn Med*. 2005;18(1):14–17.
10. Hall LL. Editorial: surviving burnout. *Am Coll Obst Gynecol Clin Rev*. 2006;11(3):1, 14–16.
11. Reis S. Holocaust and medicine: a medical education agenda. *IMAJ*. 2007;9:189–191.
12. DasGupta S. Between stillness and story: lessons of children's illness narratives. *Pediatrics*. 2007;119(6):1384–1387.
13. Engel J, Zarconi J, Pethtel L, Missimi S. *Narrative in Health Care: Healing Patients, Practitioners, Profession and Community*. Oxford, UK: Radcliffe Publishing; 2008.
14. Levinson W, Roter D, Dull VT, Frankel R. Physician-patient communication: the relationship with malpractice claims among primary care physicians and surgeons. *JAMA*. 1997;277(7):553–559.

15. Gallagher T, Waterman A, Ebers A, Fraser V, Levinson W. Patients and physicians' attitudes regarding disclosure of medical errors. *JAMA.* 2003;289:1001–1007.
16. Inui T, Frankel R. Hello stranger: building a healing narrative that includes everyone. *Acad Med.* 2006;81:415–418.
17. Delbanco T, Bell S. Guilty, afraid, and alone: struggling with medical error. *N Engl J Med.* 2007;357:1682–1683.
18. Goodrich TJ. A review of *Narrative Medicine: Honoring the Stories of Illness.* PsycCritiques—Contemporary Psychology: American Psychological Association Review of Books (online). December 20, 2006;51 (article 2). Available at: http://psycnet.apa.org/index.cfm?fa=main.doiLanding&uid=2006=21730-001, accessed April 21, 2008.
19. Lazare A. *On Apology.* New York, NY: Oxford University Press; 2004.

# Index

# I

Indiana University School of Medicine, 34, 138
informal curriculum, 33–34, 54
informed consent, 7, 98–99, 162, 224–226;
    *See also* disclosure
Institute of Medicine, 8, 19, 85, 161, 231
insurance companies, 36
insurance rates, 3–4
Inui, Thomas, 31, 32, 34

# J

Joint Commission on Accreditation of
    Healthcare Organizations, 85, 125, 137
*Journal of the American Medical
    Association*, 69
juries
    appreciation of honesty, 216–217
    as an audience, 212–213
    decision-making of, 228
    impression of the physician, 213–215
    looking at doctor attributes, 90
    looking for filled out forms, 198
    looking for preventable errors, 201
    sympathy value and, 5, 9, 186
    view on altered records, 220–221
    views on unreachable doctors, 102
    visual evidence and, 215–216

# K

Karliner, Leah et al., 94
knowledge deficit, 142, 247
Korsch, B., 85
Kotb, Hoda, 63, 64
Kripalani, Sunil et al., 137
Kübler-Ross, E., 237

# L

Laine, Christine, 43
language barriers, 66–67, 225
latent error, 37, 194
Laub, Dori, 253
Lawrence-Lightfoot, Sarah, 184
lawsuits; *See also* malpractice claims
    in the 19th century, 68
    apologies and, 185–186
    caps, 6, 9, 22
    communication and, 67–69

complexities of, 5
differing perspectives of, 244
documentation and, 92–93, 227–228
expert testimony and, 219–220
fear of, 15–16, 184
history of, 68
to obtain information, 17, 67, 170
onset of, 241–242
physicians seeing all patients as
    potential, 16
prevention of, 9–13
reasons for, 6–8, 19–20, 23–25, 48–49
recommended by a healthcare provider, 148
span of, 12, 245–246
Lazare, Aaron, 177, 178–179, 186, 188, 268
Leape, Lucien, 43, 161, 184–185, 194, 247
Lee, Thomas, 134
Levinson, W., 69, 246
Li, James, 97
liability issues, 2, 179, 185
listening
    to the entire person, 86, 257
    medical training and, 53–54
    as part of therapeutic relationship, 50
    to resolve patient anger, 83, 156
litigation. *See* lawsuits
Litvin, Cara, 125
*Lost Art of Healing, The* (Lown), 16, 57, 167
Lowenstein, Jerome, 43–44
Lown, Bernard, 16, 19, 24, 57, 167

# M

malpractice, overview of crisis in, 2–3
malpractice claims; *See also* lawsuits
    arising from delay in diagnoses, 112–113
    communication and, 23, 48–49, 76, 84
    costs of defending, 6
    defensive strategies, 20–21
    disclosure and, 171
    due to system errors, 195
    factors in decisions about, 151
    insurance and, 3–6
    "lottery" aspect, 5–6
    most difficult to defend, 224–225
    negligent events vs. claims, 17
    over untreated secondary illnesses, 201
    physician self-esteem and, 16, 17
    reasons for, 6–8, 19–20
    reducing costs in, 9–12
    reducing risk of, 195